P9-DUY-457

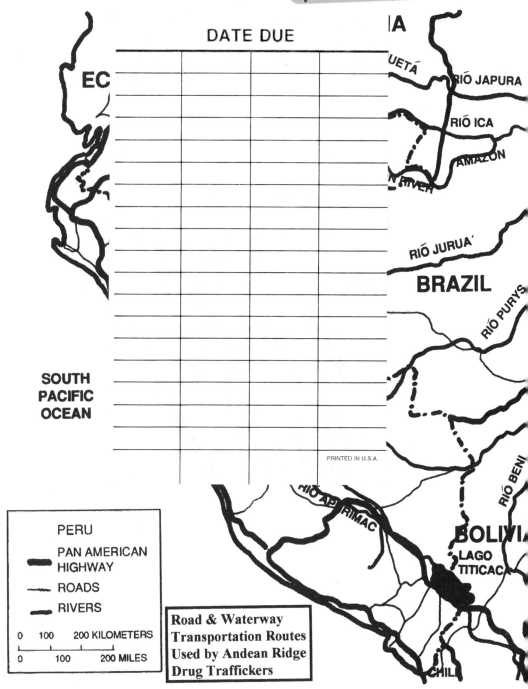

DATE DUE

EC...   ...IA

...UETÁ

RÍO JAPURA

RÍO ICA

AMAZON

N RIVER

RÍO JURUA'

BRAZIL

RÍO PURYS

SOUTH
PACIFIC
OCEAN

PRINTED IN U.S.A.

RÍO BENI

RÍO AP...RIMAC

BOLIVIA

LAGO
TITICAC...

PERU

PAN AMERICAN
HIGHWAY

ROADS

RIVERS

| 0 | 100 | 200 KILOMETERS |
| 0 | 100 | 200 MILES |

**Road & Waterway
Transportation Routes
Used by Andean Ridge
Drug Traffickers**

CHIL...

ILLUSION OR VICTORY

To Dr. Foster,

It was terrific meeting you and your associates at RCC, and we look forward to working with you on this most exciting project.

While I spent most of my time in corporate life, I noticed that more and more of the young men I coached in amateur baseball were experiencing more and more serious drug problems, and spent two years researching the severity of our nation's drug problem, which was enormous. The most important part of the book is the sizing of the "global drug problem contained in the "Author's Introduction."

With very best wishes

Richard Knopf 3/15/99

ILLUSION OR VICTORY:

How The U.S. Navy SEALS Win America's Failing War On Drugs

Richard L. Knopf

S.P.I. BOOKS

New York

Disclaimer

The author has used composite names, places, events and dates to protect his sources. Any resemblance to actual persons, living or dead, is purely coincidental.

ILLUSION OR VICTORY. Copyright © 1997 by Richard L. Knopf. All rights reserved. Printed in the United States of America. No part of this book may be used or reproduced in any manner without the written permission of the publisher, except in the case of brief quotations embodied in critical articles or reviews. For further information, contact S.P.I. Books, 136 West 22nd Street, New York, NY 10011. Tel: 212/633-2023, Fax: 212/633-2123

Library of Congress Cataloging-in-Publication Data
Knopf, Richard L.
Illusion or Victory/Richard L. Knopf

CIP

First Edition April 1997

Freedom isn't free.

*Unless we declare war on the drug cartels
we are doomed to lose this conflict....
and our freedom.*

DEDICATION

Illusion or Victory is dedicated to my parents, Ruth and Frank Knopf, my uncle Paul Rifkind, and to my brother, Bob, who taught me the values by which I have lived my life, and to my wife, Bobbie, and sons Andrew and Jonathan. It is also dedicated to local, state and federal law enforcement at every level including the DEA and Customs Service that join them in a so-called "War on Drugs" that they cannot possibly win.

I want to make specific mention of the entire Tucson, Arizona Police Department, the Pima County Sheriff's Department, as well as MANTIS, the Southern Arizona inter-agency narcotics task force, who are together engaged in a mortal battle to take that city's streets back from drug dealers and their confederates.

The book is further dedicated to my publisher, Ian Shapolsky of S.P.I. Books and Isaac Mozeson, S.P.I.'s Editor-In-Chief, whose experience, patience and wisdom helped tremendously in the writing of this book; to Richard Brown and Maurice Tremblay whose intensely private battles have demonstrated a level of courage and committment rarely seen in my lifetime; to Phil and Donna Satow, Paul Anton, Jerry Maltz, Jeff Cook, John Cirigliano, Jim Warren Rich Manoukian, Fred Hill, and Ellen Knopf, whose nearly four decades of loving friendship have taught me the true meaning of compassion, and to Steve Fehrman, Marshall Michalean, Rob Neborsky, Brian Mudd and Mode Perry, who supported me in the pursuit of my dream. Also, to FBI Special Agent Ed Hall and every other active service FBI agent, who today must face not only the daily threats of terrorism from outside the United States, but from inside as well.

Most of all, *Illusion or Victory* is dedicated to United States Navy Commander Daley T. Coulter, (ret.), who served as a Navy SEAL for more than 25 years and brought back alive every SEAL serving under him through dozens of extremely dangerous missions, and to FBI Special Agent John Gordon, (ret.), who gave this country 27 more years of service after winning the Distinguished Flying Cross as a B52 navigator in Vietnam. The bravest of the brave, Tom Coulter and John Gordon remain the two most morally grounded human beings I have had the honor to call friends during my lifetime, and neither ever retreated from the high moral ground in any quadrant of their lives. The United States was a safer place when these two men stood the watch.

Lastly, the book is dedicated to the United States Navy SEAL Team, and to the beloved memory of the 37 SEALs who perished during the Vietnam War, and those who have given their lives since in Grenada, Panama and wherever the finest young people this society produces go willingly into harm's way in the service of their nation.

I also want to make specific mention of United States Navy Rear Admiral Irve C. LeMoyne, United States Navy Chief Petty Officer Robert Brown, United States Navy Master Chief Petty Officer Gary G. Gallagher (ret.) and United States Army Captain Frank M. Muller, Jr. (ret.). Admiral LeMoyne was the only Navy SEAL to attain the rank of Rear Admiral (two star), and passed away prematurely at age 57 earlier this year.

Chief Brown was one of my instructors during BUD-S (Basic Underwater Demolition-SEAL) training in Coronado. The winner of several combat citations for bravery in Vietnam, Chief Brown saved two mortally wounded comrades. On that same mission he received a gaping chest wound that would have killed lesser men than himself. He tragically passed away before his time at age 48 due to the lingering effects of his wounds.

Master Chief Gallagher was awarded 37 combat awards and citations during a thirty-year career beginning in

Vietnam, and retired as the most heavily decorated veteran of naval service at the time.

Captain Frank M. Muller Jr. was awarded eight Bronze and Silver Stars, the Distinguished Flying Cross, and the Vietnamese Medal of Honor as an Airborne Ranger in Vietnam. He volunteered for a lone rescue mission of a downed U.S. Air Force pilot in North Vietnam, carried the horribly wounded man several miles and, while fighting off an ambush by nearly five thousand enemy troops, placed the pilot aboard a rescue heliocopter that could only accomodate one man.   This heroic action represents the single greatest act of compassion observed during my lifetime. Captain Muller survived the war and has remained a loving friend for more than 20 years.

The heroic exploits of these four men extend beyond legend, and they were consummate warriors. It has been an honor and privilege to know them.

Cardazanna, Colombia,
1985

"The narcotics trade is a revolutionary means of struggle against imperialism. Colombia drug traffickers use their vast wealth to train and arm communist guerrillas to protect them, which in turn foments revolution—a pattern emerging in other Latin nations."
—José Ocho Garriana,
Head of the Cardazanna Drug Cartel

Washington, D.C.,
February 26, 1996

"The President of the United States announced today that according to the annual State Department Survey of Drug Trafficking, $400 billion of illegal drugs were imported into the United States in 1995. While an estimated 50% of the total entered the United States through Mexico, the President refused to apply economic sanctions due to the importance of commercial trade between the two countries. Instead, sanctions were applied against Colombia."
--News reports covering the President's remarks on the State Department's 1995 Report on Drug Trafficking into the United States

New York City,
March 6, 1997

"Colombia, the world's largest producer of cocaine, today suspended all aerial eradication of drug-producing crops in a sharp rebuff to the United States"
--From a March 6, 1997 *New York Times* article about Colombia's reaction to the United States decertification of the country as an ally in the "War on Drugs".

Washington, D.C.
March 10, 1997

"Taxpayers have paid $103 billion dollars over the past 10 years for a federal drug war that has done little to stop international narcotics traffickers."
--From a U.S. Government General Accounting Office Report, released March 10, 1997

TABLE OF CONTENTS

INTRODUCTION

After nearly twenty-five years the so-called "War on Drugs" has proven to be a failure. In fact, the only real war being fought on the drug front is the one being waged against America by the governments of more than sixty of the one hundred seventy-three countries where drug cartels and allied terrorist organizations operate with near impunity. In many of these countries, it is almost impossible to separate the drug cartels from the terrorist organizations, or even from the governments themselves.

Our courts, jails and hospitals are overburdened with the results of this tidal wave of cocaine. Despite near heroic efforts by local, state and federal law enforcement, as well as the governmental organizations that support them, an estimated eighty percent of all the illegal drugs targeted at the United States gets through.

With a somewhat aging drug population, the Narcoterrorists have now targeted the youngest Americans, and there has recently been an alarming 167% increase in drug use among this country's 12 to 18 year olds, giving the drug cartels decades of future markets. In a recent survey released by the governor of Arizona, an estimated 50% of the high school seniors in his state had used illegal drugs one or more times. Similarly disturbing news emerges from surveys throughout the United States, as federal agencies report an "epidemic" of cocaine, crack cocaine and methamphetamine use among inner city youth.

Annually, the United States now loses more of its citizens to drug overdoses, secondary causes such as HIV and drug-related deaths than the annual killed in action (KIA) losses during the Vietnam War. Directly, the country spends more than $13 billion dollars fighting a fictitious war, and the indirect costs in terms of broken families, rehab centers, etc. runs into the billions of additional dollars.

The illegal drug "industry" is an enormous worldwide criminal enterprise employing more than two million people whose financial resources dwarf even the world's largest corporations.

While estimates vary, the general consensus is that international trafficking in illegal drugs generates between one and two trillion dollars a year. At the low end, this would make the drug cartels bigger than the top ten corporations listed in *Fortune* magazine's annual ranking of the fifty largest companies in the United States. At the upper end of two trillion dollars, the cartels would be larger than all fifty companies, and of course they do not pay taxes the way legitimate companies do.

More than one million citizens of the Andean Ridge countries of Colombia, Peru and Bolivia, (the region where approximately 70% of the world's cocaine supply is grown, processed and shipped to the United States and other countries) are estimated to be employed in all facets of the cocaine industry. This includes growing, harvesting and processing the coca leaf, as well as money laundering. In addition, another one million or more individuals are involved in similar activities in other areas of the world, such as the Golden Triangle and Bekaa Valley, where other illegal drugs such as heroin and marijuana are grown and processed. In Bolivia, an estimated 400,000 citizens of that nation, representing about 6% of the population, are involved; an additional 60,000 families are estimated to be active in Peru, and an estimated 400,000 of Colombia's citizens (all this from U.S. governmental data).

It is not necessary for the United States to support high employment in the Andean Ridge countries, the Golden Triangle, Bekaa Valley and other areas at the cost of killing

25,000-50,000 of our citizens a year and wounding 500,000-1,000,000 more who require either emergency room or private medical assistance due to drug overdoses.

If the entire FBI, DEA, Customs Service, as well as all local and state law enforcement officials, spent 100% of their time in counter drug activities, they would still be outnumbered by the drug criminals by ten or more to one. These incredible odds, along with the cartels' virtually unlimited financial resources, make the present "War on Drugs" unwinable, and demand an aggressive new strategy such as the one presented in this book.

In addition to the numerical human odds against the efforts of law enforcement, the cartels' profits enable them to fund worldwide development of high tech weapons systems. These are being used by the terrorist organizations which the cartels work with globally to attack the international legal community as well as the United States and its citizens.

Today, the world's drug cartels aligned with terrorist organizations within the Andean Ridge countries have, in effect, been fighting an undeclared war against the United States. This war is not only being fought with the most modern and sophisticated weaponry possessed by the cartels and their allies, it is also being fought with something that is even more powerful... the drugs that are poisoning our country on an increasing basis, and corrupting generations of our citizens. Battling such a potent and well-armed menace with education programs and occasional border seizures alone is totally unrealistic.

There is no reason for the U.S. to continue losing the drug war. The United States, with its Tier One Military Forces of SEAL Team Six and Delta Force, clearly possesses the military and technological resources appropriate to fight a real War on Drugs, down to satellite imagery that determines the precise location of the Andean Ridge coca leaf crops. The issue, simply put, is national will.

Actual research for this book began about thirty years

ago during my own BUD-S (Basic Underwater Demolition-SEAL) training. This is where I learned first hand the capabilities, particularly in and around the water, possessed by the U.S. Navy SEAL Teams, as well as the emotional, physical and other traits required to be a SEAL.

Over the years, I remained a staunch public supporter of the unit and its mission, and got to know dozens of SEALs and affiliated personnel such as those in the SEAL boat support squadrons.

I also met dozens of FBI agents and law enforcement personnel at all levels in the course of researching this book. In addition, hundreds of hours were spent researching published information from the DEA, The National Office of Drug Control Strategy, SAMHSA, and dozens of other sources. These provided a composite picture of the staggering magnitude and dimensions of the drug problem in the United States caused by the war being waged against it by the Narcoterrorists and their allies.

It became absolutely clear that the only logical solution resides in interdicting drugs along the waterways of the Andean Ridge countries with U.S. Navy SEALs to effectively stop the problems at its source. The conclusion of virtually everyone I interviewed within this county's law enforcement and intelligence communities is that 80% of the illegal drugs targeted at the United States crosses our borders, along with the terrorists who often accompany them. The problem is so enormous that it could eventually tear this country apart.

Interestingly, a recent *New York Times* article of February 3, 1997 quoted U.S. Drug Czar and retired Army General Barry McCaffery as indicating that the Pentagon is prepared to assist the Peruvian government in interdicting the Amazon Basin waterways to curb the flow of coca base destined for processing in Colombia. While the U.S. Navy SEALs were specifically mentioned, this was merely in the role of military advisors and trainers. This is an encouraging first step, but far from fighting the real War on Drugs.

The fact that Mexico's top anti-drug official, General Jesus Guttiérrez Rebello was recently indicted for masterminding the shipment of ten tons of cocaine a week into the United States illustrates how corruption at the very top of many governments, even friendly ones, makes the problem impossible to stop once the cocaine has left the Andean Ridge Countries. In addition to transporting the illegal drugs, the Mexican General, who was the equivalent of the U.S. Drug Czar, had almost certainly compromised America's counter-drug-intelligence network in that country. This also illustrates how the enormous financial resources available to the drug cartels enables them to virtually buy the assistance of entire governments, even large ones such as Mexico's.

The President's 1997 statement on America's Drug Control Strategy was announced publicly on February 25, 1997. It calls for increased spending in education, advertising and other programs that traditionally characterized this country's recent counter-drug efforts. Ironically, the only area of decreased spending was in illegal drug interdiction. This goes in absolutely the wrong direction and could result in a "Narco-Disaster" of epidemic proportions being perpetrated against the estimated fifty-two million children and young adults who comprise today's U.S. school population.

After reading this book the obvious question that will be asked is whether the events portrayed actually occurred. The most accurate answer is that the first seven chapters do, in fact, represent a composite of historically accurate events. Beyond that, the technology possessed by the U.S. Navy SEAL Team that is interwoven throughout the remainder of the book represents existing weapon systems or those now under development.

As a real War on Drugs has not yet been declared by the United States, the scenario outlined in this book for possibly fighting such a war is plausible based on the hundreds of sources interviewed by the author. It is certainly not the only scenario, but the critical issue remains this country's national will to interdict the waterways in the Andean Ridge countries using U.S. Navy SEALs and the type of weaponry and technology described in the book.

An important question involves our former, more aggressive policies. The United States had once begun a policy of crop eradication and interdiction of the waterways used to transport the coca leaf. In the beginning of 1995, a twenty-five pound bag of coca leaves priced at $25 had plunged to $5 when farmers could no longer find buyers. Before the flow to Colombia picked up, many coca growers were planting alternative crops. Why did our government move away from a successful, active policy to a passive, unsuccessful one of education, attempted border seizures, airport security measures, etc.

This is a question Americans should ask their elected leaders, unless we are prepared to accept increasingly higher drug casualties, worse than those incurred during the Vietnam War, see many sacred American Institutions undermined, and watch our natonal treasury be drained by the Narcoterrorists and their allies both inside this country and within the international community. The author hopes that *Illusion or Victory* will raise these questions to the level of a national debate, where the enormity and real cost of the drug problem can finally be confronted by the American people and their elected leaders.

Richard L. Knopf
Tucson, Arizona
March 19, 1997

FOREWORD

Illusion or Victory is Clancy-like in detail and accuracy. This true-to-life scenario is the result of extensive technical operational research by the author. Some may question the reality of the futuristic weaponry described here, *but it's real and it's now.*

The author's efforts could not be more timely. Recent administrations have adopted a policy of education to counter the continued flow of illegal drugs into the United States. This policy has been unsuccessful, and contrary to the country's efforts, drug use among teens has sky rocketed. The concept of telling teens something is illegal and may not be good for them is equivalent to daring them to experiment with drugs. As long as drugs are as plentiful as they presently appear to be, teens and others will seek them out. There are other methods.

Illustion or Victory takes a more Reaganesque approach. During that administration a policy of eradication of the cocoa leaf crop proved somewhat more successful in curbing the flow of drugs into this country. The policy was simple. The Andean Ridge countries were encouraged to burn specific amounts ef coca leaf and allowed to harvest the remaining product. For their efforts, those countries, and purportedly their farmers, received financial compensation from the United States Government.

This policy, although successful, failed to measure up to predictions of the U.S. State Department and the Drug Enforcement Agency "DEA". There were several reasons that the policy was not more successful. Those governments involved in the program did not always pass the compensation along to the farmers, causing the farmers to become less enthusiastic about the eradication program. A second cause was traced to the State Department along with the DEA not holding those countries accountable for this agreement and compensating them regardless if all the designated hectares of coca leaf were destroyed.

A third, and perhaps most important reason the plan was not more successful, was that the U.S. concentrated most of its monitoring and surveillance efforts on tracking aircraft movement, as the primary method of transporting product. The waterways of the Andean Ridge countries were all but ignored as a major source of transport for both the coca leaf and the precursor chemicals required for refinement and manufacturing.

This story identifies U.S. Navy SEALs as the instrument that would be best suited to address the drug problem from a different perspective. Surveillance, patrol and hard target interdiction are but a few of the neccessary skills SEALs would bring to the War on Drugs.

Interdiction of the drugs along the various network of rivers has been considered for some time a preferred approach by many in the intelligence community. SEALs were created and are ideally suited for riverine warfare, and make no mistake about it, we are at war. Our politicians assume we have the high technology market cornered regarding everything from thermal imaging equipment to remote listening devices and sensors. This is not the case. We have been out-spent and out-developed by the drug cartels in the areas of communications, surveillance, satellite tracking, sensors and special weapons development.

The drug cartels are legitimizing their high tech development efforts and working in conjunction with nations that are supporting terrorism to undermine the U.S. and its foreign policy. The drug cartels underwrite technological development and arm terrorist groups with the resulting technology. In return for this technology, the terrorist groups train the cartel's personnel and conduct special missions on their behalf. Effectively, the cartels have been using terrorist groups and their vilolently intimidating tactics to exend their worldwide influence.

The U.S. government has yet to meet the drug threat with the same intensity and dedication that the drug cartels undertake in their efforts. The government appears more interested in ensuring that the rights of criminals are addressed, rather than the well-being and security of the nation. If asked, recent administrations would state with some pride that our shores and borders have never been penetrated by enemy forces and weapons. This, of course, is not true, our nation is infiltrated daily by foreign forces and their weapons of mass destruction, illegal drugs. We have the means to stop them. It is a question of national will and implementing offensively aggressive programs and measures, rather than continuing with weak defensive stopgaps.

The author presents a most interesting scenario in his story line. There is little question that the scenario is plausible, regardless if the events occured as indicated. If the scenario were to be true, the SEALs are the resource that would be called upon to undertake the mission. The story reflects a change in policy that would be welcomed in many quarters but questioned in others. The operational employment used in the book reflects tactics employed by SEALs in a riverine environment. The crafts described in the book may actually exist or may represent a composite of several craft in various stages of development and testing.

The author's description of the characters in the story reflects the types of men that represent the TEAMs of the 90's. They represent a cross section of the nation, with all its inherent strengths and weaknesses. If the story were to be true, only the SEALs could succeed and only the SEALs could survive.

Daley T. Coulter
United States Navy Commander (ret.)
25-year U.S. Navy SEAL

UNITED STATES NAVY ENLISTED RATINGS AND OFFICER RANKS USED IN THE BOOK

BM1 - Boatswain's Mate, First Class
BM2 - Boatswain's Mate, Second Class
BMC - Chief Boatswain's Mate
CPO - Chief Petty Officer
MM2 - Machinist's Mate, Second Class
MM3 - Machinist's Mate, Third Class
GMC - Chief Gunner's Mate
GM3 - Gunner's Mate, Third Class
YM3 - Yeoman, Third Class
Lt. (jg.) - Lieutenant, Junior Grade
Lt. - Lieutenant
Lt. Cdr. - Lieutenant Commander
Cdr. - Commander
Capt. - Captain (sometimes called "Four Striper")
Adm. - Admiral

CHAPTER 1

UPPER HUALLAGA VALLEY, PERU
JULY 9, 1992

The four United States Navy SEALs had made their way undected from SEAL Team Four's headquaters in Little Creek, Virgina deep into the Amazon River Basin to strike a blow at the very heart of the Cardazanna drug cartel's operations. Since nearly 70% of the world's cocaine supply was grown in Peru and Bolivia, with precursor chemicals added in Colombia prior to trans-shipment to the United States, the message, delivered inside Peru itself along one of the waterways used to transport the coca paste for further processing in Colombia, would be loud and clear.

Young and strong, and all in their mid to late twenties, the men mirrored the ethnic mix of the society that had produced them. One was an Irish Catholic, one an Afro-American of the Baptist faith, one a Jew and the fourth was a WASP. Physically, each would be a match for an NFL football player, as each man had to bench press 400 pounds to even be considered as a candidate for the unit.

Unlike civilian or even military "wannabee" marksmen, a SEAL had to run twelve or more miles in full gear through soft sand, swim perhaps five more miles still in full pack, and stand motionless in icy water for several hours before firing a single deadly head shot at an adversary at long range.

It was the complete mastery of one's being this required to accomplish the stated goals that separated Navy

SEALs from all others. (This was taught early in SEAL training during "Hell Week" where the trainee must function during seven days and nights of non-stop physical and emotional duress, while sleeping a total of only a few hours. During that time, the individuals build in a mechanism to press ahead automatically, irrespective of unbearable pain, fractures, broken bones, numbing cold, exhaustion or anything else).

As ridiculous as many Hollywood stunts seemed to knowledgeable viewers, such as firing hundreds of rounds of ammunition from a magazine that only holds forty bullets, the actual capabilities possessed by today's SEALs made movie stunts laughable, as the targets of this particular mission would soon find out. This was not Hollywood, it was real life.

Lt. (jg.) Jeremy Powers held his right arm up, clenching his hand in a closed fist he gave the silent signal for his four man fire team to stop. The men were dressed in dark, jungle striped camouflage fatigues, and wore dark green bandannas over their heads in a somewhat futile attempt to keep sweat from filling their eyes.

Every inch of exposed skin was covered with camouflage makeup to match the endless shades of the flickering light and darkness of the dense jungle. The men literally blended into their surroundings. Sweat ran down the entire length of Powers' body. Even the makeup on his face seemed to turn to ooze, acting as fly paper to the swarming insects. The suffocating tropical heat and humidity of the Amazon created an almost claustrophobic atmosphere, the thick underbrush of the jungle seemingly coming alive, as though attempting to devour the four men. Brushing the sweat and bugs from his eyes, Powers' gaze strained through the dense, dimly lit moss hanging from the trees and he tried to make a positive identification of the scene in front of him. Any mistake could be fatal to his men.

Just before leaving headquarters, Powers had read a

26

highly-classified CIA intelligence report indicating the presence of several squads of Shining Path guerrillas in the region. This particular group of guerrillas had a well-deserved reputation for violent brutality. Based on the reports of their almost daily activities, this guerrilla group was second to none in the atrocities committed against its own people, a fact that was verified to Powers just two hours before. When Powers and his fire team passed through the village of Santa Rosito, they had seen what was left of the body of Father Lucien Marriana. A village in this part of the world reflected a level of poverty that could not possibly be imagined by inhabitants of the developed countries. The streets were a smelly mixture of oozing mud mixed with human and animal excrement, and the destitute human beings who lived there resided in little more than mud huts with thatched roofs.

The abject poverty was a major reason the United States and other countries had such little success convincing the Andean Ridge peasants to stop growing coca leaf, the primary ingredient of cocaine and its derivatives including the lethal new drug, crack cocaine. The handful of dollars received from the sale of a single crop could keep the villagers alive for another year. Of course, the drug cartels sold the end product for hundreds of times what they paid the peasants. As political representatives of the Andean Ridge countries repeatedly told the American public, if they would only curb their voracious appetite for cocaine, there would be no demand and therefore no problem.

Arriving in Santa Rosita, Powers had noticed something hanging from the church tower. At first glance it appeared to be the remains of a butchered animal. Only after closer study, had the form of a man become recognizable. It was well known throughout the region that Father Marriana was the villagers' primary source of inspiration for their acts of rebellion against the Shining Path. In what appeared to be the guerrilla's attempt to strip the villagers of not only

Father Marriana but of the source of their strength, the church, they committed every conceivable act of blasphemy against the priest's body. Stripped of his cloth he hung naked, crucified, high above the village where he had not only lived all these many years, but where he had spread the word of the church. Here they had come, people from all the villages in the region, for his guidance, taking away with them the strength to endure the hardships of their meager lives. Marriana had loved the simple people of these villages and they returned that love.

Powers later learned that, while still alive, Father Marriana had first been stripped of his robes, stretched spread eagle on the ground, his skin slowly peeled from his body, exposing his heart. Then, in an almost ritualistic ceremony, two of the guerrillas not only castrated Father Marriana, but later when they crucified him they nailed each of his testicles to his own hands. From what the villagers had told Powers, while hanging crucified, Father Marriana's exposed heart continued beating for almost two hours while the guerrillas purged the village.

In celebration of their triumph, the guerrillas took every female member of the village, from the age of 4 up, including the aged, to a spot just beneath the crucified body of the Priest where they were viciously raped and sodomized. When finished, in almost a conscious act of forcing the priest's last living vision to be that of the horror that had just taken place beneath him, the same two guerrillas who had castrated him pulled out their guns and shot out his eyes. With this act, Father Lucien Marriana was released from his agony.

Shaking from emotion and revulsion from the memory, Lt. (jg.) Powers brought himself back to the present and the job at hand. Despite their atrocities, Shining Path guerrillas were not Powers' primary target. As much as he wanted to avenge Father Marriana's murder, Powers' mission was to stop the cocoa base shipments being smuggled up the Amazon River. Every boatload that made it to the transit point at Los Monchios added another $250 million worth of illegal drugs to the vast quantities already being chased by law enforcement officials all across the United States. Since Shining Path and the guerrillas running river operations on behalf of the Colombian Cartels had become indistinguishable, Powers and his fire team were only too happy to kill as many of the Shining Path assassins as they deemed necessary, or appropriate, while carrying out their orders. But they had to keep their perspective on the mission: "Stop the shipments".

Peering between the foliage, the CAR 15 with a model 203 40 mm grenade launcher felt clammy and unusually heavy in Powers' arms. Less than sixty yards ahead, three Shining Path guerrillas chatted as they gathered around a small fire. Their gazes were fixed on a small blackened pot precariously balanced on the rocks surrounding the fire. Powers signaled with a slow, circular motion of his hand. Each man in the fire team knew what to do and began to encircle the guerrillas. CPO Jim "Baldy" Rodgers was about a hundred yards to Powers' left and some twenty yards behind. Hunched down, he was trying to minimize the obvious bulk of his 6'3", 228 pound frame. The M60 machine gun, the lighter and more compact version favored by Navy SEALs, looked like a toy cradled in Rodgers' huge forearms. Despite his bulk, the man's cat-like movements were those of a jungle creature stalking its prey. At this particular moment, that is exactly what CPO Rodgers had become.

Some 150 yards to the right, BMI Lawrence "Huckleby" Smith slowly began his maneuver, circling around to the right of the guerrillas. A black man, Smith, looking like an NFL tackle, was surprisingly agile for his size. He had been a football star at Grambling University before joining the Navy. Along with the camouflaged clothing and what Smith called his God-given SEAL weapon, he was almost indistinguishable in the darkness of the jungle.

He carried a highly classified automatic shotgun that could empty its six, 12 gauge, triple ought buckshot shells in less than two seconds, killing anything within a 30 yard arc. Only someone of Smith's enormous size and strength could hold the weapon and not have it ride up over his head or knock him down from the recoil.

MM2 Johnny Crane was directly behind Powers at a distance of some fifty yards. Crane looked like someone's nephew who had been invited to the big game. This was highly deceiving as Crane, only 5'9" and 185 pounds of angularly chiseled marble, could bench press 400 pounds. He had averaged almost 200 yards per game rushing as a highly recruited high school running back from Batavia, New York. But the adventurous youth had enlisted in the Navy as an eighteen-year-old, volunteered for the SEAL Team three years later, and rose to the rank of Petty Officer Second Class in the minimum time of four and a half years. Crane seemed lightly armed with the new SAW (Squad Automatic Weapon). Although weighing less than seventeen pounds, the SAW could pour a lethal amount of fire into an enemy position. Crane immediately turned to the rear, crouched down and walked backwards towards Powers. The 180° turn was done to ensure no "backdoor" ambush against the fire team. After closing to about 20 yards behind Lt. (jg.) Powers' position and scanning in a 180 degree arc, Crane took up his ambush position approximately 50 yards to the left of the Lieutenant junior grade. Both this maneuver and those of his squad mates had been practiced hundreds of times and were now instinctual, automatic reflex actions.

Little had changed in SEAL Team weapons fire doctrine since the unit's inception in 1962 and its subsequent experience during the Vietnam War: Get in close and pour as much lethal fire on the targets as possible, in the shortest period of time. The ratio of SEALs to more traditional military units, in terms of firepower, remained at ten to one (that is, ten SEALs could take on one hundred traditionally armed troops). With these four SEALs to the three Shining Path guerrillas they were about to face, there could be only one outcome.

After giving the preliminary signal, Powers opened and closed his fist twice, telling the other three men that the ambush would take place in exactly ten minutes. Everyone glanced at their watches. It was exactly 0538 hours local time.

Within eight minutes, all of the men had arrived at their pre-designated spots. Silently, they had moved to within 20 yards of the guerrillas, while remaining still hidden by the jungle. The guerrillas continued their activities, not realizing that death was all around them. The four SEALs were now positioned in a semi-circular arc around the three unsuspecting guerrillas. While well-trained themselves, the guerrillas' camp was only 20 yards from the Amazon River.

They never imagined that their enemy, the soft Americans, would come near a river overflowing with huge snakes, crocodiles and the horrifying Piranha that could devour a full sized oxen in minutes. No, the "Yonkees" were too squeamish for that.

"Huckleby" Smith had closed to within fifteen yards to ensure the ideal range for maximum effectiveness of his shotgun.

Two of the guerrillas, their weapons on the ground next to them, kneeled over the campfire laughing. The third, possibly the sentry, lit a cigarette, the butt of his weapon leaning against his thigh. As he gazed at the dawn, it was obvious his thoughts were somewhere other than in this steamy, hot, insect-infested jungle.

Powers, who now could plainly see the three figures less than thirty yards ahead, glanced at his watch. It read 0547:40, seconds from Armageddon. He proceeded quickly but quietly, moving to within twenty yards. At 0547:50 he raised his right arm. Balancing his weapon with his left, at

31

0548, he dropped his arm and in the same motion carefully placed his finger around the trigger.

Suddenly smoke, deafening noise, torn flesh, bone, foliage, dirt, dust and ejected brass were everywhere. Even with all their training the SEALs were almost deafened by the sound, particularly since they did not wish to give away their positions by the motion required to insert earplugs that would have reduced the noise to an acceptable level. It was a mixture of staccato bursts, the "varoom" sounds of exploding grenades, and a thunderous cacophony so loud that time seemed to stop. "Huckleby" Smith's shotgun had emptied its six rounds in 1.8 seconds. Not wanting to take time to reload, he stooped down, dropped the shotgun to the ground, and in one swift motion withdrew his HK SOF .45 caliber automatic pistol from its holster and began firing twelve round magazines of ammunition at what was left of the guerrillas.

Unlike the antiquated Model 1911 .45 pistol used by the United States military for decades after its development for trench warfare in WWI, advances in recoil technology made firing this weapon not much more difficult than the significantly smaller .22, so it remained on target instead of riding up. In addition, improvements in gas blow back technology made the pistol absolutely quiet when fitted with a silencer. Each 230 grain bullet fired from this weapon would tear a 200 pound man apart. Smith had completed the exchange of weapons and re-engaged his targets in less than two seconds.

A few seconds later, as if by some unseen hand wielding a gigantic machete, all underbrush, small trees and anything within 6 inches from the earth was cut clean. A clearing was formed around the guerrillas where jungle once stood. As if in slow motion, never moving from the spot they were standing when it began, each of the guerrillas' bodies was sliced cleanly from one side to the other. Never having the time to fall, each piece was then again sliced

32

until flesh, bone, entrails, skull fragments and pieces of limb were everywhere. Shreds of clothing and burned flesh ricocheted around the foliage and along the ground. More than 300 rounds of ammunition had been poured into what was just a few seconds ago three strong young men.

In a normal engagement of this type, the order to cease fire would be given after the targets stopped returning fire. Since the three guerrillas were decimated before firing a single round, after emptying two 40 round magazines and three 40mm grenades at his targets, Lt.(jg.) Powers began signaling to the other members of his fire team to cease fire by waving his arm from side to side and yelling, "Cease fire! " repeatedly as loud as he could. Not even FBI forensic experts would be able to re-assemble what was left.

As the firing subsided, a chilling silence suddenly filled the air. The SEALs said nothing, nodding at each other that it was time to go. The men returned to the jungle, disappearing into the dense underbrush without so much as a rustle. The smokey mixture of gunpowder, earth and human remains descended to earth, placing a layer of finality on the terrible scene. As time passed, crocodiles and other local predators would devour the guerrilla's remains, acting as the jungle's equivalent of a clean up service.

CHAPTER 2

LANGLEY, VIRGINIA

Nine years had passed since intelligence men Sir Robert Bretham Chapman of MI5, and General Chaim Ben Lavan of Israel's Mossad had worked together. Along with John Griswald of the CIA, the two had tried to stop development of the so-called "Islam Bomb" in the 1970s. Sir Robert, now in his late fifties, had become Deputy Director of Britain's Security Service. General Ben Lavan had gone on in 1982 to become the head of the Mossad. His identity was the most closely guarded secret in all of Israel. Now the two had been requested to attend a meeting at CIA headquarters in Langley with John Nesmuth, the newly appointed director.

At 6'3", Bretham Chapman was still an imposing figure, although his graying hair and slightly bent gait mirrored a graceful aging. Being the type of individual who was "too busy" to worry about wardrobe, and with the attitude that "a suit doesn't fit his personality", he compromised convention by wearing his usual dark-brown checkered slacks and a camel-hair jacket with leather elbow patches. The one signature of dress he had become famous for was his bow tie, which he had carefully hand tied around the somewhat frayed collar of a washed-out blue shirt. Impatiently waiting outside the Director's office, he sat tapping his pipe lightly against the edge of the Queen Ann mahogany sidetable.

General Chaim Ben Lavan was about three inches shorter than Sir Robert and sat next to him. Unlike Sir Robert, he was a man who liked to dress. Image was extremely important to him and his choice of wardrobe today spoke volumes. Impatiently, Sir Robert changed the subject from grand-children and economics to the agenda at hand as he addressed Nesmuth, "So, John, what brings us together today?"

Nesmuth's demeanor changed from that of light conversation to a man deeply concerned, his furrowed brow reflecting the depth of emotion this particular subject elicited. So much depended on just how much of an impact he could make on these two men with the information he was about to give, that the mood must reflect the content. Slowly, with a deliberate, hushed voice he responded, "Nothing short of a direct threat to the survival of all free nations, their interests, institutions and societies throughout the world."

General Chaim Ben Lavan interjected, showing only a slight trace of his Israeli accent and more than a trace of the sarcasm for which he had become known. "International threat?...Which one? The list goes on, or is there something new I can add?"

Nesmuth continued, ignoring the General's tone, "No, I wouldn't say it was something new. I am referring to the Narcoterrorists. What is new and becoming more and more dangerous to us all are the in-roads they have carved throughout the world. The progress the alliance among their ideologies, allies and money has made toward destroying everything we all stand for. Also, our government has become convinced at the highest level that the ordinary citizenry, to say nothing of most people in our government, are oblivious to what is actually going on. During World War II, everyone knew where each country stood. Those behind Hitler were members of the AXIS. Everyone else, with few exceptions, was part of the Allied Coalition arrayed against him. The Cold War was the same. Today, dozens of countries pursue ambiguous policies on the surface while seeking to slowly destroy us, in ways more deadly and with more of a long-term effect than any all-out war could. Their choice of weapons—drugs and the money it brings. Using the very weakness that is shared by all people, of all countries....greed, they create a breeding ground for a disease that literally causes the global society to destroy itself from within."

With that, Nesmuth swung his chair to the left, stood up and walked to a large screen that had been behind him. Standing next to it he picked up a small control box which was attached to the screen by a long chord. Never looking up, he faced the two men, whose eyes were transfixed to the screen which contained a large map of the world, flat and one dimensional. Both Sir Robert and General Ben Lavan noticed the presence of one small light bulb located within the outline of each country. The only difference appeared to be the color of each bulb. A quick glance indicated three different colors with no particular pattern. Before beginning to speak, Nesmuth rotated a circular control button that dimmed the overhead lights.

The CIA Director continued, "The West is under direct attack as never before by an enemy more insidious than any Adolph Hitler, or any Joseph Stalin wannabe. They, at least, announced their aim to take over the world, by violence if necessary. The Narcoterrorists and their allies do not announce any such goal. They cloak their assault in the rhetoric of all revolutionaries. Their bestiality and disregard of all legitimate laws and judicial authority are legitimized by the alleged decadence of their victims."

Sir Robert grinned and in a somewhat jocular voice spoke to Nesmuth, "So, John, is this an ideological lecture held over from your days at Yale University?" He turned to the Mossad General who seemed to share in his humor.

Nesmuth hesitated and smiled himself knowing that within the next few minutes this attitude would suddenly change, "No, Sir Robert, it is not. Let me get to the point."

"That might be a good idea," quipped the Mossad General.

With that, Nesmuth pressed the first control button. Green lights suddenly lit up all across the panel. The startling impact of the bright color contrasted against the darkened room had a visible reaction on Nesmuth's two guests.

Nesmuth explained, "The green lights represent countries that support, directly or indirectly, the illicit drug traffic aimed at the West. I must tell you that more than one third and perhaps as many as 50% of the countries in the world support illegal drug activities and therefore, in one way or the other, are involved in the drug war being waged against us. Therefore, they must be considered our common enemy, no matter what pro-western rhetoric their diplomats broadcast around the globe. They believe that by flooding our societies with drugs we will be destroyed from within. Drug-related crime will become rampant, our citizens will demand strong countermeasures and we will be forced to sweep aside constitutional safeguards and become totalitarian governments ourselves. This, in turn, will create revolution from within. In order to maintain objectivity and not present this as a one-sided ideological issue, I must tell you that in many instances drugs are these countries' primary source of foreign exchange. That makes the problem even more complicated. Why, for example, should a starving peasant in Peru or Bolivia refuse to grow cocoa leaf when he could feed his family from his share of the proceeds of one drug crop for a year? Today, economics seem to take precedence over ideology. The concept of a common good, such as used to rally the Anti-Fascist forces in WWII against Hitler and his stooges no longer exists. That is precisely why this threat is so insidious."

Nesmuth continued studying the faces of the two men in front of him. He was right, their expression had now taken on a look of intensity. While the other two men intuitively knew most of the countries involved, both were startled to see just how many and how large and significant some of them were. The green lights covered nearly one-third of all the countries in the world powerfully demonstrating Nesmuth's points.

For the first time during this presentation, Nesmuth looked up at the board and began to list the countries, in no particular order, but generally by group within a specific geographic region, such as Latin America or Southeast Asia, "Colombia, Peru, Bolivia, Brazil, Chile, Argentina, Mexico, Nicaragua, Cuba, Panama, Costa Rica, Guatemala, Syria, Lebanon, Libya, Iran, Iraq, Pakistan, India, China, Laos, Cambodia, Burma, Thailand, Vietnam, North Korea, virtually every state within the former Soviet Union, Bulgaria, Rumania, Hungary, Yugoslavia, Czechoslovakia, Nigeria,...."

His voice droned on as he reeled off another ten or so countries. In this phase no one country created any particular incantation in his voice. Nesmuth's guests listened for the slightest clue as to which country or countries received greater emphasis, but could not detect any lesser or greater enthusiasm from Nesmuth. This conveyed a feeling to his guests that the sixty countries just named should be considered to be part of one general class. Sir Robert mentally calculated that since there were presently one hundred seventy-three independently constituted countries in the world, the sixty comprised about one-third of these. This constituted a substantial number and certainly defined a major problem for the other countries of the world. The symbolism of green light bulbs was one thing. The impact of one third of the countries in the world being involved in the illegal drug and currency trade was quite another.

Pausing, Nesmuth looked back at his two visitors, than turning back towards the board he pressed the second control button. Amber lights lit up on less than a handful of countries. It was the location of the amber lights that was so startling to the two men. Looking to Nesmuth they anxiously awaited the explanation of their meaning.

Nesmuth continued, "The amber lights represent countries where the drug lords exert influence at the top levels of government and, in some cases, like Italy and Canada, have even infiltrated to the very tops of their intelligence services." The amber lights covered Canada, Italy and Spain.

General Chaim Ben Lavan's voice mirrored the intensity of his concern, "John, you are saying that the so-called drug lords, or narcoterrorists, or whatever we choose to call them, are not just actively working in Latin American countries like Peru, or in areas such as the Golden Triangle in Southeast Asia, but in large, industrialized countries as well? My God!...Canada, Italy and Spain? I thought countries like were impregnable!"

Nesmuth's voice rose with the increased urgency and tempo of the subject, "That's exactly what I am saying. The Mafia in Italy controls much of the worldwide trafficking in heroin and, if we are not vigilant, could take over that country, including completely controlling its parliament and other major governmental institutions. Many members of the Italian legislature are already on the Mafia's payroll. An individual at the very top of Canada's intelligence service has been on Ocho Garriana's payroll for twelve years. He has been providing top secret NATO flight plans to the drug cartels, enabling them to fly plane-loads of cocaine worth hundreds of millions of dollars into remote areas of Canada's north and land them at infrequently used NATO airfields. The situation is the same in Spain. Basque Separatists have allied themselves with local drug lords and the two groups pose a direct threat to the survival of the Spanish government. We are seeing the beginning of enormous influence and pressure on the governments of the former Soviet Republics by organized crime groups with incredible sums of money, certain to be major participants in worldwide drug trafficking."

Sir Robert interrupted, "How much money is involved, John?"

"More than a trillion dollars a year. That would make

the illegal drug business about fifteen or twenty times the size of IBM or seven to ten times the size of the General Motors Corporation, and, remember, unlike legitimate companies such as IBM or GM, the cartels don't pay taxes. Let me put it another way. If all the drug money in the U.S. banking system were suddenly taken out, we would have a depression that would make the crash of 1929 look like a boom time," Nesmuth answered.

The two men sat rigidly, anticipating what would come next. Nesmuth pressed the third control button, and red lights went on in almost every country on the map not yet covered by a green or amber light.

"The red lights indicate those countries of the world that are in imminent danger if we do not collectively do something," he said.

The United States, United Kingdom and Israel were among the large group of Nations that had red lights. Silence engulfed the room; a pin dropping would have sounded like an explosion.

Sir Robert made a mental note that the two largest countries which remained unlit were Norway and Sweden. He shuddered at the idea that these countries, with such small populations, might be all that remained of a "free world".

Only after several minutes did General Ben Lavan, now leaning forward with both elbows on his thighs in intense concentration, speak, "What can we do, John?"

"That's what we're here to talk about. MI5 has extensive contacts throughout the world, particularly in Africa, Asia and the Middle East, from the old glory days of the Empire, and Mossad must have a major network in Latin America since you have been chasing the Nazis down there for years and you managed to catch Adolph Eichmann in Argentina."

The meeting continued. The unwritten rule against never revealing sources overrode all else. Nesmuth again spoke, "We even have some, let us say, influence at the very top of the Colombian Cartels. Remember, 70% of the world's cocaine supply is grown in Peru and Bolivia. Chemicals and other ingredients used for cutting or thinning the drugs are added in Colombia and distribution takes place from there. Colombia is where further processing into the white powder of cocaine also occurs in very sophisticated processing facilities. By totally controlling the Panamanian government, and having enormous influence on the governments of almost every country between themselves and the United States, the Colombians have an uninterrupted land and sea corridor directly into the United States. Notice on the map where Cuba and Haiti are located. They provide almost unrestricted access into the United States by sea."

The reality behind headlines that usually had to do with the illegal takeovers of ostensibly legitimized governments by illicit elements, such as in Haiti, never ceased to amaze even the hardened heads of these major Western intelligence services. Control the government, control the sea lanes. Control the sea lanes, flood the United States with illegal drugs. No matter how much objectivity each of the three wished to apply to his analysis of the data being presented, random chance could not possibly account for the patterns placed before them. Nesmuth's presentation of the land and sea lanes into the United States that provided the highways for both drugs from Latin America and money flowing both ways was particularly strong.

Sir Robert asked a question that had been nagging at him for many years, "John, where does all the money go? Does it really get stuffed and wrapped into little cellophane bags, I think called 'baggies' as the international press would have us believe, and then get carted to and deposited in bank accounts all around the world? How many lunch bags would be needed to hold a trillion dollars in small bills? How many human beings would be required to carry it all? How many suitcases would be necessary to stuff it all into?"

Everyone in the room already knew the answer, but none of the men were quite prepared for that truth to be spoken out loud. Nesmuth replied, "It comes back through most major banks in the world, including the Who's Who of banking in our own countries, with the assistance of a number of major corporations as well. The stuff about ghetto gangs and all their involvement is pure fluff. They are merely the final link in the distribution chain. The problem is with those wearing the suits, that is the executives of several major banks and corporations, who must be included in our expanded list of narco-terrorists. The severity of the problem is made crystal clear when, you see First Global Bank, one of the largest banks in the United States and among the biggest in the world, appearing at the top of the list of most wanted narco-terrorists!"

As Nesmuth allowed the two men to study the map and digest all they had just heard, a long silence fell over the room, interrupted only by the sound of General Ben Lavan's tea cup crashing back into its saucer.

Sir Robert finally spoke, "I will certainly pass all of this along to the Prime Minister and assume General Ben Lavan will do the same at the top of the Israeli government. What should we do next?"

"After you both have passed on this information, and assuming we can all convince our governments that our survival is at stake, why don't we meet again in a few weeks to coordinate our response?

This cannot continue to be a lopsided fight between our nations' over-burdened law enforcement agencies and individuals with private mercenary armies or criminal organizations that have the full support of corrupt foreign governments, or, in fact, are actually part of those governments. The law enforcement agencies cannot possibly win. What we are engaged in is more like World War III. This law enforcement struggle must become elevated to the governments of the major industrialized nations versus those governments being controlled by the narco-terrorists. In other words, we must finally conduct a real world war against the drug cartels, not just a limited police action by a disjointed group of nations going through the motions. Our efforts must be further elevated from the realm of law enforcement to full fledged overt and covert military action.

Certainly, we will have to calm the very real fears of our countries' leaders about entering the realm of committing our armies, navies and air forces to military action, but the problem has become so life-threatening to the survival of our Nations that nothing less will have a chance. Constitutional safeguards and rights must override all else in normal situations, but the war launched against us by the narcoterrorists has already gone way beyond that. If they prevail, constitutional protections will cease to exist anyway."

While his two visitors slowly nodded their assent, both had lived with the realities of balancing their respective constitutions against the harsher realities of war with limited restrictions, and each realized that in this particular situation, finding the right compromise would be no easier than it had ever been. Both also realized that, once a certain line had been crossed, the governments of the free world would have to fight the narco-terrorists according to the rules of War, not the rules of Law.

General Lavan nodded his consent and spoke, "I'm sure I can speak for Sir Robert in saying, 'You can count on us, John.' Since a codename in this type of situation is best for use in future communications, why don't we call this 'Operation Snow Bird'?"

Sir Robert interjected his interpretation of the name, "White will symbolize the color of our enemy's weapon, cocaine, and the winged bird the desire to free ourselves of this poison."

It was more symbolic than the general had intended, and not exactly what he was thinking, but, for diplomacy's sake, he decided to agree with the analysis.

CHAPTER 3

AMAZON RIVER BASIN, PERU

After the ambush of the Shining Path guerrillas two days before, Lt. (jg.) Powers' fire team made its way eleven miles north along the winding, slimy banks of the Pastaza River to intercept and destroy the boat-load of coca base that would be making its way up the river the next morning.

During the initial phase of the production of cocaine, coca leaf harvested inside Peru was mixed with chemicals in laboratories located very close to the coca leaf fields themselves . This was accomplished using local residents who prepared the coca base by walking through the pasty mixture of coca leaf and chemicals and moving their feet up and down as firmly as possible, much like the process used in Italy and elsewhere to stomp up and down on grapes to produce wine. Unfortunately, the constant exposure to the chemicals resulted in serious damage to the exposed legs of those involved in the process, but this was considered a small price to pay for the riches the drug cartels accumulated by selling the end product of cocaine. Once the coca base had been prepared, it was shipped along the waterways in the Amazon River Basin to more sophisticated processing plants located inside Colombia, where other chemicals called "precursor chemicals" were added, and further refinement occured to create the white powder known as cocaine.

It took the men nearly three hours to reach their destination as the thick foliage and water-soaked muddy banks made the going extremely difficult and slow. Nobody spoke during the three hours, except for a brief electronic transmission to check the team's position by satellite. BM1 Smith, the radio operator, also radioed the report of the team reaching the site of the ambush to a SEAL Team Four support position located sixty miles away near the remote village of Los Ronias. The ambush position itself stood near the "S" shaped curve in the river, where the sharp curves, shallow water and narrowness of the river itself would cause the boat to slow to a virtual crawl. Powers and his men stopped and made a hasty camp. The men rested as much as they could, spending the night looking out over the murky, moonlit, quiet water. The tranquility was disturbed only by the hum of the ever-present swarms of insects that tested a man's sanity and the ripple of an occasional crocodile silently sliding down the river bank into the water, leaving a trail of rings on the water's surface that quickly dissipated into the darkness. The men, in turn, were being watched by a sixteen-foot spotted anaconda that slowly slithered along the overhanging branch of a nearby tree, his tongue flicking in and out, tasting the air for his next meal. Through the seemingly endless silence, now and then the men could hear violent splashing as a school of feeding piranha devoured some unsuspecting animal unfortunate enough to wander too far into the river for an evening drink.

Lt. (jg.) Powers could remember the "war stories" exchanged over several drinks with Vietnam War SEALs as they described ambushes in North Vietnam in remarkably similar terrain. He reflected back on a story he heard about a Navy SEAL who, while standing motionless in an ambush position, waist deep in a swamp, came face-to-face with a twenty-foot boa constrictor. The snake hung motionless from a branch, inches from the man's face, and, never changing position, the two stared into each others eyes for nearly sixteen hours. After the arrival of the eight NVA (North Vietnamese Army) soldiers, the targets of the ambush, the SEAL quickly wasted them with several bursts

45

from his M63-A1 Stoner machine gun, then, in the same motion, reached up and, grabbing the snake with his bare hands, broke its neck with one powerful twist.

Then there was the memorable confrontation where a SEAL, and two of his comrades were seriously wounded in an ambush attack. One was hit squarely in the chest with a .50 caliber machine-gun round and the other SEALs, receiving even more fatal wounds, went into shock. Despite the gaping hole in his chest, and the weakness brought on by blood loss, he managed to tow the two unconscious men three miles out to sea. Battling rough water and strong currents, through the darkness of the night he delivered himself and his two comrades to the safety of a waiting destroyer. As a result of his devotion to his fellow SEALs and his heroism, this Navy Chief Petty Officer received the Silver Star. Both stories had been told to Powers in the tradition of passing on the lore of the SEAL Team from generation to generation.

In his mind, Jeremy Powers always pictured his father, a former SEAL, as the SEAL depicted in the stories and if not, he knew that his father carried on the same values and strength of character these men had displayed. The young officer possessed great admiration for his father, who had been a major influence on the direction Jeremy took in his own life.

But the sudden splash of a crocodile entering the far shore of the Pastaza River reminded Powers of his mission. The fire team's pre-determined plan was relatively simple and would take advantage of recent technology developments in the field of acoustic mines. Numerous pre-armed acoustic mines would be planted along the Pastaza River in the area where the drug cartel's boats, filled with the cocoa paste, passed on a regular basis. There was little concern about destroying the boats of innocents, since Shining Path units, working closely with José Ocho Garriana (head of the Cardazanna Drug Cartel), had cleared the river for several miles of any normal boat traffic. This was done by hideously butchering more than a dozen Andean peasants who violated their orders and trespassed on the river. Even the search for enough food to sustain life was no excuse to disobey the rules set by the drug smugglers.

The mines would be placed by SEALs on the river bottom, and the sounds of a boat passing over them would trigger a release mechanism causing the mines to float up, stopping just below the surface. The next boat to pass over a particular spot, seemingly safe during the last transit, would then hit and detonate the mine. Other mines, similarly floated near the surface, would sink other ships at random times and locations along the river. When this happened, perhaps days or weeks later, the SEALs would not even be in-country. The mine technology had originally been developed for sinking Soviet warships sailing in open seas, as they traversed the world's oceans in repetitive patterns. While many expensive weapons systems developed for major wars had to be scrapped or set aside due to the end of the Cold War, acoustic mines and other technology could be readily adaptable to the type of covert action that Navy SEALs would embark on now and in the future. Jeremy Powers smiled to himself at the thought of these acoustic mines finding their way to this remote area of the Amazon and now being used to blow José Ocho Garriana's coca base-loaded boats into oblivion.

The four SEALs remained in their concealed positions until nightfall. Already set-up in a defensive position some twenty yards from the river, they remained motionless until the appointed hour of 1830 local time, (6:30 p.m. civilian time) at which point they were to enter the river and place the mines. The river's dangers did not escape the men's attention. It wasn't the fear as much as the reality that was on the men's mind. There were the flesh-eating fish. A school of piranha has been known to clean the meat off of a man's bones within minutes, leaving only his skeleton. Even if random chance allowed them to elude the piranha, there were still crocodiles. Of even greater concern to the SEALs in Powers' fire team, while not life threatening, were the large, black blood leaches prevalent in the area. The mere thought of these creatures latching on to you brought feelings of revulsion to the men. They seemed to appear from everywhere, attaching themselves to even the smallest area of exposed skin. The only way to remove them was to burn them off. Unfortunately, the hissing sound and smell of burnt flesh this caused might reveal a man's position. As bad as the leaches were, when you were close to a target area you had to suffer with them on your body as they weren't worth dying for.

The four men had come prepared for the dangers of the Amazon. They wore black neoprene wet suits and carried LAR V Drager self-contained breathing apparatuses. These oxygen re-breathers prevented any telltale sign of their presence by not generating bubbles or disturbing the natural ECO system. The neoprene suits would keep the loathsome leaches from attaching themselves to the men's skin, and for increased protection, the men wore their shirt sleeves rolled down and buttoned at the wrist, also buttoning them at the neck. While impossibly hot, the constant damp, gooey feeling was far more preferable than having something akin to a vampire sucking the blood out of you.

Two of the SEALs considered the most adept at swimming in these waters and placing the mines, dressed in the diving gear they each carried, while the other two set a defensive perimeter at each location to handle any uninvited guests, such as squads of Shining Path. Lt. (jg.) Powers knew the guerrillas could be expected, since Sendero Luminoso (Shining Path) always provided security for the Cardazanna Cartel's river operations. BM1 Smith and CPO Rogers had been assigned the diving duty. At each of the predetermined spots, approximately one half mile apart, the two divers silently entered the river, descended to the bottom, and worked in the blackened, slimy water. About a mile from the first location, back from the "S" curve in the river, the two other men, Lt. (jg.) Powers and MM2 Crane, crossed the river at a shallow point, wading in chest-high water.

"No wonder Garriana's boats only have 30" drafts," Powers thought to himself as he forged the dark river. Had the drafts been any larger, the boats would have continuously run aground on the slimy riverbank.

Powers pushed on, fighting to sublimate the fear of what was going on in the water around him. By placing himself on the opposite bank of the river with MM2 Crane on the near shore, both sides of the river were protected against surprise or ambush, allowing the divers to go about their delicate tasks uninterrupted. Only the mine at the "S" curve was initially placed near the surface. It would detonate upon first impact by the boat scheduled to carry the next shipment of cocoa base in the morning. The other six mines would be released to the surface by sound waves at different intervals, thus providing a randomly impossible pattern for Ocho Garriana's men to defend against. The second mine, for example, would not detonate until the fourth ship passed over it, allowing it to ascend to the surface, and so on. Since approximately one contraband boatload a week came up the river, the SEAL operation could shut down the initial transit of the cocaine to the processing plants in Colombia for several weeks, or months.

In a real war on drugs, any cartel boat that escaped the mines could be detected either by satellite or some form of remote motion sensing device and blown out of the water by a single 105 MM shell fired out of the rear of an airborne AC 130 gunship. These aircraft are flown by the Night Riders of the U.S. Special Operations Command.

The fear factor and unknown elements of the attack could add additional days to the down time. When measured against any standard the U.S. Government or U.S. Navy wished to apply, the cost effectiveness was enormous.

For a cost that did not exceed several tens of thousands of dollars, hundreds of millions, perhaps billions of dollars of cocaine would be prohibited from reaching its ultimate destination. In the future, the billions spent on weapons, such as submarines and aircraft carriers, with dubious results in the post Cold War era, would have to be measured against the considerably lower cost of covert actions of this type, conducted against a real versus imagined enemy.

Hours later, the 170 foot "Ocho Gar", named after the Colombian drug kingpin himself, with its cargo hole fully loaded with coca base, the crew, and two dozen of Ocho Garriana's best hand-picked security men, approached the "S" curve. Suddenly, the normal sounds and songs of the river basin were interrupted by an explosion that could be heard 20 miles away, as it echoed through the jungle.

From this point forward, this type of covert mission would increasingly be utilized by the government of the United States in the on-going war against drugs. It appeared to those at the top who call the shots, that this was one of the only tactics that could truly get to the heart of the matter and deliver tangible results. Veiled threats against the cartels, diplomatic pressure against the governments involved, and random arrests of relatively low-level participants such as the human "mules" who transported the illicit drugs, all seemed to be getting nowhere.

Finally, the resounding echos of the mines' explosions were carried to the "powers that be" in the drug cartels, along with the clear message that things were getting serious. At the exact moment of the sinking of the "Ocho Gar", the men of Lt. (jg.) Jeremy Powers' fire team were enjoying the clear blue skies of a new day, well on their way out of the country. "Plausible denial" remained a key element of every highly classified SEAL Team operation.

How could the Navy SEALs have been responsible if "officially" they were not even in the area, or the country for that matter?

CHAPTER 4

WASHINGTON, D.C.

The daily meeting of the President's National Security Council (NSC) had only one major agenda item outside of the normal review of the national security issues confronting the United States around the world. Present at the meeting would be the President, the Secretaries of Defense and State, the National Security Advisor, and the Directors of the FBI and CIA.

The meeting was held in a highly secure conference room located just a few steps down the hall from the Oval office. There was to be a general review of U.S. policy towards Latin America, largely due to major expansion of the violent shining Path Guerrilla movement in Peru, and an evaluation of policy options in Peru itself. No longer just a threat to the outlying Indian peasant communities, the insurgency had spread from the Andean Highlands and Amazon Basin throughout the countryside, and was now threatening to engulf the major population centers including Lima, home to nearly one-fifth of the country's citizens. The ongoing confluence of issues that always seemed to affect U.S. foreign policy was present in spades, as were several new elements. While this remote spate of intense violence was not understood by many, its rapid escalation contained frightening implications for the United States and other countries that were not yet prepared for the inhumanity of Shining Path's violent Marxist ideology.

The meeting began at precisely 9:30 am with a briefing by the Under Secretary of State for Latin American Affairs, Jane Greenhouse. She had been introduced by her boss,

Secretary of State Randolph Johnson. Next to her was a three-dimensional map showing the individual countries of Lation America.

"Before we begin, I have had a copy of a document entitled 'Peru's Brutal Insurgence: Sendero Luminoso' given to each one of you. This document is top secret and was prepared by the Assistant Secretary for Inter-American Affairs, as his statement before the Subcommittee on Western Hemisphere Affairs of the House Foreign Affairs Committee on March 12, 1992. It outlines the atrocities being perpetrated against the Peruvian citizenry and foreign visitors by Shining Path. I ask that you read it now," said Greenhouse.

An envelope was handed to each attendee, silence filled the room as the documents were read, and Greenhouse returned to her seat.

The document partially read: *"Sendero Luminoso's Aims and Activities". Sendero Luminoso is unlike any other insurgent or terrorist group that has ever operated in Latin America. Put out of your mind the FML (Farabundo Marti National Liberation Front) of El Ssalvador which just signed a peace agreement, the Sandinistas in Nicaragua who allowed themselves to be voted out of office, the M-19 of Colombia, and other South American insurgencies that have ended their violent struggles to take advantage of the political space open to the peaceful, democratic left. Sendero Luminoso is in a category by itself.*

There are other communist insurgencies, but only Sendero saw the fall of Eastern European communist governments as a positive step where the people overthrew decadent, bourgeois communism; Sendero bombed the North Korean commercial office in Lima and believes Fidel Castro is a U.S. lackey. Latin America has seen violence and terror but none like Sendero's, where children are forced to commit acts of brutality as part of their in-doctrination and where entire towns are forced to witness the so-called trial, torture, and killing of nums or municipal leaders. Latin America has seen many variations of the

52

Marxist vision but none so sweeping as Sendero's war against "Western culture." A Sendero victory would compare not to Cuba under Castro or Nicaragua under the Sandinistas but to Cambodia under Pol Pot. In the words of (Sendero's leader) Abimael Guzman,

'We start from a principle established by Chairman Mao: violence is a universal law with no exception...without revolutionary violence we cannot replace one class for another...'

The revolution will triumph, according to Guzman, after the Peruvian people 'cross over the river of blood' to the other side.

Make no mistake: If Sendero were to take power, we would see this century's third genocide. Luis Arce Borja, Sendero's representative in Europe, told a Lima newspaper last November that the current stage of the war—'strategic equilibrium',—will cost 1 million Peruvian lives.

Sendero began its armed campaign in 1981 just as Peru returned to democratic government. It is a movement of the 'unreconstructed' Peruvian left born in protest against Peru's return to democracy. When most of Peru's left decided to re-enter the democratic process, a small, fringe, university-based Marxist elite cried 'treason' and evolved into Sendero Luminoso.

Its founders, especially the undisputed leader Abimael Guzman, also known as Chairman Gonzalo, were deeply influenced by Chinese communism during the Cultural Revolution and brought a strong Maoist orientation to Sendero, hence the strategy of a rural, peasant-based movement that hopes to capture the cities as its final objective.

Sendero takes advantage of two factors unique to Peru. In its ideology, it plays on the sharp division of Peruvian society between white descendants of the Spaniards, the mestizos, and the rural indigenous Indian population, much of which speaks only Quechua, the language of the Incas. In its finances, it profits from Peru's key role in cocaine production. We do not believe that Sendero receives significant material or financial support from foreign governments or revolutionary movements, but it

53

*does raise funds from gullible publics in Europe. Roughly esti-
mated, we believe Sendero has 3,000-5,000 full-time armed fighters and up to twice that many part-time militia. Including political cadre of various types, Sendero may be able to count on as
many as 25,000 supporters. In addition, 15%-20% of Peru's
population lives in 'pink' or 'red' zones under significant or pre-
dominant Sendero influence. Some of these citizens provide support out of intimidation and fear.*

*In response to the combined threat of Sendero and the Tupac
Amaru (MRTA) guerrillas, about one-third of Peru's 183 prov-
inces and nearly half of its people have been placed under 'emergency zones' where civilian rule is suspended and the local military commander is effectively in charge of government and security.*

*Sendero knows that in the past 2 decades, the expansion of
participatory democracy in Latin America has delegitimized revolutionary movements. From El Salvador to Chile, violent revolutionaries lost their raison d'etre as democracy grew and citizens gained a real role in governing their own affairs.*

*Sendero's strategy, then, is to use violence to destroy demo-
cratic institutions, to stop citizens from participating in local
government, to destroy the functioning economy, and to cripple
programs which provide aid and services to the population. This
form of terror often succeeds. Mayors and municipal leaders
refuse to run—or take office—because not only will they be targeted by Sendero, but their families and the entire community
will be subject to Sendero's terror. Sendero's intimidation caused
a round of municipal elections scheduled for 1989 to be delayed
until 1991. When the balloting was held last August, guerrilla
intimidation prevented candidates from running on 104 towns.
Overall, elections had to be annulled in 220 out of 498 jurisdic-
tions because either no candidate ran, the winner resigned after
being elected, or too few people cast ballots.*

*In Sendero's mind, any Peruvian or any foreigner who takes
up the democratic cause, tries to ease human suffering, or resists
terrorist threats is hampering the development of revolutionary*

54

consciousness and delaying the day when the people will turn to armed revolt. That makes them targets for terror:

- *Last May 18, Sendero terrorists publicly shot to death an Australian nun, Sister Irene McCormick, of the Catholic relief organization Caritas, who worked to help the poorest of Peru's poor in the Junin region. Her body was left lying where it fell for 24 hours on orders from Sendero.*

- *Sendero has bombed Catholic and Baptist churches and murdered religious workers. On August 22, 1990, Sendero killed two young Baptist missionaries in Junin, one with a knife thrust through his neck.*

- *Norman Tattersall, a Canadian working in Lima with the Protestant social services organization World Vision, lost his life in a Sendero attack last May 17, as did his Colombian associate José Chuquin.*

- *In January 1990, a Sendero group, mostly of children under 16, shot two French tourists they took off a bus passing through a rural area. The youngest member of the group was made to beat one of the victim's skulls with a large rock until it was completely crushed.*

- *Two other tourists were taken off a bus, tortured, and shot in November 1989. In this killing, Sendero slashed a young woman's chest and stomach so badly that it had to be bound to hold in its internal organs before she could be moved.*

- *Sendero killed two Polish and one Italian priest who worked with poor children in Ancash department last August.*

- *Last July 12, Sendero murdered three Japanese development workers near Huaral. The Japanese have withdrawn most of their aid workers in response to this and other attacks.*

- *On February 15, Maria Elena Moyano, Vice Mayor of Lima's largest shanty town of Villa El Salvador, was leaving a neighborhood barbecue party with her family. She had met Senator (Mark) Hatfield and Assistant Secretary of State for Human Rights Richard Shifter in Lima last fall. She bravely, vocally, and actively resisted Sendero terror, even after they bombed the local community food warehouse. Sendero assassins shot her point-blank then threw a dynamite charge that scattered pieces of her body over 100 yards away.*

- *Juana Lopez directed the Glass of Milk feeding program in Callao, north of Lima. Sendero killed her and others last fall in attacks against food distribution and emergency aid projects.*

- *Andres Davila Arnao organized a local self-defense force to protect his neighborhood against Sendero brutality. He was killed February 17 just outside of Lima.*

- *A Catholic priest from the Ayacucho area told of ritual murders of peasants who refused to cooperate with or tried to escape from Sendero during its early years of terror. After so-called people's trail, victims were stripped and tied to a post in the town square. Every person in the town—men, women, and children—was forced to cut a piece of flesh from the living body. The Sendero torture went on for as long as an hour before victims died from shock and loss of blood.*

- *Peruvian police found the body of a fellow officer in the summer of 1989, completely eviscerated and filled with human feces — Sendero's work.*

- *Sendero assassins machine-gunned the mayor of one small town, then set off a dynamite charge in his lap, while they forced his wife and four children to watch.*
- *Sendero's campaign against Peru's Ashaninka Indians in 1990 and 1991 was terrifying in its brutality: A 14-year-old stuck in the head with a machete, shot, stabbed, and dumped in a river; victims doused in gasoline and set afire; children forced to eat their parent's tongues.*

- *A November 1991 Sendero attack on a village near Ayacucho left 37 dead, including 9 children.*

- *Since 1980, Sendero has killed 42 Peruvians working with U.S. Government development projects.*

On February 14 Sendero climaxed a bombing campaign against government offices, banks, diplomatic missions—including U.S. Ambassador Quainton's residence, where a bomb killed three Peruvian policemen and severely damaged a security wall—and other targets with an 'armed strike' in Lima. Armed strikes are a long-standing Sendero tactic in which the guerrillas seek to enforce compliance with the strike through waves of killings against those who dare to go to work. Despite numerous bombings in last month's strike, Lima citizens tried bravely to go about their business.

This past decade of violence has cost Peru 24,000 lives and about $20 billion in economic damage—about 1 year's GNP." [*]

After all of the attendees, visibly shaken, some ashen, had looked up signifying completion of the document Under Secretary Greenhouse stood up, walked to the front of the room and continued, alternately moving a long pointer around on the map. To get a feel for their response, she

[*] Excerpts from actual testimony given to the U.S. Senate Sub-Committee on Latin American affairs.

periodically looked over at the President and around the room studying the faces of the others present. The general feeling of moral and emotional outrage was obvious by the look of horror in their eyes. The President concentrated intensely on what Jane Greenhouse had to say next.

"As you can see from the area of Peru covered in red, Shining Path has considerably extended its area of control within the country. It now occupies approximately sixty percent of the land area and controls nearly fifty percent of the population. For any of you not quite up to speed on this, Shining Path is a hard-line Marxist organization dedicated to the violent overthrow, not only of the Peruvian Government, but any government in the hemisphere that gets in the way of its aspirations. That would include about every country in Latin America. There is a definite immediate threat to contiguous countries including Bolivia, Colombia and Ecuador. Ultimately, even Venezuela, Argentina and Brazil would all be in mortal peril. At some point in that scenario, the direct threat to the United States becomes unmistakable.

While this session is primarily centered around Sendero, and we only briefly mention Tupac Amaru, we must also monitor the activities of that group as well. They are the pro-Castro communist organization." (They had not yet attained the notoriety of the Shining Path, but at the end of 1996 their fame spread when they occupied the Japanese Ambassador's residence in Lima during a party. They held hundreds of hostages and demanded the release of hundreds of their jailed comrades).

After she finished, Under Secretary of Defense for National Security Affairs, Max Palmer, followed her to the map.

"Ladies and Gentlemen, there are other serious dimensions to this. The guerrillas are providing much of the armed security for the Colombian drug lords who acquire cocoa leaf in Peru and Bolivia. As far as we can tell, the two groups have almost merged and become one. It's like facing an army of fanatics armed with guns and cocaine. It is very clear to us that one or more of the Colombian drug cartels is financing the movement and providing it with the absolute latest in weapons and technology from around the world. Shining Path's tentacles reach to the far corners of the world and it has sent agents to foment revolution and support its cause in Asia, Europe and here in the United States itself."

The President asked for a clear statement of the possible threat to America's national security interests which Palmer answered as directly as he could.

"Sir, we could talk about the immorality of the illegal overthrow of democratically elected governments and all of that, but we all understand the controversy that always starts, particularly in Latin America. For once, we could just be forthright and direct with the American people. Imagine what could happen if seventy percent of the world's cocaine supply fell into the hands of an illegally installed Marxist government whose number one policy issue is the violent overthrow of all democratically elected governments, including that of the United States? Imagine further that the primary methods employed by that government were a widespread policy of genocide more inhumane and brutal than those of even Hitler, Stalin and Pol Pot."

The clarity with which Under Secretary Palmer answered the question and defined the threat to the United States shook everyone into a sense of terrible reality.

The discussion continued for another hour, before the NSC meeting was adjourned. All who attended left with the clear priority that these atrocities and the immediacy of the threat to the delicate balance of power throughout the world, must be stopped. The fear of the exploding power of the drug cartels, along with vivid pictures of the brutality, stayed in their minds, and caused many sleepless nights. Having gone from the abstract of normal diplomacy to the absolute horror of this threat, nobody present could remain in denial about any dimension of this problem. In this situation, at least, issues were being presented in far less abstract and far more vivid ways to avoid much of the ambiguity that seemed to characterize U.S. foreign policy in the present day.

CHAPTER 5

CARDAZANNA, COLOMBIA

José Ocho Garriana, the leader of the Cardazanna Drug Car tel, paced back and forth across the length of his study. His palatial 26-room estate was located in the remote highlands, seventeen miles outside the center of the modern skyline of the city of Cardazanna. Ocho Garriana, a handsome, olive skinned man of 48, presided over a worldwide network of cocaine trafficking that brought the Garriana Cartel profits of more than $75 billion dollars a year. Ocho Garriana had started 26 years before as a contract killer for the Rio Orsála family in his hometown of Valendella, Colombia. He won high marks for the vicious brutality with which he dispatched his hapless victims, no questions asked. All of the names were simply given to him by Andreas Rio Orsála and his injustice was meted out quickly, usually within 24 to 48 hours.

In order to make examples to prevent further slights, real or imagined, against the drug lord's family, the killings were ritualistically bestial. Torture, beheadings, gouging out eyes and sawing off limbs were all common practice. Finally, not content in the role of a henchman, Ocho Garriana murdered the Rio Orsála brothers, their wives, children, top advisors and bodyguards and took over the cartel some seventeen years earlier, in 1975.

His meteoric rise since that time knew no bounds. He became ever more brutal as he climbed each rung of the ladder until he reached the pinnacle of his chosen profession. *Forbes* magazine had recently listed him as the sixth wealthiest man in the world with a personal net worth estimated to be between six and seven billion dollars. Colombian intelligence files indicated he had been directly responsible for more than 450 deaths and had played an indirect role in nearly 500 others. Once he had blown-up a cruise ship with 215 innocent passengers aboard. Those who were not killed instantly by the blast, were lost in shark infested waters. All of this to get at just one man who had become an enemy, and who ironically had escaped the attack by unexpectedly leaving the ship at a previous port. There was no reaction by Ocho Garriana, other than "next time", when news of the "miss" was conveyed to him. He then turned and shot the man through the head who had brought the news of the failed mission to him, handing his pistol to an underling next to him before leaving for the opera with his wife. As he left, he wiped the splatterings of his victim's blood his off his tuxedo with a white silk handkerchief.

The CIA also had a very thick file on José Ocho Garriana. He had a bewildering array of visitors. Emissaries of Shining Path, Tupac Amaru, and FARC (Revolutionary Armed Forces of Colombia) visited him at his estate weekly. The IRA sent Brendon O'Toole, one of their chief foreign operatives. The PLO sent Omar El Khalil, number three to Chairman Arafat himself. Most distressingly, several members of the KGB and other East Block intelligence services were also frequent guests at the house. Syrian, Iranian and Libyan intelligence agents dropped by. The term "Narco-terrorism" had recently been developed inside the U.S. Intelligence apparatus to label the cocaine assaults against the United States, and its infiltration into America's commercial and political institutions. Their goal of disrupting much of the U.S.' infrastructure, was now considered the most dangerous form of terrorism within America's intelligence community, and Ocho Garriana its most violent and dedicated practitioner.

Ocho Garriana's trusted Lieutenant, Juan Espinoza, sat silently watching his boss' every step, fearing the news he had delivered was about to set-off an uncontrollable rage that could result in Espinoza's own death. Espinoza was hardly the suave, debonair drug dealer portrayed in the movies. Standing only 5'7", and weighing more than 250 pounds, Espinoza waddled like a duck. Due to his massive weight, the expending of even the slightest bit of energy caused him to sweat profusely, making it less than pleasant to be within 10 feet of him. Even his closest and most trustworthy henchmen, who knew better than to offend him, tried to avoid any type of close contact. An extremely violent man, he had personally murdered more than 150 victims, most hacked to pieces with a machete. Espinoza enjoyed making his victims suffer for as long as possible before loss of blood mercifully brought on death. His enjoyment was displayed by his chilling laughter, as each stroke of his machete separated another portion of a human's body from its torso. His sadistic humor was brought out with one of his favorite games. He would bet with his men on how long a man, or woman, or child, could stay alive while having portions of their bodies hacked off while hanging upside down by their feet from a beam or a tree limb.

"What the fuck happened to my boat!!?" Ocho Garriana screamed at the top of his voice.

"The Yonkees sunk it with a mine, boss." Espinoza's voice went up an octave reflecting his fear. The high pitched squeal could have been a Freudian anticipation of being castrated by the even more violent and sadistic Ocho Garriana.

"How in the hell did they know where and when to hit!!?" Ocho Garriana's anger became increasingly intense, aggravated by the obvious fear shown by the man sitting in front of him. Any display of weakness inevitably enraged the man even more. It was the classic "no win" situation.

"We don't know boss. We eliminated anyone who knew anything about the schedule before the boat left." The fat man was sweating profusely, and kept dabbing at his face with an already wet handkerchief.

"Go get me one of the secure phones and get out of my sight before I conclude that *you* are the piece of shit with the big mouth."

Espinoza quickly left the room and returned less than three minutes later, carrying a metal clad carrying case about the size of a large, thick briefcase. Ocho Garriana took the case, unsnapped the metal buckles and opened it. Inside was the latest in scrambler telephones from the KGB communications laboratory outside St. Petersburg, Russia. It had been given to "El Patron" by Lt. Col. Oleg Kamanoski, a senior operative in the service of the KGB who worked out of the Soviet Embassy in Cardazanna. While not even America's NSA (National Security Agency) satellites could intercept its signals, Ocho Garriana knew that surveillance satellites could certainly pick up ship movements all along the Amazon River Basin. He dialed in the six digit code that would connect him directly with Col. Kamanoski. He immediately recognized the Colonel's voice on the phone.

"Good evening, Colonel, this is José Ocho Garriana." Since both assumed their conversation was not being monitored, neither coded words, encrypted messages or aliases were used.

"Ah, my good friend the banker. How are you this evening?", was Oleg Kamanoski's greeting, with hardly a trace of an accent. He could, and in fact had on many occasions, pass for an English country gentleman.

"Not so good. The American pigs sank another boatload of Gringo medication," Ocho Garriana sadly responded.

Col. Kamanoski, an ideological zealot, winced when he realized the repercussions. Several hundred new addicts, the resulting street violence, crime and increasing damage to American institutions such as its banking system had been delayed. Col. Kamanoski's tone became serious...

"The Americans have a naval unit called SEALs who operate in and around water. We also happened to be listening while one of the psychotic warmongers in the Pentagon bragged about a recent operation. It definitely was a group of these SEALs. I say that because our Speznatz commandos' instruction is patterned after theirs and covers training for many of the same missions".

"I must make an example to ensure that this never happens again. How can I find out who the responsible individuals were and where to find them?" Ocho Garriana's tone was ominous.

Col. Kamanoski reassured him, "Do not worry yourself, my friend. I know exactly how to get the information we need. We will get the Americans who did this wherever and however necessary."

"I leave it in your hands." Ocho Garriana's mind had been put at ease. This was one problem that was going to be resolved, and resolved soon. "Good night, Colonel, and I expect to hear from you soon."

Both phones went dead as one hang-up click followed closely behind the other.

Col. Kamanoski immediately sent out the following highly classified message to his lengthy list of KGB posts at Soviet embassies worldwide and to all of his intelligence services around the world. The message was encrypted and sent via the most secure electronics emission frequencies available:

TO: ALL KGB POSTS
         ALLIED SECURITY SERVICES

FROM: COLONEL OLEG KAMANOSKI, KGB
         CARDAZANNA, COLOMBIA.

URGENT RECEIVE ANY INFORMATION INTERCEPTED REGARDING U.S. NAVY SEAL OPERATION, HUALLAGA REGION, PERU, ON OR AROUND AMAZON RIVER, 3 JULY, 1992. NOTIFY ME MOST RAPID MEANS AVAILABLE. IMPERATIVE TO ASSIST ALLIES IN FIGHT AGAINST IMPERIALISM.

CHAPTER 6

PARIS, FRANCE
SEPTEMBER, 1992

1462 Rue de La Cheval looked like most of the other buildings in the modern industrial section located seventeen miles West of Charles De Gaulle Airport. It was relatively non-descript, low slung, with a faded white brick exterior. The antennas on top of the building appeared to be little different from those similarly situated atop the adjacent buildings, although there seemed to be more of them. Relatively glassless, with a main entrance at the front, a loading dock against one side and an emergency exit door to the rear, there appeared to be no other way in or out. A sign in the front identified the facility as The Désparit Electronics Corporation. Other than highly placed officials of the French Intelligence Service, few realized that 1462 Rue de La Cheval was, in fact, the top secret headquarters of France's Electronics Intercept Service which is a division of France's CIA. It was the equivalent of America's National Security Agency, the most secret of all U.S. intelligence operations.

France's CIA was referred to as Le Sedec. No electronic emission escaped the detection of their Electronics Intercept Service. Every phone call in or out of France was monitored. So were phone calls inside the country between all persons working at the various embassies located within France. Even top secret encrypted messages sent into or out of the country by U.S. intelligence services did not escape the Agency's ever vigilant surveillance. While the United States used every means possible to avoid detection of its most secret messages by obvious enemies such as the Soviet Union, why should it be suspicious of a longtime ally and fellow NATO partner?

This bit of naiveté by U.S. intelligence agencies proved to be disastrous for Lt. (jg.) Jeremy Powers. Unlike any other major power on earth, the French government has simultaneously been both friend and foe to most countries for decades. This hypocritical, self-serving foreign policy enables France to prosper financially, especially through arms sales—often to both sides of the same conflict.

The French government's willingness to collaborate with the Nazis during World War II, especially concerning their ambiguous stance toward their own citizens of Jewish descent, was a constant reminder of the duality of its agenda. The iron hand with which the government enforced its Nation's policies in former colonies, such as Algeria, was yet another.

French Legionnaires, operating under classified orders from the very top of their government, had no equal among the West's counter-terrorist operations in terms of the viciousness with which they engaged France's enemies. They truly operated under the credo of "an eye for an eye." Entire villages were burned to the ground, whole families were butchered and anyone perceived, correctly or not, as having helped the country's enemies were slaughtered without pity. Even France's staunchest allies recoiled in horror at the moral duplicity with which the country pursued its foreign policy objectives.

Inside the intelligence agency's building, the constant low level din of the seemingly endless array of computers and almost infinite variety of futuristic looking electronics equipment could barely be heard above the sound of the air conditioning. Technicians scurried about, tearing off pieces of paper, moving from one screen to another and always avoiding conversation. Any distraction could mean missing some bit or piece of information that could prove harmful to the nation. Personal vigilance must occur around the clock to protect the country against all enemies, real or imagined. So anxious were the employees to win favor with their superiors, that they competed amongst themselves to deliver some tidbit of information manually before the giant computers that analyzed the data on an ongoing basis delivered the results.

Jacques Broughes, a youngish looking man in his thirties, was scanning a printout of intercepts of top secret transmissions between the Pentagon and the United States NATO military command, located in the Paris suburb of Dormand. While appearing relatively innocuous, Broughes was a paid informant of the Syrians. Although Broughes' superiors had an inkling of his pro-Arab sympathies, they really didn't care. France had for decades been a major trading partner to many countries in the Middle East, and French companies had recently secured a handful of multi-billion dollar contracts with the Syrian Government. Since French commercial interests overrode the nation's rather fluid and self-serving ideological concerns, why wouldn't they want to occasionally pass along helpful classified information to trading partners and allies such as the Syrians?

Syria, as a major backer of the violent forays of Middle East terrorist organizations, also might recognize France's assistance to their cause and continue to leave French citizens alone. It had long been rumored in Western intelligence circles that France looks the other way as terrorist murderers transited its soil, coming and going from attacks against citizens of other Western countries.

Broughes was compensated to automatically pass along to the Syrians anything classified "TOP SECRET FLASH", the highest level security classification of any messages. As Broughes continued to fix his gaze on the screen, messages translated in real time from electronic intercepts scrolled by. The first top secret flash message of the day came across the screen. It was logged in at 6:20 a.m., Paris time. It had been extrapolated from military euphemism to more standard language:

TO: ALL MILITARY AREA COMMANDS

FROM: JOINT CHIEFS OF STAFF

SECURITY ALERT

ALL COMMANDS ORDERED TO HIGHEST LEVEL SE-
CURITY IN ANTICIPATION OF POSSIBLE RETALIATION
FROM SENDERO GUERRILLAS AND CARDAZANNA DRUG
CARTEL FOR SEAL TEAM OPERATION AGAINST BOAT
LOAD OF COCOA BASE ON AMAZON RIVER. SINKING OF
SHIP COST CARTEL $250 MILLION IN LOSSES. SEAL TEAM
FOUR OP LED BY LT (JG) JEREMY POWERS MET WITH OUT-
STANDING SUCCESS. SENDERO GUERRILLAS HAVE APPA-
RATUS. TO STRIKE U.S. TARGETS ANYWHERE IN EUROPE,
LATIN AND CENTRAL AMERICA, CONTINENTAL U.S.,
MIDDLE EAST, SOUTH AND CENTRAL ASIA. FEW AREAS
SAFE. SENDERO ALLIED WITH EXTREMES OF VIOLENT TER-
RORIST ORGANIZATIONS.

SIGNED:
CHAIRMAN, JCS

Jacques Broughes printed a hard copy of the message and
proceeded to an encryption machine located only a few steps
away. He took a small key from his pocket, unlocked the machine, which looked like a cross between an old fashioned type-
writer and a stenography machine. Broughes pulled out the card
containing the matrix of that day's encryption characters, and
carefully entered the letters representing the cryptography sym-
bols as he read from the message. The message was received at
the headquarters of Syrian Intelligence in Damascus and trans-
mitted almost simultaneously to KGB Headquarters in Moscow.
Within two minutes the message was on the desk of Colonel
Oleg Kamanoski in Cardazanna.

CHAPTER 7

THE SOVIET EMBASSY
CARDAZANNA, COLOMBIA

Colonel Oleg Kamanoski could hardly contain himself. Only the vanity of the Americans would permit a security lapse of this magnitude. Anyone responsible for a breach like this within the KGB or any part of Russian intelligence would be summarily executed. Making public the name of any Russian soldier involved with a classified mission or secret unit was automatically punishable by death.

Hollywood and the news media were providing a forum even for American intelligence to make their positions known to the American public. Long the exclusive reserve of American politicians, the media was now becomming a public forum, even for classified matters of the most sensitive kind. This had resulted in more and more security lapses, even causing the deaths of American military personnel and intelligence operatives.

Colonel Kamanoski picked up his scrambler phone and punched in the six digit code that would connect him to José Ocho Garriana. The man answered immediately.

"Good evening José Ocho Garriana. Is the banking business any better?"

"Not really, we must avenge the losses."

"I have some information that should help you. Can we get together?"

"When?"

"Now. Can you pick me up in about 10 minutes at the usual place?"

Ocho Garriana could hardly contain his joy. Revenge was just around the corner. "Of course!" Both men hung up, trying to minimize every second that could delay the meeting.

Ocho Garriana pressed the intercom button in his study and when the green light went on began to speak, "Pull up the car now. We must go to meet Col. Kamanoski at the appointed place. I will be down in two minutes."

The man pressed another button and the green light went off, indicating the transmission has been completed. He got up from his chair. As he did so, his two personal bodyguards, Manuel Garcia and Jorgé Echuera, politely entered the room, each taking his appointed place on one side of the door. Ocho Garriana put on his white linen jacket, sunglasses, and placed his beige Panama hat on his head. He was dressed in white shoes, white slacks and a pale yellow shirt tucked into the pants. A white belt circled around his waist, a silver handled, engraved, Walther PPK 9mm automatic tucked into the belt on his right hip. The inscription, "To His Magnificence, El Patron," and signed by José Rodriguez Guttierez, the President of Colombia, appeared on the handle.

Neither of the two bodyguards fit any particular stereotype with the exception that each man was over six feet tall, broad shouldered and both obviously were bodybuilders. Both had been Colombian Naval Commandos before joining the Ocho Garriana organization, and each had come from one of the country's finest families. The only rationalization for their joining the cut throat world of Ocho Garriana was their hunger for something neither their social standing or money could buy. That was the power that only fear brings. It was an addiction all its own, not brought on by the cocaine itself, but by the infinite power, excitement, intrigue and danger that characterized it. The process of rationalization had to also be strong enough to overcome the resistance to commiting almost every crime known to the civilized world, particularly in this situation, where murder and ritualisitic executions were commonplace. In the case of Manuel Garcia and Jorgé Echuera, they satisfied themselves with the fact that they were only defending the great man, not committing murder in his name.

Manuel Garcia, a former member of Colombia's Olympic weight lifting team before joining the Colombian military, stood 6'1", weighed nearly 220 pounds, had dark skin, and long shiny black hair pulled into a ponytail. Standing to the left of Ocho Garriana, he wore white slacks and a short sleeved Hawaiian shirt in a red, yellow and blue pattern. Jorgé Echuera was very tall for a Latin at 6'5" and weighed nearly 250 pounds. He wore tan slacks and a green short sleeved Polo shirt. The man's bulk forced the shirt to stretch around his enormous, bulging upper arms. He had close cropped brown hair and wore dark sunglasses. Echuera walked to the right of Ocho Garriana.

Both men were highly trained in the martial arts, expert marksmen, demolition specialists and licensed pilots. Each had become expert in the use of numerous types of weapons. Only U.S. Navy SEALs, British SAS units or similar organizations would be a match for them. Normal State or Federal police units wouldn't stand a chance.

Despite Western Intelligence's denial, Ocho Garriana had the connections to purchase, through the "backdoor", any weapon and much of the security technology, including the latest in frequency hopping, spread spectrum communications equipment, produced anywhere in the world. Both men carried an HK MP5 submachine gun and had Sig Sauer 9mm automatic pistols tucked into their belts. The bodyguards, wearing their shirts outside their belts, had tucked several extra clips for the submachine guns into the military belts encircling their waists. The military style belts were the major indication that the two men's primary responsibility was security. As they walked down the hall towards the front door, they were joined by four other body-

71

guards. Two walked in front of Ocho Garriana and two behind him, the formation moving with all of the precision of a well drilled military squad. Luis Echoverra and Pablo Luis Gonzales walked to the front. Guillermo Cruz and Gabriel Sanchez followed in the rear. The four men looked like the first two and were dressed and armed in much the same way. Heavy fire power, including anti-tank weapons, were available with backup units only a cellular phone call or high frequency radio transmission away.

As the first two men reached the front door, everyone else stopped as it was opened. Outside, four men stood on each side of the front walk facing to the outside, looking for any sign of trouble. Every man knew that part of his job was to take any bullet intended for the top man himself. At the end of this phalanx of bodyguards, Ocho Garriana's Chief Lieutenant, Juan Espinoza, sat inside the back of the white limousine and discreetly held the door open for his boss. Two helicopters patrolled overhead as they crisscrossed the area looking both in the air around them and down at the ground for any potentially dangerous interlopers. These were not merely commercial helicopters, but were the latest in U.S. military cobra gunships acquired from the Colombian Army, each complete with a 50 calibre machine-gun on the aircraft's left side.

The man began to walk briskly towards the car as he saw the back door open. The limousine itself was a fortress. Built in the Federal Republic of Germany by the Daimler-Benz Corporation that produced the Mercedes Benz automobile, the car was specially fitted with tons of armor-plated steel, and bulletproof glass with fire ports that could accommodate up to six automatic weapons. Neither the President of the United States nor the Pope had anything close to this. Besides the driver, one man sat in the front, two in the rear facing the back seat and a fifth man followed Ocho Garriana into the car and occupied the place to the left of him. Juan Espinoza sat to the right. An identical car with six bodyguards waited in front of Ocho Garriana's limousine and a third to the rear. Eight motorcycles, identical to those used by Colombia's national police, waited outside the curved driveway to pull up in front of the caravan and eight more were to pull up to the rear. Four more helicopters joined the first two. In all, Ocho Garriana's normal compliment of protection consisted of six military aircraft, sixteen motorcycles and three armored limousines. At least fifty highly trained bodyguards protected the man at all times. Backup units mirroring the primary security groups were located less than two miles away. They were on standby for any offensive or diversionary tactics that might be necessary.

As the caravan proceeded left onto the main highway leading to the appointed meeting place, Ocho Garriana leaned back in the cushioned comfort of his seat feeling untouchable. He had built a protective wall around himself that put him well beyond the reach of anyone or anything that might jeopardize not only his life, but his position of being one of, if not the most, powerful and influential men in the world. He was protected from the inside by the best trained, most loyal men he could find, all of whom would gladly die for him, as many had in the past. In evaluating his climb to power he felt his greatest satisfaction and accomplishment was obtaining external protection that included the highest levels of the U.S. government, a fact that was unknown to the rest of the world, with the exception of only five other living human beings.

As the caravan sped along at 65 miles per hour, it came to a "Y" intersection in the road. All of the motorcycles and cars went to the left, as a diversionary tactic, while Ocho Garriana's car alone went to the right. Exactly 3.7 miles ahead, the limousine came to a screeching halt.

Col. Oleg Kamanoski stood leaning against the white Russian embassy limousine, tapping a cigarette against a sterling silver cigarette case. He was protected by six hulk-

73

ing KGB guards. As Ocho Garriana got out of his car, carrying a briefcase handed to him by Juan Espinoza, he walked towards the Colonel. Together, his seven bodyguards and the six KGB men fanned out in a circle around the two cars, no more than fifteen to twenty yards away. Col. Kamanoski was dressed in the same style as Ocho Garriana, although he had on blue slacks, a white Polo shirt, wore sunglasses and had no hat.

Ocho Garriana put the briefcase down next to him. "So, Colonel, what do you have for me?"

"Nothing much, just the name and location of the American who commanded the naval operation against your boat." Reveling in what he had accomplished, Col. Kamanoski put the cigarette in his mouth and lit it with an expensive, solid gold lighter. He angled his head back as he blew out the first puffs of smoke.

"And who is this pig?!" shouted Ocho Garriana, momentarily losing the cold emotional neutrality for which he had become famous. Ocho Garriana would make love to his wife in the same tone of voice he used while cutting someone's head off with a machete. It was the first time Col. Kaminoski had heard the man speak in anything but a cold monotone. Several of his KGB guards instinctively raised their weapons to the firing position in response to the agitated tone. Col. Kamanoski handed him a slip of paper, while motioning to the security men to put their weapons down. On it was written...

Lt. (jg.) Jeremy Powers
SEAL Team Four Base
U.S. Naval Station
Little Creek, Virginia

Ocho Garriana stared at the paper for several seconds to insure the information on it had been forever committed to his memory. He then held it out, knowing what came next. Col. Kamanoski, who still had the gold cigarette lighter in his hand, pressed the fire switch with his right thumb and lit the corner of the paper. Ocho Garriana held it in his hand until the flames were unbearably hot against his hand, although he made no sound, then dropped it onto the ground. By the time the flame went out, only a few blackened ashes remained. They were gently scattered by the humid breeze that never quite subsided in this part of the country. Ocho Garriana reached down, picked up the briefcase and handed it to the Colonel. Neither man showed any emotion.

"A small gift, to show my gratitude, Colonel."

Inside were three million American dollars in cash. While an ideological zealot, Colonel Kamanoski had become used to the finer things. He had a high standard of living adopted from the decadent West. Although his possessions would be the envy of any wealthy American, the Colonel felt that he alone had not been corrupted by them. Being an ideological zealot would forever remain at the top of his own personal list of priorities, and although misplaced, one could not help admiring his loyalty. Even his bevy of some of the world's most socially prominent and beautiful women could never cause him to stray from the path of ideological and moral absoluteness. It was this trait that made him renowned within the world's best intelligence services, including his own.

The two men shook hands and both sets of guards returned. The men entered their limousines, each departing in different directions. Inside his limousine, Ocho Garriana turned to Juan Espinoza, who leaned over to receive his orders. Ultimately, in every terrorist organization, final orders were given verbally to avoid detection on communication lines by NSA satellites. Receiving such an order directly from Ocho Garriana himself had actually become an enormous badge of prestige within the Garriana organization. After repeating the information contained on the piece of paper, Ocho Garriana continued, "Murder this man as brutally as possible. Spend millions if you have to. Spare nothing and no one. I don't care who or how many die with him. This must be accomplished at all costs, do you understand?"

Nodding his response, Juan Espinoza knew that if he failed this mission, death would be preferable to the torture that would await him at the hands of Ocho Garriana. He would be the one hanging by his feet from a tree limb, methodically having his limbs hacked off until the mercy of death arrived.

He immediately began mentally planning the operation, realizing that success had to be the only possible outcome. Lt. (jg.) Jeremy Powers must be slaughtered, without mercy or pity. Anyone dying with him would simply be part of the job.

CHAPTER 8

LITTLE CREEK, VIRGINIA

Juan Espinoza sat in his rented car in the parking lot of the Burger King restaurant located two blocks along the North Avenue main road leading to the entrance of the Little Creek Naval Amphibious Base. The dark blue Ford sedan was unobtrusive among the several other cars entering and leaving the parking lot. Next to him sat Paulie Rivera, a trusted associate.

The two-million dollar bribe paid to their state police informant had been well spent. All they had needed was the license plate, registration number and car description of one Jeremy Powers and now they had them. The orders given by Ocho Garriana were unambiguous in terms of the money Espinoza could spend to carry out the assassination. He had flown thirty of the nearly one thousand Ocho Garriana henchmen scattered across the United States to Little Creek. Since this city contained a major military installation, no undue attention would be drawn by the dozen different states represented on the license plates of the killers: all except Espinoza and Rivera had driven their cars into the city, their arrivals spread over several days. The men checked into a dozen different hotels in the city. The two Colombians had flown directly from Cardazanna to Miami, using false identification and diplomatic passports provided by Bolivian loyalists. The men rented the car at Miami, Florida International Airport, and drove to Little Creek. Their associates were organized into four-car watches and posted near the main gate between the hours of 4:00 am and 8:00 pm, since Espinoza believed that their vigil

77

would be too obvious if continued throughout the night. Staggering the brands and models of cars, colors, inhabitants, times and locations would make their operation difficult to observe by anyone watching. This random pattern was the basic element of any such operation. Repetition and consistency were to be avoided at all costs.

Two of the men, permanently residing in Jersey City, New Jersey were car bomb demolition experts. They had prepared the massive 500-pound bomb by bringing in plastique high explosives in 50-pound increments from twelve different locations around the country. The extent of the cartel's infrastructure within the United States, much like those of other worldwide terrorist organizations, was only now beginning to be understood by U.S. law enforcement and security organizations. Once again this country was paying an enormous, though as yet undefined, price for asking far too few questions of people who entered the United States through its porous borders. Their ability for inflicting enormous damage against United States citizens and property within this country were staggering. The bombing of the World Trade Center in the near future would only represent the beginning, the so-called "tip of the iceberg".

The hit squad brought along an extra hundred pounds of explosive, just to be sure they had the necessary backup. It had been meticulously assembled inside a 1989 red Toyota sedan stolen in South Carolina the week before. The bomb would be detonated by remote control from a distance of several blocks. It would level anything within a block and one half radius. It was as large or larger than anything used in Beirut, Belfast, Cairo or other trouble spots of the world.

For weeks Espinoza had been waking up in the middle of the night from frequent nightmares, screaming and in a cold sweat. Nightmares that were caused by his fear of what would happen if he failed to successfully complete the mission given to him by Ocho Garriana. Anything was prefer-

78

able to the hideous death that would befall him if this Lt. (jg.) Powers were left alive. Espinoza originally believed a two-hundred pound bomb would do the job, but mentally increased it to five hundred pounds after waking up from one of the nightmares, during which he could almost feel his testicles being ripped off by a pipe wrench. The fact that the extra three-hundred pounds of explosives would kill hundreds of additional innocents was of no consequence.

Each man had the latest and best in optical and communications equipment, including night vision, infrared binoculars. It was possible to minimize the danger of being seen by passers-by, since they knew Powers drove a red 1988 Chevrolet Camaro and would only have to lift the binoculars above the car door to look at the license plate numbers whenever a red Camaro entered or left the base. Espinoza knew he would need some luck, because if Powers' unit were not at the base, away either on training or deployment, he could be gone for weeks or months. The longer the surveillance, the greater the risk of detection. In order to determine a pattern of Powers' driving, it would be necessary for them to observe him over several days. This could be problematic since he would most likely be using random evasive tactics himself, so the car bomb would have to be detonated the first or second time the Camaro was spotted or they might not get another chance. Extremely rapid response to the sighting would be necessary. Accordingly, three cars on each watch were assigned to locate the Camaro and the inhabitants of the fourth car would detonate the bomb. The car containing the explosives had to be driven several blocks each night to a hotel and returned in the morning, no matter how great the risk.

As far as Espinoza was concerned, the other men were far more expendable than himself. Cars and locations were rotated on a daily basis and the men changed hotels at least every other night. Espinoza always stayed at least two miles away from where the car bomb was parked for the night.

While his safety was paramount, that of his men meant nothing.

About two weeks into the watch, the red Camaro was finally spotted leaving the base.

Humberto Ruiz, in one of the three cars, anxiously called Espinoza on his secure cellular phone to let him know Powers was coming. Fortunately for Espinoza, the red Camaro turned onto the street where the Toyota containing the car bomb was parked. Espinoza gave the final go-ahead, shouting, *"Que esplote la pinchi bomba!"* (Detonate the fucking bomb!) into his remote phone.

While not the coded stuff of James Bond movies, it generated the desired result. As Powers' car moved along the North Avenue Road, the car bomb was detonated. The explosion looked like something out of Beirut, as vehicles, buildings and human beings were all incinerated by the fiery blaze. The centers of Hiroshima and Nagasaki had looked little different from the area immediately surrounding the blast's epicenter. The fire bombings of Frankfurt and Dressden by the RAF during WWII were better analogies, and more closely resembled the pattern of destruction caused by the car bomb. Thick, black smoke enveloped the entire city and the stench of burning debris was everywhere, with the cinders forming a column rising to the sky.

Everything within a block-and-a-half radius was reduced to debris, ashes, dust and molten steel. The fact that twenty of Espinoza's henchmen also perished in the blast was of no concern to him. What Juan Espinoza could not have known was that the Camaro had gone a half a block further than expected prior to the explosion. Several feet from the car, where he had been thrown by the force of the blast, Lt. (jg.) Jeremy Powers was alive, although seriously hurt. He agonizingly dragged himself away from the carnage, hoping for help. Trained to be stoic, it was perhaps being a SEAL that would save his life. He went on "auto pilot", forcing himself to physically function though horribly wounded.

Juan Espinoza was well on his way to Miami before police roadblocks were set up around Little Creek. He had not shown up in any of the FBI's immediate screening of all suspected terrorists entering the United States during the past several days. He was, after all, passing himself off as the Bolivian Diplomat, Alberto Cheralla. About two hours south of Little Creek, Espinoza could no longer contain himself. He took out his secure phone (which, taking into consideration buy-outs, pay-offs and hush money cost him forty thousand dollars) and dialed the pre-arranged number that would connect him to Ocho Garriana. As soon as he heard someone pick up the phone at the other end, he shouted the signal, *"El puerco esta muerto! "* (The pig is dead!)

In Cardazanna, Colombia, Ocho Garriana hung up the phone grinning from ear to ear. Yes! He was the most powerful man on earth. No human being, not even the superpower United States or its Navy SEALs could stop him, and no place on earth was beyond his reach. Powers would never be back to screw up his plans again! Not only did he, Ocho Garriana, eliminate an embarrassment, he made a statement to all who know him in the world...Ocho Garriana is power. A power to be feared!

CHAPTER 9

PHOENIX, ARIZONA

The shrill ring of the phone jolted David Powers awake, and he instinctively reached across his wife, Maggie, to answer it. Glancing at the red digits glaring at him from the face of the GE clock radio on the bed table next to her, he noticed it was 5:45 am, 45 minutes before he normally awoke to the strains of Phoenix station KBZY. Maggie seemed asleep as Powers fumbled for the phone, which he almost dropped before it reached his ear. He was half-way between sleep and semi-consciousness.

A firm female voice began, "Mr. Powers, this is Yeoman 3rd Class Ferraro calling for Admiral Blankenship. Just a moment, sir."

David Powers bolted upright in bed. He was all too familiar with this type of call.

Vice Admiral William H. Blankenship, III was the Senior ranking Navy SEAL. A much decorated combat veteran, Admiral Blankenship had seen action in most major SEAL team operations since the unit was first commissioned by President John F. Kennedy in 1962. The call was the one every parent of a serviceman dreads.

"Mr. Powers, this is Admiral Bill Blankenship. We regret to inform you that your son....'

Powers' heart sank and his stomach churned so hard his vision became blurred and a violent shudder ran the length of his body. He started wretching as though to vomit.

'.....has been seriously wounded as a result of an encounter with hostile forces outside of the United States...."

David Powers could not have known that "the encounter with hostile forces" was a euphemism for the detonation of a 500-pound car bomb less than a block from the younger Powers' car as it passed by the gate at the United States Naval Amphibious Base in Little Creek, Virginia, and that the resulting multiple injuries included burns over twenty percent of his son's body, multiple fractures, a substantial loss of blood, deep cuts and numerous dislocations. While this concluded the preliminary injury list, further examination by the specialists at Walter Reed Hospital might uncover more.

Nor did the Admiral divulge that two hundred and eleven innocent victims, mostly civilians, died in the blast described by the press as "an explosion at a propane gas storage facility". However, behind the headlines, FBI counter-terrorist experts were already hard at work on numerous theories and, due to the obvious "car bomb" signature, one theory included the strong likelihood that it was the work of foreign terrorist operatives. Now, the job would be to find our as quickly as possible which terrorist operatives and on whose behalf they had carried out this operation that had resulted in such unimaginable carnage.

Powers was too stunned to respond. Suddenly, a deep, visceral scream erupted from deep inside him. "Oh my God!", he shouted as he flung the phone down, subconsciously hoping that it would make what he had heard go away.

Maggie, who had begun to stir at the first rings of the phone, instinctively grabbed Powers' right arm so hard that he could feel her fingers all the way to the bone. It was a grip of someone consumed by fear. Powers, terrified and sweating profusely, was screaming incoherently. He had flung his head back and was yelling at the ceiling. The phone, tangled in its cord, lay on the bed beside him. Maggie could hear Admiral Blankenship yelling, "Hello! Hello! Is anyone there?!", at the top of his lungs. She reached down and while still holding her husband with one hand, grabbed the phone and placed it against her own ear. Anxiously, she asked,

"This is Maggie Powers, with whom am I speaking?"

"Hello, Mrs. Powers, this is Admiral Blankenship, the Commanding Officer of the Navy SEAL Team."

No matter how many deaths he had seen and no matter how many letters he had sent to the parents of the brave young men who had died serving under him, the Admiral could never get used to the inexplicable mixture of sadness, rage, disappointment and fear felt by everyone on both ends of the line.

"My God, Admiral! What happened?" Maggie asked, almost pleadingly, as she stared sympathetically at her heartbroken husband, trying to shake him back to a coherent state.

"I cannot say much. Your son has been seriously wounded and will be airlifted to the Walter Reed Hospital in Washington as soon as he stabilizes."

Maggie had a thousand unanswered questions that raced through her mind. She felt as though she were looking at a scroll on the screen at the end of a movie, the words passing by too rapidly to permit concentration or coherence.

"I'm sorry, all of this is very highly classified and I am not at liberty to say much more. Please call area code...."

"Just a minute Admiral, I could not possibly remember that in the condition I'm in. Let me get a pencil." She turned, opened the top drawer of her end table and flinging the contents in all directions, found a pen. "Please continue."

"Area code 804-741-9800 and ask for YM...excuse me....Yeoman 3rd Class Stephanee Ferraro. She will make arrangements for you and your husband to fly to Washington on a military aircraft as soon as possible to see your son. We will all pray for Jeremy and everyone in your family. We believe he will live, but there could be serious long term complications. God bless you!"

Maggie could hear the deep, genuine sadness in Admiral Blankenship's voice, reflecting the heavy burden, unknown to most, that goes with having to notify immediate family of a brave young man's death or crippling injuries. She gently hung up the phone and turned to face her husband.

Although David Powers was now forty-seven years old, he still had the trim appearance of a much younger man; he had gone to great lengths to keep himself fit through the years. Without a single gray hair, only the lines on his face reflected that he was well into middle-age. He had become Extremely successful and financially secure while running a seven-hundred-million dollar a year division of a large New York Stock Exchange company for a decade. He, his wife and young son lived in an expansive twelve-room home located on four acres in the Phoenix suburb of North Scottsdale. After taking a year off when Modular Products, Incorporated had closed in 1978, he went to work as Executive Vice President of the Thompson Electronics Corporation and rose quickly to the Presidency, ascending to his present job as Chairman and Chief Executive Officer only two years before. Thompson manufactured high-tech electronics gear for the United States Government. Its products were renowned for reliability and technical performance. They were used throughout the military, including for the latest generation of NSA satellites as well as the USAF reconnaissance planes.

Thompson Electronics technology was also utilized by the SEAL Team itself, particularly in a highly classified, new area known as Low Observable Technology. Thompson employed 17,000 workers at its nineteen manufacturing plants located across the United States, Canada, Singapore, France and the United Kingdom. The company's research and development facility was located in the same complex as its world headquarters on the Northwest side of Phoenix.

David Powers met Maggie six years ago after moving from San Diego when his first marriage ended in 1980. His first marriage had failed largely as a result of the intrigue-laden roller coaster he had ridden during his tenure at a company called Modular Products. While there, Powers had inadvertently become entangled in a national security matter involving attempts by a country on the sub-continent to acquire a nuclear weapon. Realizing it could easily fall into the hands of terrorists seeking to damage or destroy the United States, he desperately tried to stop his company's technology transfer from taking place. Feeling that his lone crusade had largely fallen on deaf ears inside this country's intelligence services, he almost got himself killed desperately trying to stop those involved in this illegal technology transfer from getting what they needed to assemble a nuclear bomb. Only one other person, FBI Agent Bob Lewis, believed him and joined in his desperate crusade to expose what was secretly going on in what turned out to be the "front company" for a group of extremely dangerous nuclear terrorists.

Powers had come to realize through the years that he was not paranoid, that countries hostile to the United States had succeeded in acquiring nuclear technology and other weapons of mass destruction, although not through the company he had worked for. The war waged against these nuclear terrorists by himself and FBI Special Agent Bob Lewis, did indeed stop Modular Products from being used as one of the dummy front companies to export crucial nuclear components. Even though the foreign agents had merely gone elsewhere and acquired the components they needed from less patriotic sources, Powers felt at peace with himself. Although physically and emotionally spent he had walked away from Modular Products with his head held high.*

After a year of solitude in the high country of Colorado, David returned to the world he knew best....the cor-

* This true story of nuclear terrorists trying to use an American corporation as a "front" for stealing nuclear technology is revealed in the author's forthcoming book, "Nuclear Countdown" (S.P.I. Books, 1997).

porate world. Despite offers to run two other larger NYSE companies, he felt comfortable with the Thompson company and its people and accepted the position of Executive Vice President.

Maggie Powers, forty-one, had also been married once before. The Harvard Law School graduate brought her nine year-old son, Casey to the marriage. Maggie was an outdoor enthusiast and an avid mountain biker who also enjoyed mountain climbing. Although forty-one, she looked years younger. She could be called statuesque, standing about 5'7", slender, stunning to many, with dark brown—almost black—hair and hypnotic, radiant green eyes. Maggie was the center of attention wherever she went. A nationally recognized expert on Intellectual Property Law, she was a partner in the Phoenix law firm of Squires, Mason and Gwynn. The two were introduced to each other by mutual friends, and had never been happier since they married. Casey was now David Powers' adopted son. With Jeremy, 24, a Navy SEAL gone all the time to far off, dangerous corners of the world, and daughter, Julie, 21, a senior at MIT, young Casey had become the center of their private world.

After a half-hour, Maggie was still unable to calm David Powers down. He paced back and forth across the room, almost smashing into the walls as he gestured wildly with his arms. He began throwing clothes into the suitcase he had removed from one of the many spacious walk-in closets lining "His" side of the "His & Her" dressing room. The dressing room, large master bedroom suite and bath area containing the spa and sunken whirlpool bath were surrounded by a private flower-ladened arbor.

Maggie realized it was time to stop, to gather their combined energies and resources, and make a plan of what to do next. Sitting on the divan, she motioned for David to sit next to her. She pleaded, "David, please. We have to talk. You know from your past that the irrationality lurking just below your surface can be a terribly dangerous thing."

"Maggie, they've killed my son!" David responded slowly, in almost a whisper, lowering himself next to her. They were both looking at a collage of photographs on the wall above his desk. There was Jeremy's high school football portrait next to his picture as a star running back at Yale, and next to that a graduation picture of his entire SEAL Team class. There were several local newspaper clippings of Jeremy's record-setting exploits at Scottsdale High School and his selection as an all-state halfback. Standing 6'1" tall and weighing a heavily muscled 208 pounds, the boy had added the 3" in height normally associated with a second generation. Jeremy had been the source of enormous pride to his father who was proud of all his son's accomplishments. In addition to his selection as an all-state football player in high school, he became an all ivy league running-back at Yale. While considered too small at 208 pounds to be selected in the National Football League draft, he had been invited to try out as a free agent by the New York Giants. While at Yale he had finished as runner-up for selection as a Rhodes Scholar before being commissioned as an Ensign in the United States Navy. He was named number one in his Naval Reserve Officers Training Corps (NROTC) unit.

Jeremy, however, thought of no other immediate future after college other than becoming a Naval officer like his dad, and a SEAL at that. He turned down the chance to tryout with the New York Giants to enroll in his Basic Underwater Demolition—SEAL (BUD-S) training class. All this brought great pride to David, but most of all he was proud of the man Jeremy had become. A man with enormous character, ethics and compassion for his fellow man. Yes, David was proud.

Maggie reached over and placed her hand on his thigh, feeling him tremble with emotion. "David, nobody is dead. Why don't we call the admiral back and find out how quickly we can get to Washington?" Going to the desk Maggie dialed the number Admiral Blankenship had given her.

"Admiral Blankenship's office, Yeoman 3rd Class Ferraro speaking," spoke the young woman with the tone of military authority.

"Hello, Yeoman Ferraro. This is Maggie Powers. May I speak with Admiral Blankenship?"

"One moment, M'am" came the response, but the voice had softened. Maggie, looking at David and seeing the pain on his face, waited impatiently. She heard the voice of Admiral Blankenship. He sounded firm yet sympathetic.

"Mrs. Powers....I'm very glad you got back to me so quickly. Are you and your husband okay? I know that all of this has been a terrible shock to both of you."

"Yes, it has Admiral," Maggie tried to keep her voice as calm as possible. "How soon can you arrange for us to come to Washington?"

"Right away. At the time of my first call, my information was a few minutes old. Since then I have learned Jeremy's condition has stabilized and he is at Walter Reed Hospital. I can arrange military transportation for you."

David had moved to eavesdrop on the conversation. The burst of emotion he had allowed himself for one of the few times in his life had subsided. The logic and reason of his trained mind, that had not only kept him alive in the past, but enabled him to achieve what he had in life, kicked in. He got on his other phone, and called United Airlines. Maggie knew it would be best if her husband could feel as though he were doing something, anything to make things happen. She could hear him discussing flights as she cupped her hand over the speaker and momentarily glanced over at David. Replacing the phone to her ear, she rejoined her conversation with the Admiral.

"Thank you Admiral, but knowing my husband he won't want to wait." Despite all the pain being felt at that moment, Maggie could not help the feeling of warmth and pride that surged in her as she overheard her husband winding-up his conversation with the airlines. Obviously, David was again in control.

"I understand. Please call me the moment you get to Washington. Mrs. Powers, my prayers are with you, your husband and your family."

With that, Admiral Blankenship hung up. Maggie walked over to her husband and embraced him. He felt her warmth, love and support. There was silence between the two until it was broken by David's now quiet and controlled voice, "There's a non-stop United Flight from Phoenix Sky Harbor leaving in three hours. I've made reservations. I'll call Bob Lewis and have him meet us in Washington. He's in New York on business."

Lewis, now fifty, had retired from a distinguished twenty-five year career with the FBI seven years earlier. Standing six foot two, Lewis was a marathon runner whose trim physique was about the same as it had been twenty years ago. While the FBI insisted that its agents run four or five miles a day to remain in top notch physical condition, Lewis had regularly participated in twenty-five mile marathon runs and continued to do so even after retiring as an active service agent. He had dark brown hair, piercing blue eyes and was one of the most upbeat human beings Powers had ever known. While he was still on active service, unlike other agents who kept their weapons discreetly hidden, Lewis always wore his .357 magnum revolver openly in plain sight of anyone he was around.

Lewis often explained how in earlier times, the .357 magnum was selected as the in-service personal weapon by FBI Director, J. Edgar Hoover. Today's agents could carry seventeen round automatics, if they wished. This was the result of the infamous shootout in Miami between former FBI agents and domestic terrorists, when the Bureau suffered its greatest single day loss of agents). Lewis simply preferred the compact feel and enormous stopping power of the .357 magnum, whose bullets could penetrate a car's engine block.

90

Considered too brash by other agents, Lewis' point was that he was not afraid of either the complexity of the cases he worked or of the perpetrators involved. He was the FBI Agent involved with Powers while he was the President of Modular Products in Downey, California. The two had developed tremendous respect for one another during those difficult times and became lifelong friends. To Powers' delight, and later it would be proven to his great benefit, Lewis accepted the position Powers offered him as Security Chief for Thompson Electronics after he retired from the FBI three years later. While there did not appear to be any terror-ist plots afoot at Thompson, it was imperative that the highly classified electronics components at the company not fall into the wrong hands. If they did, they could provide enemies of the United States with many of the same capabilities possessed by the United States Military and intelligence agencies' most highly classified operatives. Lewis had broken-up two such attempts, one by a ring working for a Colombian drug cartel and the other for Communist China, during the past three years.

Powers soon reached Lewis in New York. Explaining noth-ing, he briefly gave him the in-flight information and asked that he order them a limousine and pick up Maggie and himself at the airport. During the conversation, Lewis sensed something faintly familiar and frightening in David's voice. It was a tone he had not heard since the days at Modular Products.

After hanging up from his short conversation with Powers, Lewis felt a slight twinge in his chest. It was the same twinge that warned him of coming danger when he was an agent in the FBI and a twinge that was often responsible for saving his life. Slowly he opened a metal clad case containing several handguns and started cleaning one of his guns. Somehow it gave him comfort. Knowing Powers, something told him he was going to have use of a weapon sometime soon. He started working on cleaning up a second weapon for his friend, and now boss, David Powers.

CHAPTER 10

SAN DIEGO, CALIFORNIA

Betty Powers had remained in San Diego after her divorce from David nearly ten years before, and her life had returned to some sense of normality after the seemingly endless ups and downs of her life with him. Now approaching fifty, Betty still maintained the trim, youthful appearance of her earlier years.

With hardly a gray hair, standing only five feet, three inches tall, her jet black hair, piercing brown eyes and radiant smile could turn a roomful of people's mood from glum to happy. She was the principal of a local high school, having earned a doctorate in history at San Diego State University. While having her share of an active and varied social life, she had never remarried, although a long standing relationship with a San Diego internist had resulted in three postponed marriage dates. The two, who cared for each other deeply, eventually decided that based on past experience, marriage could destroy the underpinnings of their shared love. Certainly the realities that life had handed to them had dulled their optimism. Dr. William Forrest had also been married once before, and his two grown children lived with their mother in Cleveland, Ohio.

While the present level of contact between Betty and David Powers was somewhat sporadic, their son Jeremy was a shared treasure. Betty and David Powers had both decided years before that they each loved Jeremy and, for his sake, agreed on a shared, or joint, custody arrangement, while he was growing up. Jeremy spent summers and most vacations with his father, as well as at least two weekends a month, before deciding to move to Scottsdale with his father and attend high school there. Neither he or his parents ever had to make a decision that would exclude anyone from his life. Despite the roller coaster emotions of any divorce, in this case the parent to child or child to parent relationships remained civilized and largely in tact.

It was 7:00 am in the morning when the phone rang in Betty's two-bedroom ocean townhouse in the neatly-manicured city of La Jolla, just north of San Diego. Betty had eaten breakfast, cleaned-up the kitchen, and was almost out the front door when the phone rang. For some reason, she decided to answer it, turning back into the house and grabbing the phone before her answering service picked up. Her ex-husband's nearly hysterical voice on the other end of the line instantly returned her to the terror of the Modular Products situation nearly twelve years before.

"Betty, they've killed our son!" The words spilled over in a gush of emotion and Betty's purse and keys dropped to the floor.

"My God, David, who killed who? It can't be Jeremy!" Betty could hear Maggie in the background trying to calm her husband. Within a few moments David, realizing that he might be giving Betty a heart attack, regained enough composure to be both more coherent and accurate.

"Betty, Jeremy was seriously injured in a highly classified SEAL Team operation. He was brave." David's words trailed off into uncontrollable sobbing, and Betty stood mute, holding the phone to her ear, staring off into space and hearing little of what her ex-husband was saying.

The sound of a wave crashing against the rocky seawall below reverberated in her brain and seemed to return her sensibilities. She asked David to keep her closely informed as he continued to monitor the situation and said she wanted to visit Jeremy as soon as possible. The two agreed to remain in close touch and hung up. Betty Powers headed for school, her mind thousands of miles away at the place where her son lay mangled but stabilized, promising herself she would make phone contact with Jeremy, if not visit him in person, at the earliest possible moment.

CHAPTER 11

WASHINGTON, D.C.

David and Maggie Powers rapidly approached the doors separating them from the road outside of the arrival area at Washington National Airport. Since they only had carry-on luggage, they had quickly disembarked the United Airlines 757 jet, that had taken them from Phoenix to Washington. Using one of the new in-flight phones, the two had learned that Jeremy's condition, while still categorized as critically serious, had indeed stabilized. Unfortunately, with David's voice rising on the phone, everyone on the plane seemed to know what was happening, although the couple found solace in the concern of fellow passengers.

Maggie struggled to keep up with David as he raced through the airport, his thoughts single-mindedly on Jeremy. Suddenly, it seemed, they were outside the airport, blinking in the strange light and there was Bob Lewis leaning up against the opened passenger door of a white stretch limousine, his eyes scanning the area, more like a presidential bodyguard than a waiting friend. As the three embraced, Lewis noticed how truly beautiful Maggie was, yet he also noticed the look of extreme anguish on his two friends' faces. At the same time, both David and Maggie Powers somehow felt more secure in the presence of this man, and their spirits could not help but be uplifted by Bob's always upbeat mood.

"You folks have a good trip?" asked Lewis.

"Yes, Bob, we did. David almost flew here by himself, with no need of the plane." Maggie had taken David's hand

94

in both of hers and with a loving smile gave it a little squeeze.

"Dave, you have a message here from an Admiral Blankenship. It was relayed to me from our Phoenix office. He asked that you stop by the Pentagon right after you visit your son. He gave me directions from Walter Reed. It's less than a twenty minute drive. Maggie, no offense, he asked that David come alone."

"I'm not offended. But what's all the secrecy about, Bob?" Maggie couldn't hide a hint of bruised feelings.

"Honestly, Maggie, I don't know. I'm just relaying what the admiral told me." Lewis was feeling a little defensive. He really liked Maggie and did not want her to feel left out.

But Maggie knew when to leave something alone. Within 15 minutes, Lewis brought the limousine to a stop in front of Walter Reed Hospital. Before Lewis got around to opening the passenger door, David was already halfway up the dark gray concrete steps of the hospital entrance, and disappeared through the revolving doors. Entering the hospital, he suddenly turned around to wait for Maggie, and saw Bob Lewis handing her something.

Lewis was telling Maggie, "Why don't you page me after the hospital visit and I'll be in front within five minutes. The number is on the card, 703-351-9756. After dialing you will hear a tone. After the tone dial your home number finishing with the pound sign (#) and I'll know it's you. Send Jeremy my best and I'll see you soon."

Powers began looking impatiently at his watch, wishing it would get Maggie up the stairs faster. Thanking Lewis, she turned and hurried toward her husband. By the time she reached David, Lewis had already driven to the visitor's parking lot.

Inside, David and Maggie walked up to the large information desk located inside the cavernous lobby of the world's largest military hospital. An elderly black man, dressed in a gray uniform, looked up at them. Doctors and nurses wearing white gowns over their military uniforms hurriedly passed by in all directions. Visitors in military uniforms hurried past as well, the men with their hats tucked under one arm as is customary inside a military hospital. David and Maggie were among other civilian visitors in this odd mix of military patients and personnel. Every branch of the military and several foreign military organizations were represented. The two felt small and insignificant in the vast, sterile atmosphere of the building. Maggie felt a cold chill. Looking around she attributed it to the stark emptiness and enormity of the room in which they were standing. The walls and hallways, branching out in various directions from the main entrance, looked like vast beehives of activity. With the exception of the few furnishings that were absolutely necessary, decorative touches were noticably absent.

David addressed the officer at the Information Desk, "We are here to see Lt. (jg.) Jeremy Powers, USN, military service number 856413."

The man flipped pages of a large ringed binder containing lists of patients' names.

"Ah, here we are. Just a moment, Sir."

The desk officer turned his back, leaned his head down and proceeded to dial a number. Neither David or Maggie could make out what he was saying. He placed his hand over the speaker on the phone and turned to the couple. "Who may I say is here, and do each of you have at least three forms of identification?"

David reached around and began to remove the wallet from his rear pants pocket. Maggie started fumbling through her purse to retrieve her wallet. David questioned all the formality....

"We're David and Maggie Powers, Jeremy.....Make that Lt. (jg.) Powers' parents. Yes, we have identification. Why all the fuss?"

Ignoring the question, the man took the couple's driver

licenses and two credit cards from each. He again turned his back and spent nearly 5 minutes engaged in a conversation with the person at the other end. David's feelings of annoyance were mixed with an unnerving sense that something was wrong. Why would parents have to provide proof of their identities to visit their wounded son? Something was definitely wrong, and because of Powers' instincts in such matters, he knew it was serious. Just as the man turned back to them, Powers noticed a Naval officer and two enlisted men with the black arm bands and yellow MP block-letters that signified military police, walking down the hallway towards them. The officer, a tall, youthful, athletic looking young man, walked in front. The two senior enlisted men, one a Chief Petty Officer and the other a Petty Officer Second Class, walked next to each other and a few steps behind the officer. The three men all had their hats on and walked with military precision. Powers also knew instinctively that their arrival must have something to do with his son. The desk officer had stopped talking and by now Powers had turned completely towards the three men.

"Mr. Powers? I am Lt. Michael Jansen," the young man addressed David, extending his hand.

As they shook hands, David replied, "Lt. Jansen, I'm David Powers and this is my wife, Maggie."

Lt. Jansen removed his hat and backed up a couple of steps answering, "Pleased to meet you, Ma'am." He was now standing at attention, his hat tucked under one arm.

"Mr. & Mrs. Powers, this is Chief Jones and Petty Officer Second Class Kinkaid."

Powers shook hands with each of the two men and Maggie extended her hand to them as well. The Lieutenant's response was polite yet firm, and as he put his hat back on he addressed Powers.

"Sir, could I please have a few words with you?"

He motioned David towards an empty room normally reserved for visitors. Maggie smiled politely, her eyes following the men as they walked away. The two Petty Officers stood rigidly motionless and neither one spoke. Maggie walked over to a nearby couch and sat down. Jones and Kinkaid did not follow her. She was confused, scared, worried and nervous, all at the same time.

Inside the rather small room, furnished sparsely with a couch and two chairs, with nothing on the walls but an old faded calendar, the lieutenant spoke in subdued tones that could only be heard by the lieutenant's visitor....

"Mr. Powers, this is a very highly classified matter. I have been instructed to escort you to see your son. Please do not consider me rude for not being able to answer any of the thousand questions I am sure you would like to ask."

Powers' suspicions now came to the surface, something was very wrong, and while tempted to say a thousand things, he said very little.

"Should we just follow you, Lieutenant?"

"Please, Sir."

David followed Lt. Jansen back to where the two Petty Officers stood. Maggie got up to join her husband and stood next to him as the Lieutenant walked by. Looking up at him, he softly squeezed her hand, silently communicating to her that neither of them should say anything. It was clear they should follow closely behind Lt. Jansen and the two Petty Officers fell in behind them moving with military precision to the elevator.

Powers' suspicions and concerns mounted as he noticed Lt. Jansen turning a pass key that restricted the elevator from stopping anywhere until it reached the designated destination. Nobody spoke. David Powers' anxiety level was so high that the blinking lights signifying each floor as the elevator passed from one floor to the next, appeared as one continuous glow. His anxiety level seemed to rise in cadence with the flashing lights. On the seventh floor, Lt. Jansen inserted the key, giving it a one-half turn. The elevator doors opened revealing four Navy SEALs standing at attention, facing the elevator passengers. David and Maggie thought they had stumbled onto an NFL training camp. The four were enormous and dressed in crisply-pressed camouflage uniforms with rolled up sleeves (starting exactly 1 inch above the elbow and with the width of the roll measuring exactly 4 fingers), and the square cap for which the unit had become famous. All had sidearms strapped on, and two carried HK (Heckler and Koch, the world renowned German manufacturer of advanced individual weaponry) MP5 submachine guns with straps slung over their shoulders.

This particular weapon was a favorite of Navy SEALs due to the fact that it was waterproof, fired 9mm bullets at extremely high cyclic rates of fire, was concealable and could be fitted with a silencer, laser aimed sights and a simple light that enabled a SEAL to begin firing as soon as the light hit the target. Since a split second could often mean life or death in a fire fight, the fact that the light was matched precisely to the trajectory of the weapon's 9mm bullets gave the SEAL just such an advantage. Often carried with an over the shoulder sling much like a woman's handbag, and fired from the hip when on single fire, the SEAL merely had to point the light at a target and fire. The adversary would require four such motions, one to find the target, a second to acquire the target, a third to sight, and a fourth to pull the trigger. In most situations, the individual would be dead before reaching the second motion.

The two guards held their deadly weapons pointed away at hip level. Powers noted that the safeties were off, and each weapon had fully loaded clips inserted. The man in charge, Lt. (jg.) Walter Benson, saluted Lt. Jansen and addressed the man, who had stepped out into the hallway. Powers started to follow, but was gently held back as Lt. Jansen, speaking softly to Lt. (jg.) Benson, pushed his hand back against Powers, signaling him to stop. Lt. Jansen turned to the couple as the two Petty Officers, after saluting Lt(jg). Benson, stood rigidly against the back of the elevator.

99

Lt. Jansen spoke, "May I have your three forms of identification, please, Sir?"

David and Maggie again took the required items out of their wallets, handing them to the Lieutenant who again addressed them, "May I also have your Social Security Cards and/or numbers?"

These were promptly handed over to Lt.(jg) Benson. He checked them against information previously provided by the Office of Naval Intelligence (ONI), and checked the couple's appearance against photographs provided by Admiral Blankenship's office. He then addressed David Powers, "Would you kindly step over here, Sir, and give us your fingerprints?"

Powers was astonished, but complied. He would cooperate in any way to get to see his son. Thinking back, he realized his prints were on file with the Navy since he had to provide them on his military identification while a Junior Officer in 1964. After completing the process, which Maggie watched silently, but with astonishment, Lt. (jg.). Benson moved further out into the hallway and asked the couple to follow. Powers observed at least a dozen similarly dressed and armed SEALs lining the hallway as far down as he could see. The hallway appeared to end several yards ahead in a sharply angled turn. The men were stationed about every twenty feet and stood motionless, their arms cradling the automatic weapon each carried. Six plain clothes FBI counter-terrorist agents were also present, as well as a dozen uniformed Washington Police. Powers grew increasingly perplexed and did not know what to say or do. While his son Jeremy meant the world to David, he did not think he was this important to the world at large.

Finally, Lt. (jg.) Benson introduced himself. He stood 6'3", weighed 223 pounds, was square jawed and extremely eloquent.

"Mr. and Mrs. Powers, I am Lt(jg) Benson. I am a SEAL Team Four officer serving proudly with your son. As you know, he has been seriously injured, and we will ensure that the responsible parties who did this do not get another crack at him. They will be suitably bashed!! David Powers momentarily lightened up and almost smiled at the SEAL Team euphemism for doing somebody in.

Another crack at him? What in the world was Benson talking about, Powers thought to himself, returning to his nearly crazed state. David Powers could not speak even if he wanted to, as every possibility swirled around in his brain. Lt. (jg.) Benson led David and Maggie down the hall, past the nearly three dozen men obviously on guard duty and promptly turned right at the point the hallway appeared to end. A concrete-lined, bomb proof corridor extended about twenty yards ahead of them.

Lt. (jg.) Benson anticipated the question, "Sir, this is for the protection of the people who come here. It protects our guests from any threat to their well being."

The three continued walking along the corridor without uttering another sound. About five steps beyond the point where the re-enforced concrete ended, the group again turned left.

Two more SEALs stood outside of the door to a single, large room. A third continued the vigil inside. As the couple entered the room, their hearts leapt to their throats. There lay what they thought was their son. He was hard to distinguish, since both legs were encased in plaster casts and suspended from the ceiling; his left arm was heavily bandaged, his right arm was also encased in a cast; the middle of his body was tightly bandaged and his face was completely covered by bandages, obviously over serious burns. Open slits showed his eyes, mouth and ears. Intravenous fluids entered his body through multiple tubes inserted inside his bandaged arm and chest. An array of instruments monitored vital signs. The only sound came from the instruments themselves. The boy's chest moved slowly up and down. At least his father knew he was alive. Tears glistened in David's eyes as he tried to subdue the sobs that rose up from the depths of his soul.

101

Maggie wept silently at the pain she saw.

Silently, Lt. (jg.) Benson reached over to the box of Kleenex and offered a handful to each of his two visitors. He tried to hold back the combination of rage and sorrow he felt as he looked down at his fallen comrade witnessing the pain and endless grief that this had caused both to his friend and Jeremy's parents. He silently swore revenge, much like when he and several other Navy SEALs carried a picture of Zahid Fawazza, the PLO killer who had murdered the Navy diver aboard the hijacked TWA plane in Beirut years before. The young man's brother, also a Navy SEAL, had publicly sworn to avenge his brother's murder, so long as Lebanese authorities continued to do nothing. Somewhere, some-day, one of the members of "The Teams" would cross paths with Fawazza and he would no longer be a threat to them or anyone else. It was that simple. This was the loyalty and "right over evil" philosophy of one who was a member of a military unit that did not allow its fellow members to leave a fallen comrade behind, dead or alive. Not one SEAL had ever been left behind to suffer the tortures of the Juan Espinozas of the world.

Jeremy Powers was barely conscious. The morphine made the horrible pain bearable, and he instinctively knew his father was there. The young man made a slight motion with his head, agonizingly moving it to his left and back. David Powers, seeing his effort, gently squeezed his son's hand. Feeling the slight pres-sure back became more than Jeremy's father could stand. He re-leased his grip, smiled, uttering..."Son, I love you"....and then turned to leave the room, bursting into uncontrollable tears.

Maggie walked over to Jeremy's frail, broken body. She kissed him gently on his bandaged head and told him she loved him. Then she hurriedly left the room to catch up to her husband. Outside, in the hall, she found the elder Powers. Unable to con-trol his emotions any longer, his scream resonated down the crowded concrete hallway, tearing at the souls of his fallen son's comrades,

"What the Hell is going on here??!!"

CHAPTER 12

WASHINGTON, D.C.
THE NEXT DAY

David Powers and Bob Lewis greeted each other in the coffee shop located just off the lobby of the elegant Willard Hotel. The hotel, a Washington landmark for generations, had provided lodging for many of the city's most important guests, starting with George Washington. Maggie and David had stayed in a suite on the fourth floor, and Lewis in similar accommodations at the other end of the hallway. It was 7:30 am and the two men greeted each other warmly before proceeding to their table. Maggie was sleeping in and would be visiting with two of her law school classmates who were now partners in the famous Washington firm of Frost, Stone, Anderson, Laudenbach and Dressler.

Lewis spoke first, "I am praying for the speedy recovery of your son. After what you told me last night, I wanted you to know that he will be in my prayers until you tell me he's out of there and back at home. I hope you slept well Dave, and I'm glad you got my message. I'm sorry you and Maggie had to take a cab back, but I needed to visit with some old friends over at the Bureau and I didn't realize you were going to be so tied up with all of the security checks you had described, before meeting with your son. It was great seeing the old gang and from what I saw, it doesn't seem to have quieted down much, or changed since I was an agent. Same old problems. You know, I was really honored the guys still trust me enough to give me such a detailed tour of the old place, since I've been away for so long. Oh well, enough reminiscing. Tell me more about how is your son is doing?"

Powers, his eyes red and glassy from worry and sleeplessness, gave Lewis the detailed run-down on everything that they saw at the hospital.

"Jeremy's doctor, a four-striper named McDermott, spoke to us for nearly an hour after we saw our son. He answered every medical question we had, but would say nothing about the incident, or where, why or how.....I'll tell you, Bob, something stinks about all this. Why would the military and FBI guard my son like some kind of national treasure if he wasn't targeted by someone? Someone that they have a definite interest in."

Lewis appeared anguished, "Dave, old buddy, this is starting to sound suspiciously like conversations you and I had nearly ten years ago. Even though you were right, and perhaps I down-played the seriousness early on, I thought we had left all the conspiracy theories back at the Modular Products plant."

Looking into his friend's eyes, and having the knowledge learned from past experience, Lewis knew that this conversation could have no conclusion and let the remark drift away.

Bringing Powers' attention back to his original question, Lewis asked, "What else did the doctor say?"

Powers started to relate more of what he and Maggie had been told by the doctors. As he recited each point his voice began to reflect his pain and frustration.

"He'll recover, and probably with no permanent damage. That's the maybe good news. The bad news is he has severe burns over 20% of his body, one broken leg, a fractured fibulae in the other one, a dislocated elbow, four fractured ribs and he suffered a concussion. Thank God, there is no brain damage and no internal injuries. He's lucky to be........."

Powers broke down and putting his head on the table, wept openly and uncontrollably. Lewis reached his hand across the table and placed it on his friend's shoulder. Through the sobs, he could hear Powers utter the word "alive". After taking several minutes to regain his composure, David wiped his eyes with a white linen napkin. Both men lowered their eyes and proceeded to complete their meals in silence that was only broken when, after completing his meal, Lewis excused himself, leaving to claim the limousine from the valet parking service. He had a feeling that the two of them had returned to the vigilant days when David and he were involved in exposing the nuclear terrorists at Modular Products. He began emotionally gearing himself up for the "wartime footing" that he sensed lay ahead. It was frightening and exhilarating, both at the same time.

Powers sat at the table, staring at his coffee for a while before signing the check, and leaving the restaurant. Exiting the hotel he found Lewis waiting in the car with the motor running. Walking around the car to the passenger side, Powers got in and snapping on his seat belt stated, "It's too God damned officious to sit in the back, Bob. You're my friend, not my chauffeur!"

Bob noticed that some semblance of humanity and humor was returning, David Powers was shifting out of his depression and into overdrive.

Heading out of the hotel driveway, Lewis turned the car sharply to the right off Main Highway Thirteen to the Pentagon Exit at Route Ninety. The huge building was now straight ahead of them. Both men always felt a little awed when they saw this symbol of America's global military power and prestige. Glancing at the directions that had been given to him by Admiral Blankenship's aid, Yeoman Ferraro, Lewis read aloud,

"It says to pull up to the Main Gate, ask for Admiral Blankenship, and they'll tell us where to go from there."

Slowing the limousine, Lewis rolled down the window

as he came to a stop at the guard house. They were greeted by a sharply dressed Marine sentry in the classic uniform of blue pants with a red stripe down each outside pant leg, khaki shirt and tie and white hat with a highly polished black bill. The .45 automatic inside the black leather holster attached to his waist by a khaki dress web belt was plainly in sight. The sentry leaned towards the open window. He glanced past Lewis to Powers and, apparently sensing no immediate threat, spoke to Lewis,

"Yes Sir, may I help you?"

Lewis, quite used to such protocol from his days with the FBI, glanced up at the sentry and announced, "David Powers to see Admiral Blankenship."

Powers had anticipated the next request, and began assembling the same identification he had provided at Walter Reed Hospital to Lt.(jg.) Benson. The sentry backed up a couple of steps, reached into the guard shed and withdrawing a clipboard, scanned a pad containing the names of several expected guests, including Powers. Pointing to a building about 20 yards to the left with a sign above the door, identifying it as Building-17, Guest Passes, he gave Lewis his instructions.

"Sir, Admiral Blankenship is expecting Mr. Powers. Please drive over to Building-17, located over there. You will see a large parking lot marked "Visitors Parking", please park your car there. Then go through the main door to the front desk. They will issue you a visitor's pass. Please have your identification ready. Have a nice day Sir."

Pulling into the almost full visitors parking lot, next to Building 17, they were unable to find a parking spot that would accommodate the length of their limousine. Lewis decided to drop Powers at the front of the building, giving the same instructions he had given to Maggie the day before on how to page him when he was out of the meeting.

Entering the building David presented the requisite three forms of identification at the front desk. He was again put through the finger print ritual. Finally, after much paper shuffling, he was given his guest pass showing the number "11", and he was firmly cautioned that this pass was restricted and would give him access only to the section where he was to meet the Admiral.

While he was fastening the clip on the back of the pass to his lapel, the sentry assigning Powers the pass called Admiral Blankenship's office to announce that his guest had arrived for his 9:30 am meeting. After hanging up the phone, the Marine Sergeant directed Powers to the Admiral's office.

"Sir, please proceed to Entry Gate Six." The Marine said, pointing to its location. "Yeoman 3rd Class Ferraro will meet you there."

Powers thanked the man and started walking to Entry Gate Six, plainly visible about a hundred yards to the left and about two-thirds of the way down the dark, gray stone fortress. After walking about three quarters of the way, he could make out a female sailor dressed in a khaki uniform. Stopping a few feet away from where she stood, and since she was the only female Naval person in the area, he had correctly assumed it was Admiral Blankenship's aid.

"Yeoman Ferraro?" he asked.

She glanced at Powers' visitor's badge. "Yes, Sir, Mr. Powers?" responded the somewhat plump Yeoman. Crisply turning around, she gave what sounded more like a command than a request.

"Please come with me, Sir, the Admiral is expecting you."

They began to walk down the seemingly endless hallway, the linoleum floors shimmering with wax. Military personnel of every rank, branch, country and gender all over. The people spoke in hushed tones and moved swiftly down the hall, occasionally stopping to enter one of the rather modest appearing wooden doors leading into one of the thousands of offices that seemed to fill every square inch of this giant edifice. Dozens of Marine sentries, noticeable everywhere, were standing at ease, though rigidly.

As he looked around, Powers mused to himself about what backup security must exist at this "inner-sanctum of global U.S. military might." All of a sudden he came to an abrupt halt. Reality had hit with such a force that it caused him to momentarily slow his march up the hallway. Yes, it was true! Despite everything, his son's pain, his pain and all the unanswered questions, he could not suppress a swelling pride. Pride that he and his family, and particularly his son Jeremy, were known at the highest levels of the American military. The old Navy man in him had come out and here he, Lt. David Powers, was being escorted to, and at the request of, the office of Admiral Blankenship. David loved his son deeply, but there was also a love of his country that went to the depth and breadth of his soul. During the Vietnam War he never questioned why he was there. His country had asked that he do his job, and his reward was saving many young men's lives. Shaking his head as though someone outside was speaking to him, Powers hurried to catch up with Yeoman Ferraro.

The two said virtually nothing as they proceeded toward Admiral Blankenship's office which was located near one end of the first floor in Office 1165. He could see the office door a few yards up on the right. Yeoman Ferraro stopped and opened the door for the visitor.

"Admiral Blankenship's office, Sir. Please go on in."

The Marine sentry posted outside the door snapped to attention. Powers entered a reception area that was furnished with standard military, bare essential furniture. As he waited, he perused the dozens of plaques, mementos and citations that filled the walls. He could tell that the man he would meet had enjoyed an extremely distinguished career, and several signed photographs gave ample testimony to the fact that Admiral Blankenship was no Pentagon desk pusher or bureaucrat. He was a highly decorated combat

108

veteran. Hearing footsteps, Powers turned to find the Admiral had appeared in the doorway on the opposite side of the reception area. He was dressed in an immaculate khaki uniform, his brown shoes shined to perfection. Several rows of combat ribbons adorned his chest, including the Command Star and SEAL Team trident. The gold shoulderboards attested to the rank of Admiral. He stood a couple of inches taller than Powers and had the lean physique of a twenty-one year old, although he had just celebrated his fifty-first birthday. No gray was visible in his closely cropped, reddish-brown hair. He walked with the somewhat stiff gait of someone in command, and at 6'4" tall, was an imposing figure. He walked over next to Powers and joined his guest in looking at one of the photographs. As he did so, he spoke, with only a slight trace of his original Texas accent remaining.

"That's me as a Lieutenant Commander in Vietnam with several of my men from SEAL Team Three."

The admiral pointed to the men and smiled, "Only Lieutenant Black, third from the left, didn't make it. He won the Silver Star in 1966 for saving four of his men and refusing evacuation until *they* had been evacuated. There simply was not enough time to save him....." The Admiral's voice softened to almost a whisper, "he was too seriously wounded." He then added, as if to himself, "Good man that Black."

The somber, almost mournful tone told Powers just how seriously this man took his awesome responsibilities of command. He reached out his hand and introduced himself, "Admiral Blankenship, I'm David Powers, Jeremy's dad. It's truly an honor to meet you."

Powers, not intimidated by very many people, was in awe of this man. The two men shook hands warmly and Admiral Blankenship motioned his visitor into his office. "I'm delighted to meet you, Mr. Powers. Your son is a fine, young man, among the best we have."

Powers refused the offer of coffee, taking the seat the Admiral had designated. Closing the door, the Admiral took a seat on the chair next to Powers, rather than behind his desk. Looking Powers straight in the eye he addressed him softly, "Mr. Powers, this is the worst part of my job and it's something I'll never get used to. The pain is real and often overwhelming to me...."

Powers drank in every word. He had a full appreciation of the consummate warrior part of this man, yet he also had an infinite respect for his intellectual prowess and sensitivity. It was the combination of the two characteristics, present in so few human beings, that set men like Admiral Blankenship apart from most others.

The real cadre of Navy SEALs, particularly those at this level of command, had no need to convey the misplaced bravado and machismo often inappropriately portrayed in the press and in some recently published inaccurate and self-serving books about the unit. Except for a handful of instances, such feelings resulted from the misguided perceptions of jealous outsiders. "I" became "we" on the first day of SEAL training, as it had for Admiral Blankenship more than thirty years before, after his graduation from Harvard, where he had been captain of the football team, graduating second in his class. Having earned a Masters Degree in International Affairs from Georgetown University, he had a very broad perspective of the world and America's role in it.

The Admiral continued......

".....I am deeply sorry about your son, Mr. Powers, and want you to know we will do everything humanly possible to see that he fully recovers. The Navy will spare nothing to insure he receives the best medical care available. While I wish I could tell you more about exactly what happened, he was involved in an operation which was highly classified, and in a highly sensitive area of the world. Due to national security interests, it would be best to leave it at that, except for one thing. You should know your son did his duty above and beyond even the standards of the SEAL Team and he performed bravely and selflessly. His primary interests were mission objectives, his country and the men with him."

Powers thought to himself that the Admiral's words sounded like those that would appear on the citation accompanying a combat medal, such as a Bronze or Silver Star. Since Jeremy had not been awarded any medals for the engagement in which he had become so horribly mangled, it could only mean that he had not been involved in a confrontation with hostile forces. Powers was growing more suspicous with each passing moment. Why was his son being cared for and protected under the supervision of a Navy Admiral?

While bursting with pride at his son's behavior, and performance of his duty, as well as the magnificence of all that he heard, Powers still knew something was terribly wrong. An endless stream of additional questions swirled around in his head. Why the guards? Why the silence? How could his son have possibly been airlifted, probably thousands of miles, while in the condition he was in? Didn't this happen about the same time as the propane explosions outside the Little Creek Naval Amphibious Base, that made news headlines all around the world? Why the FBI? As tactfully as possible, Powers tried to open the door to some answers.

"Admiral, thank you for those heartfelt and gracious words, and while I have utmost regard for national security, isn't something wrong here?"

Admiral Blankenship did not flinch as he responded. His remarks had achieved the desired result, "And what might that be?" The question was asked firmly, but not challengingly, nor was it in any way condescending.

Powers, looking into the Admiral's eyes and seeing his jaw set, decided not to pursue the matter further and got up to leave without answering. Offering his hand, Powers instead responded, "Thank you for caring so much Admiral and for taking care of my son. You and the SEAL Team will always have our enthusiastic support. Our hearts and thoughts remain with you always."

Admiral Blankenship stood up as well, and warmly shook hands. "Please take care of yourself, Mr. Powers. I'll be in touch."

David Powers knew he meant it. The Admiral himself felt a surge of emotion as he did not like lying, particularly to someone whose feelings obviously ran as deeply as this man's.

Powers turned and walked through the outer office into the hallway and followed Yeoman Ferraro towards the gate. As soon as the outside door closed, Admiral Blankenship picked up the receiver from the red telephone on his desk which gave him direct communication to each of the Commanders of the nine Navy SEAL Teams directly under his command. He dialed a four digit number,

"Commander Thomas, this is Admiral Blankenship. David Powers just left and, knowing his record as we do, he will not roll-over and let us stonewall him. Commander, he will get into the middle of this. I understand the point of 'in the interest of national security', but remember, if we continue to stonewall him it could cause more problems than if we give him just enough information to satisfy him, but not jeopardize our work. Dale, you know this guy.....do something."

"I see your point, Admiral," the Commander responded. "I'll look into how this can best be handled and get right back to you."

"Just get it done! The last thing we need right now is this guy blowing up on us...out here." With that the Admiral hung up. The old sick feeling, that prior to just a few months ago, he hadn't felt since "Nam" started again deep in his gut. Going over to a small cabinet and taking out some

Alka Seltzer, the Admiral fixed himself what had lately become his daily refreshment. Above all, he too was human. As he regularly told intimate friends, while he often swam in the stuff (water), he could not walk on it, nor did he intend to even try.

At that same moment, in Little Creek, Virginia, at the headquarters of SEAL Team Four, Commander Dale Thomas hung up his end of the red phone hotline. He was well aware of the point the Admiral was making about Powers' character and the situation that could be caused because of it.

Commander Dale Thomas, III, now forty-seven, had been a Navy SEAL for twenty-seven years. The commander stood six feet tall, weighed a trim yet muscular 197 pounds, and was considered one of the strongest men in the SEAL Team. Growing up in the Boston area, he was a high school hockey star whose nose had been broken so many times that he looked like a boxer. He had enlisted in the Navy at seventeen, spent two years on an aircraft carrier and became a SEAL in 1965 at the age of nineteen. He was sent to Officer Candidate School where he became an officer and earned both an undergraduate college degree and Masters degree in Mathematics. He had once remarked that he had become an officer to look out for the interests of the men he directly commanded. A highly decorated combat veteran himself, he had served in the top secret counter terrorist SEAL Team Six and now commanded the two hundred forty officers and enlisted men of SEAL Team Four. His own definition of his sacred responsibility was, as he put it, "To train brave, young men to go into harms way and have them come back alive."

The Commander had just returned from a highly classified mission in the Persian Gulf and had extensive experience in, and intimate knowledge of, Latin America. He was no stranger to the true national interest and had served in the middle of several Top Secret operations for years. He had also worked closely with the President of the United States, having been directly connected to him via a secure phone line while actively participating in another classified mission years before. He was the consummate SEAL.

Commander Thomas had met David Powers two years ago at the dedication ceremony of a new community gymnasium funded through Powers' charitable efforts in Phoenix. The elder Powers had insisted on dedicating the gymnasium to the SEAL Team. He had written to the President to request the participation of a senior officer in the SEAL Team and the President had forwarded the request to the Admiral. Admiral Blankenship, in turn, sent Commander Thomas as their representative for the dedication. David Powers and Commander Thomas had become fast friends in one of those rare instances where a wide variety of common interests and shared values leap-frog the many years normally required to develop such a lifelong friendship. Powers had come to revere the man.

Back in Washington, Powers spotted the white limousine as he came out of the security building after dropping off his guest pass. Bob Lewis had been standing next to the limousine and spotted him the moment he exited the building, and had already pulled up to the front entrance. After Powers had gotten into the front passenger seat, Lewis asked, "How'd it go? Did you get the answers you wanted?"

"No," Powers stated in a sharp tone that exposed the frustration he was feeling. "The Admiral is a terrific man, but other than some nice things about Jeremy, he said absolutely nothing. It seems there is a black-out because of so-called 'national security'."

That seemed to strike a chord with Lewis who had heard that very same thing many times during his years with the FBI.

"Whenever you hear that 'national security' crap, you can bet something *is* very wrong. I'll make a few calls. What time are we supposed to meet Maggie?"

114

Powers looked at his watch. "We thought since we're in Washington we should go to the Watergate Hotel. Maggie wanted to go back home and be able to say "she was there". You know, "inquiring minds want to know." I'm not sure Bob, after this meeting I don't think I need to be made *more* aware of the behind the scenes issues of our government. OUR GOVERNMENT...I always believed in that term. Uh oh, Bob. Watch out. I'm starting to throw out clichés and get philosophical. Chalk it up to exhaustion."

Lewis looked at Powers and knew that, although he had tried to lighten up his last comment, he was starting to again question the reality of *"our* government".

Powers continued, "I told Maggie we would meet her in the lobby at 12:30 and have lunch at the Cafe El Parador. Our flight home is at 4:30 so we should have plenty of time to get to the airport and return the car. How does that sound to you?"

At that moment, former FBI agent Bob Lewis was reminded of just how hungry he was, "Sounds good to me," was his quick response.

CHAPTER 13

ANDEAN HIGHLANDS, PERU

The two hundred year-old mission in the sleepy hamlet of San Girard looked much as it did nearly two centuries ago. The old stone block church stood as a lasting monument to the villagers' veneration of their religion. The old Catholic mission had withstood the test of time. Local peasants religiously attended church services every Sunday under the pastorate of Father Dominick Sanchez. Father Sanchez had been their priest for as long as many of his parishioners could remember. The Father had been born in Nicaragua and committed himself to God nearly fifty years before when he was admitted to the Catholic Seminary in Santa Cristobal, Nicaragua as a seventeen-year-old student. Father Sanchez had some basic medical knowledge and, since there were no doctors within miles of the village, the people of the village had come to rely on him for not only the health of their souls, but of their bodies as well. He assisted them in improving their crops by utilizing some basic farming techniques he had learned while at the Seminary. Their needs and goals were simple: family, God and their crops were the most important things in their lives. They worked hard, tilled the land and with great pride and joy watched as their children grew up and their children had children.

So went the cycle, each generation living their lives in much the same way as the generation before them. For many generations, theirs was a life of peace and tranquility. The elders of the village were able to isolate themselves from the ideological wars that raged around them. But, despite the

Father's repeated warnings about the evils of the loathsome, immoral drug called cocaine and the dangers associated with the drug lords that controlled its growth, he helplessly watched as many of his young parishioners were being actively enlisted into that dark, seedy world. The youth were romanced with the promise of the great things the white powder could bring them: wealth, enormous power and an exciting life away from the quiet little village. Often it brought only horror and death.

It was a warm, sunlit day. This particular morning Father Sanchez was tending his small vegetable garden which provided much of the evening meal to the occupants of the mission. He was cloaked in his traditional black Priest's robe tied at the waist with a black knotted belt. As he worked, he glanced up and noticed a lone figure walking towards him along the seemingly endless dirt road that ran from the Andean Highlands that passed in front of the mission and ended in the village of Saint Christopher. It would take several minutes for the figure to reach the mission so Father Sanchez went about his work and did not immediately concern himself with the approaching peasant.

John Nesmuth, the Director of the CIA, actually enjoyed his forays as an Andean peasant. He was dressed in tattered clothing, a torn washed out green shirt flopping loosely over his dusty tan overalls. His only compromise to civilization was a decision to not walk barefoot. Tattered leather sandals protruded from under Nesmuth's pant legs. The raggedy, wide brimmed straw hat the world had come to associate with the destitution of many Latin American countries sat at a slightly tilted angle on his head. Playing this role seemed to return Nesmuth to the relative simplicity of his younger years, when he felt unencumbered by the materialism and absolute values of his adulthood. Even the tall grass and slight floral odor of the Andean countryside re-enforced the purity of what he felt. It was as though his soul was removed from his body, washed, purified and again

117

returned to his body.

Letting his mind wander, he never lost sight of the reason he was here. The sensitivity of his contact was so great that Nesmuth traveled alone. Only two people at the Agency knew exactly where he was and what he was doing there. Two others knew only what was necessary for them to do their job in assuring that the regular payments (totaling millions of dollars) were made to the right people. The "Need to Know" list did not even include the President of the United States, nor the CIA's Senate Oversight Committee. Having too many people aware of the mission would only increase the chances of a leak that could blow the cover of the most important CIA source in twenty years, if not in the agency's history. With the lack of awareness of Nesmuth's whereabouts, the reasons for his mission and the protection it could give, his danger and isolation increased. There was virtually no backup that he could count on. No, Nesmuth was totally alone on this one. Such was the loneliness and isolation of being at the top of the most powerful intelligence service in the world. But at that moment, Nesmuth's thoughts were not on the dangers, but on the tranquility of his surroundings.

At the same moment, a second man could be seen coming down the road from the other direction. He was dressed much the same as John Nesmuth, except his clothes were even more tattered and he carried a handmade cane. Bending slightly forward, he alternately pushed the pole towards the ground, using it to help pull himself along at a halting, almost painfully slow gait. He appeared to be affected by a serious injury, perhaps by a miss-aimed machete while working on a coffee bean plantation, during harvest time. His clothing was faded, with no hint of the original color being distinguishable. Caked with the dirt of the road and weeks of sweat and grime from the fields, they were filthy, omitting a strong, pungent odor.

Father Sanchez did not look up from his work as the

first man stopped, opened the creaky door of the weathered wooden fence and entered the yard of the mission, closing the gate behind him and entered the building. Ten minutes had passed when the second man, limping past the mission, continued making his way slowly along the road for almost a mile. He looked up, scanned in all directions for signs of anything unusual, then turned and walked back in the direction of the mission. At no time did he accelerate his painfully slow pace. As he approached the gate, he hesitated for a moment and glanced towards the direction from which he had originally come. He then opened the gate and slowly walked through the yard and into the structure. After the stranger had closed the imposing, ornately carved wooden doors of the mission behind him, Father Sanchez got up from his garden, walked to the outside gate, closed it and returned to his vegetables. Peaceful serenity again dominated the scene, as though the visitors had never existed. A mule drawn cart containing a husband, wife and child, passed by and noisily creaked its way along the road. Father Sanchez visually followed the cart until it left his line of sight. Nothing else seemed to disturb the natural order of things.

Upon entering the church, John Nesmuth had proceeded to one of the three wooden confessionals which lined the hard clay wall stretching down the right side of the church. Entering the second cloth draped door, he took the place normally reserved for the Priest. The man with the cane then entered proceeding to the same booth. He, however, entered on the right side of the confessional booth. Sitting down on the hard wooden seat, he closed the curtain behind him before speaking in a soft, whispered voice,

"So, Father Gabrella, is all in order?"

Both men were leaning toward the thin gauze screened window that separated the two compartments, each staring at the obscured figure on the other side of the screen. While satellite surveillance would find nothing unusual in two men entering a church in the Andes only a few minutes apart, the crippled stranger had heard rumors that American NSA spy satellites could even pinpoint individual human conversations, enabling them to eavesdrop directly on private conversations from space. These were reported to be directed at specific conversations, not randomly at any civilian going about their daily lives, using their regular or cellular phones. He did not wish to take any chances. José Ocho Garriana, the man with the cane and one of the most powerful men on earth, did not feel like a peasant. Unlike Nesmuth, he found the peasant garb so constricting and dirty that it made his skin crawl. After all, he had spent every day of his life putting more and more distance between himself and the poverty he experienced in his childhood in the streets of Cardazanna. While Nesmuth certainly knew the capabilities of NSA spy satellites, he could never convince Ocho Garriana that his paranoia was misplaced. Then again, was it really?

Nesmuth spoke, also in a quiet whisper, "Yes, my son, all is in order, but I must ask you a question. FBI forensic experts have clearly identified the device that blew-up half of downtown Little Creek as a car bomb of the type frequently used by Cardazanna based drug organizations. In fact, the Director of the Counter Intelligence Division of the FBI has privately told our President that he believes you.....Oh excuse me, one José Ocho Garriana was almost certainly implicated. Voice prints of someone yelling in Spanish, "The pig is dead!" were filtered out of a frequency hopping telephone conversation that was placed between the outskirts of Little Creek and Cardazanna minutes after the blast."

Nesmuth could not see the expression on Ocho Garriana's face. If he could, he would have seen the anger rise up and his jaw tighten as he thought to himself how Daniel Vivas, his highly paid technology consultant, had escaped a summary death sentence only because Ocho

Garriana had personally been assured by an American inventor that his frequency hopping, spread spectrum telecommunications were the most secure anywhere on earth. In addition to all his other costs, he had invested seven million dollars in the man's company. Ocho Garriana made a mental note to make sure the inventor's telephones went to his enemies and then to burn Juan Engueras, Viva's assistant, as a warning. He answered Nesmuth,

"Father, we have an agreement. I provide you with intelligence information that is absolutely vital to the national interests of, let us say, your church, and I must function as anyone in my position would to insure I appear beyond reproach to my followers. One of my boats was sunk, causing tens of hundreds of millions of dollars in losses to my legitimate business interests, and those responsible must pay. It is that simple."

Nesmuth knew that megalomania was a global phenomenon, although he had begun to sense that this man had exceeded any known clinical limits. What once seemed like an absolutely black and white moral choice was now becoming increasingly gray. A few hundred deaths of mostly thugs, with an occasional innocent, was one thing. So was some peripheral damage to the American banking system, to say nothing of the economic degradation of thousands of American companies and banks. Nesmuth found the banking system flawed anyway. He could even tolerate the fact that hundreds of CIA trained pilots flew the drugs into the United States and Cartel money out. After all, if America could buy a country or two and prevent them from joining the enemy Communist camp, what was the harm in dealing a few hundred kilos of cocaine? This, however, was going too far. Two dozen school children had been killed in the Little Creek blast. He answered, in an increasingly agitated tone.

"El Patron, my son, yes, we had a deal. But, killing two dozen American children is crossing the line in a big

121

way. If the President knew about this....."

Nesmuth was interrupted and could detect a sneer in Ocho Garriana's voice as he shot back, "Your President will not find out and if he does we will know who told him. It doesn't matter anyway, you surely can not tell him. You will do nothing to jeopardize your precious career."

Nesmuth realized he may as well have been talking about dead plants as dead children, they all meant the same to this man. All of them started out like this. Ruthless, ambitious, greedy, arrogant, and articulate. In the end they believe themselves bigger than all men and all governments. The next generation anxiously waits behind the scenes to take their place, each generation more murderous than the one before. Since they all had more money and power than any man could use in a lifetime, they could only distinguish themselves from the others by being the one known to be the most ruthless. First it was the Mafia, then the Colombians, and more recently the Jamaicans, Haitians and Asian groups. There were no limits to their individual depravity and the vicious cycle would never end. Nesmuth realized he would get the same response to a moral discussion from an inert rock. He now understood he had also failed to realize that what he considered his own absolute morality, placing the so-called national interest above all else, had now been called into serious question by his dealings with such a monster as Garriana.

In a moment of soul-searching, Nesmuth wondered to himself if perhaps abiding strictly by the U.S. Constitution was in the true national interest after all, not its individual creative interpretation by patriotic men like him.

Dropping the subject, Nesmuth asked, "What new information do you have for me?" Having paid a high price, he might as well get something useful from this meeting in return. He was also having a hard time restraining himself from ripping the other man's throat out. Nesmuth's voice was aggressive with rage.

Ocho Garriana pressed his face closer to the window as he spoke, "The guerrillas will soon attack Caracas."

Caracas, the capital city of Venezuela, was one of the largest, most prosperous cities in the hemisphere. Its two million inhabitants enjoyed one of the highest standards of living in that part of the world. Even Nesmuth was taken aback, as the CIA did not know that Shining Path's reach extended beyond the Huallaga region, or perhaps to Peru's peripheral cities. Venezuela did not seem possible.

"Sendero?", Nesmuth asked in surprise.

"Si, Sendero! They are everywhere! Your country will be next!"

With that, Ocho Garriana got up and hobbled out of the church, taking the same road back from where he came and at the same slow, painstaking pace.

While this information had momentarily taken priority over Nesmuth's rage, he knew a line had been crossed from which there was no return. This man had to be eliminated. His usefulness was now a thing of the past and he would have to be relegated to the garbage pile reserved for all overused "assets". The "national interest" required nothing less.

Nesmuth slowly rose. He had waited a good five minutes after Ocho Garriana left. Quietly, he walked back along the same path from where he came.

Nesmuth returned to Langley as secretly as he left, philosophically resigning himself to the fact that the Ocho Garrianas of the world would forever be the necessary creations of United States Intelligence.

Shortly, the world would learn of another American intelligence agency creation, a certain Manuel Noriega.

CHAPTER 14

NEW YORK CITY
SEPTEMBER, 1992

First Global Bank, or FGB as it was known in international financial circles, was one of the ten largest banks in the world. With nearly three hundred billion dollars in assets, the bank was a financial powerhouse. FGB's fifty-seven story glass and steel headquarters, in the heart of Manhattan's financial district, shimmered in the sun and its size dwarfed everything around it for blocks. In the business world, it stood for everything legitimately powerful in the aristocratic world of banking. Major transactions were carried out by highly educated young men and women from the finest schools, often sons and daughters of the financial elite. The bank had been founded nearly one hundred years before by the scion of a wealthy New York merchant family that had emigrated from France. Discretion and privacy were the bank's major trademarks. In a sense, it could have been any bank carrying a famous name. In another respect, it was.

This particular morning, in the lavish boardroom on the fifty-seventh floor, an emergency meeting of the bank's Board of Directors had been called. Following the tradition of grandeur expected of a financial institution such as FGB, the boardroom was overwhelming in its size and opulent decor. The richly paneled walls were covered with portraits of the twenty-two previous presidents of the bank. An enormous oval mahogany table stood in the center of the room, centered on a richly woven, antique Persian rug that would be considered a gem by any dealer. The sixteen burgundy leather, high backed, swivel chairs for FGB's directors and guests were placed neatly around the table with a leather case engraved with gold FGB initials set at each place. The case contained the meeting agendas, copies of financial statements, pads, pens, and other documents that would be utilized in the course of the board meeting. Period antiques including small tables and priceless vases from the Ming Dynasty accented every wall and corner of the room. No expense had been spared to convey the sense of discrete opulence desired by the bank's founding fathers. At one end of the room, a door led down a hallway to the palatial office of the chairman, Mr. Jon Paul Chaubenais.

The twelve Directors began filing into the room several minutes before the appointed starting hour of 10:00 am. They represented the "Who's Who" of world business, a veritable cross section of the top echelon of power, influence and prestige in the international world of commerce. The emergency board meeting had been convened by three Directors who were particularly concerned with the precipitous drop in earnings reported by FGB for the latest operating quarter, a trend that had begun several quarters before.

At twenty minutes to ten, the Bank's President entered through the private entrance at one end of the boardroom. He walked around the room greeting each of the board members, in turn. They stood individually or in small groups of two or three, energetically chatting, sipping coffee, and nibbling on the donuts and pastries being served on a silver tray ornately inlaid in gold and platinum. At five minutes before the hour, Jon Paul Chaubenais, descendant of French royalty, took his place at the head of the table, signaling to the rest of the Directors, who immediately took their seats, that the meeting was about to begin. Vincent Carlucci, Executive Vice President, Finance and Administration, and the Secretary of the Corporation, prepared to take notes. At precisely 10:00 am, Eastern Standard Time, the fateful meeting began as Chaubenais announced, "The special meeting of the Board of Directors of First Global Bank is hereby called to order."

All of the Directors simultaneously opened the leather cases before them, preparing to take their own notes of the meeting as they scanned through the agenda. FGB had three female and nine male Directors. Included were the former presidents of six *Fortune 100* companies, the existing presidents of two others, the managing partner of one of the world's largest law firms, the managing director of one of America's largest consulting firms and the presidents of two other major banks.

In order to insure proper ethnicity, there was one black, one Jew, one Hispanic, a Japanese-American and several WASPs. The Board seemed to represent a cross section of America at its highest levels of power. The integrity of this institution would appear beyond reproach to all.

After the meeting was called to order, Rick Palmer, the Vice President and Treasurer, prepared to give the financial report. The lights were dimmed in the room and colorful slides that graphically depicted the bank's operating results were flashed on a large screen that had descended from the ceiling at Palmer's touch of a button. He had a monotonous voice that often put one or more of the directors asleep. But not today.

Palmer began, "As you can see, results for the second quarter, ending June 30, were highly disappointing. Revenue decreased thirty-seven percent to $22.8 billion, expenses increased forty-six percent to $22.7 billion, generating an operating loss of eighty-four million dollars......"

The gasps of most of the directors could be heard above the droning of the man's voice. After the initial reaction, silence. Myron Fishback, one of the directors, asked,

"Without spending a whole day on this, precisely why did this happen? How could revenue decline so much, while expenses increased this dramatically?"

Palmer looked over at his boss and deferred to the president. Chaubenais spoke in his most authoritative tone, his aura of feigned superiority apparent to all.

"Our considerable portfolio of real estate loans has caused us to set aside huge reserves for bad loans. Several commercial loans have also been classified as non-performing. In addition, we have had to pay enormous legal fees to deal with these matters......"

After 15 minutes of line-item explanations, it was apparent to everyone in the room that the underpinnings of this major financial enterprise were indeed in serious jeopardy. Almost 5 minutes passed in silence, as the directors were too stunned to even speak, although they continued to flip through the pages of the material given to them, feverishly taking notes about items of particular interest. However, with a few joining in at a time, and gradually building to a crescendo, they all contributed to a bombardment of endless questions. The president would barely finish giving one answer before the next question began. Eventually his voice grew raspy and increasingly impatient as the questioning became ever more accusatory. Checking his watch, he was relieved to see the noon hour, and promptly adjourned the meeting. The directors were escorted by the president's secretary to the adjoining, lavish executive dining room located directly across from the president's office. A large buffet of fresh fruit, various imported cheeses, an enormous roast beef, caviar, shrimp and various other delicacies awaited them. Most of the directors were in no mood for a pretentious luncheon ceremony, and all of them impatiently threw various delicacies onto their plates, quickly returning to their seats to continue what was now an inquisition. Chaubenais only managed a couple of bites of his sandwich during the one hour mid-day break as the questioning continued.

After lunch was concluded, the meeting was formally

reconvened. Several directors continued their relentless assault, boring into the man with the impartial sharpness of a drill bit into wood. The verbal assaults continued into the night without the normal courtesy of breaking for an evening meal. Finally, with both the inquisitors and their victim spent, the meeting drew to a close. Chaubenais' normal aura of superiority had been reduced to a dulled monotone. The man was out of what to him were legitimate explanations, but which came across to his directors as thinly veiled excuses. In a normal situation, the man's job would have been in jeopardy. To his co-conspirators in running one of the largest drug-related money laundering operations in the world, the punishment could be far worse, including death.

Mirriam Wilson, the first female President of a major bank, had said little. She finally spoke, using the somewhat snide tone for which she had become famous, "Mr. Chaubenais, thank you for answering our questions. I must tell you, however, that they are not totally satisfactory. Speaking for myself, I will expect a major turn-around by the end of this quarter, and certainly no later than the fourth quarter."

Chaubenais was enraged, but dared not show it. The hypocrisy of this woman was beyond belief. There was silence. A couple of the directors looked at their watches, now concerned about catching their flights home to various parts of the country. That was Chaubenais' clue, "Do I have a motion to adjourn?"

Fishback, the Director who began the assault, slowly raised his hand, "I make a motion to adjourn."

Mirriam Wilson casually raised her hand, still looking at the notes she had taken during the meeting, "I'll second it."

Chaubenais immediately followed, "All in favor?" One hand at a time was raised until all twelve of the Directors showed their agreement, the slowness of the motions testifying to the exhaustion that each felt. Chaubenais continued,

"This meeting is adjourned."

He then folded his papers, never looking up from them or speaking, got up from his chair, turned and walked out of the room through his private entrance. Within 5 minutes, most of the directors had left, saying very little to one another. Mirriam Wilson was the last to leave. She had waited a discreet period of time until she was certain her absence from the departing group would go unnoticed. She walked down the hallway to where the private express elevator was located. Checking the lights located above the now locked doors, the letter "G" stayed lit for three to four minutes, indicating the directors were now on the ground floor and had all departed the elevator. It was now nearly eight o'clock in the evening. Turning from the elevator she could hear the sound of the large commercial vacuum cleaner being used by the building's janitors. Seeing no one else, she turned down the hall, passing the locked doors leading to the executive suites. She hesitated halfway down, noticing a light shining under the door of Roberto Felipé, the Senior Vice President for Latin American Operations. He was apparently working late tonight. Continuing a few steps further, she stopped and quietly knocked on the mahogany, double-doored entrance to Jon Paul Chaubenais' office. As Chaubenais opened the door he was greeted by Mirriam's broad smile.

Chaubenais, not returning the same enthusiasm at seeing her exclaimed, "What was all that bullshit about turning around the operating results by the end of the next quarter?" He stood aside allowing the woman to enter. He stepped out into the hallway, looked down each end of the hall then followed her back into his office locking the door behind him. At 46, Mirriam had what might best be described as a cold beauty about her, although her hardened features, and especially the coldness of her eyes, exposed the life she had led those 46 years. Mirriam did have the body of a 25 year-old, and moving across the room her hips

129

moved rhythmically from side to side, making Chaubenais' anger slowly turn to lust. Reaching Jon Paul's desk, she suddenly swung around and faced him. She knew just how to work her body to her best advantage, leaning against the desk, she struck a pose that announced her availability.

"Mirriam, we have to talk," Chaubenais continued, clearing his throat and trying to return his concentration to business and away from the smell of her perfume and the resulting reaction of his own body.

"Really?" She answered in her most demur, pouty, coy voice, totally unlike the icy professional tone that was heard during the meeting.

That was enough. Jon Paul quickly moved toward her, grabbing her in his arms he began kissing her on her lips then worked his way down her neck. Sitting on the desk, she pulled her skirt up and wrapped her legs around his waist. The two began feverishly groping each other. Clothing, almost being torn in the struggle to remove them, was thrown aside. Not a word passed between them. Only the sounds of abandoned passion came from them both. Suddenly the phone rang.

Reaching across his desk, Chaubenais knocked the headset off of its cradle. While still attempting to remove his clothing, and after much fumbling, he retrieved the headset and in a breathless voice almost yelled, "Yes!"

Speaking to the party on the other end, Chaubenais' voice showed his irritation at being interrupted, "Ah....Roberto, yes we will still get together in about thirty minutes. I'll call you."

While Chaubenais was trying to talk, Mirriam had been removing his pants and was in the progress of tugging at his jockey shorts. Hanging up from his short conversation, he grabbed her arms, pinning her down onto the top of his desk. Dropping his shorts to his knees, like a stallion he mounted her. This was a meeting between two separate, naked bodies, each intent on satisfying their own animal passions, not a relationship of shared joy or tenderness. Several minutes later, their passions spent and still without a word or look passing between them, they dressed. While sharing immense business interests and endless sexual passion, they shared little else. In fact, neither one had time in their lives for much else.

After dressing, Mirriam, her voice now controlled, asked, "What is this business we must discuss?"

Chaubenais' tone had also regained that of professionalism, "We have to dramatically increase our monetary recycling efforts." He continued getting dressed. Straightening his tie in front of the mirror in his private washroom, he returned to the interior of his office and retrieved his jacket from the floor. Having returned to his original, neat, aristocratic appearance, he returned to his desk. Mirriam, meanwhile, straightened her clothing, returned herself to her normally impeccable look, and took one of the two matching chairs across the desk from Chaubenais. Chaubenais picked up the phone, dialed Roberto Felipé's extension and asked the man to come in. Mirriam had unlocked the outer door and left it ajar.

Robert Felipé reflected the demeanor of his heritage, as a member of the Brazilian royal family. He was a very trim, stately man, six feet tall and 165 pounds, wearing a $2,000 Savile Row suit. A graduate of the National Académe De Brasillia and the Harvard Business School, he had risen from Assistant Branch Manager in Saõ Palo, Brazil, to Senior Vice President for Latin America, including responsibility for the countries of Colombia, Peru, Bolivia and Venezuela. He had established substantial banking and business contacts in many of the hemisphere countries throughout his tenure at the bank.

Moving to the side of Mirriam's chair and extending his hand in greeting, Felipé inquired, "Good evening, Senorá Wilson, you are well, I trust?"

The woman could not stand the deferential tone with

which Felipé always spoke to her. Not acknowledging his extended hand, she responded in kind, "Yes, I am quite well, thank you. Too bad the bank's operating results aren't as healthy as I am." Her tone was mockingly disgusted.

Felipé, dropping his gesture of greeting, sat in the chair next to Mirriam. Chaubenais ended the awkward silence. "Roberto, I'm sorry to keep you this late. As you know, the bank's operating results for the quarter were....let us say....highly disappointing. Results in Latin America, of course, helped offset this by increasing nearly twenty percent."

Chaubenais glanced over at Mirriam and continued, "The Board has instructed me to turn things around by the end of this quarter. Can you help me? From your contacts, could you get us the thirty million in additional fees that are needed to do this? Could we do more work for Mr. José Ocho Garriana, the Colombian business man? Roberto, it is imperative that we accomplish this. All of our careers depend on it."

"I will certainly talk to him, Jon Paul," Felipe responded, He has always been a good friend of ours. He parcels out a lot of his currency trading to others less loyal than we. I will contact him and get back to you as soon as possible. Is that all you wish to speak with me about?"

"Yes, Roberto, thank you for staying. Good night," Jon Paul answered, dismissing him.

Felipé got up from his chair, giving a slight bow to Mirriam, offered his farewells.

"Good night, Señorá Wilson."

Mirriam stiffly acknowledged his departure, "Good night Roberto." Whenever these two were together the disdain for each other always lurked just beneath the surface, despite their periodic yet awkward exchanges of social graces.

After Felipé had left, Jon Paul fixed his stare at Mirriam. In an almost desperate voice he asked, "Mirriam,

132

what the hell am I going to do? What are we all going to do?"

Mirriam, not particularly interested in how, or even if, Chaubenais solved the dilemma he found himself in, quipped, "You mean besides making love?"

Chaubenais did not share in her humor and was no longer in the mood for a roll on the floor. It was time to deal with the severity of the problem he was now facing.

"How are the other banks doing? Are they holding together?" Chaubenais brought the subject back to the business at hand.

Sitting back in her chair, again emanating her aura of feigned superiority, she began reeling off figures and answers as though she were offering a rehearsal presentation. Her voice changed from the flirtatious tone of just a second ago to the icy business tone he knew so well.

"Our group is doing fine. Thirteen of the top twenty banks in this country will help, and by pooling our branch resources and using wire transfers, we can increase the amounts of money we are moving back to Cardazanna from $5 billion a month to $7 billion. Based on the two points we get as our share, that's another forty million a month, net. Our bank's half is twenty million, leaving FGB twenty million. That's sixty million this quarter which is still a little short of what that bitchy Director wanted! Why don't we increase FGB's share to the full point for the quarter and you can pay us back later? We'll hide it at our end by listing it under advances to affiliates. There will be plenty of loan documents, certificates and whatever else is necessary to pass any bank audit or examination. How does that sound?"

By that time, and *not* unknowingly, the woman's skirt had slid up exposing the garter belt she was wearing, the top of her nylons and the smoothness of the skin on the upper portion of her thigh. Chaubenais, having been fighting to keep his concentration on what she was saying, lost the battle.

"Mirriam, I get so horny when you talk like that." He said teasingly. Knowing the importance of the information she had just passed on to him, including the possible answer to his problem, Jon Paul could relax a little. Looking down to the point of his attention, Mirriam slid her skirt up another few inches and swung her leg over the arm of the chair. She found that danger, intrigue and the brilliance of her own mind had an intoxicating, sensuous affect on her and she had always found it to be a turn-on. In almost a monotone voice she continued talking.

"Our customers are helping as well. Between us, the syndicate of banks we have assembled does banking for seventy-one of the *Fortune One Hundred*. We don't need Ocho Garriana's air force because we have our own. Together, these companies own and maintain a combined fleet of nearly three hundred aircraft. Instead of flying the boss's wife's dogs around, they get to fly Garriana's cocaine in and his money out! Sounds a little more worthwhile to me."

Mirriam, having become caught up in the self-admiration of the brilliance of her plan, had lost any sense of logic, reality or decency. Her voice slowly increasing in volume with excitement, she had become intoxicated with the power of it all. Addicted by her self image as a world-class financial wizard, her eyes lost the usual cold emptiness and had taken on a wild gleam. Listening to Mirriam and watching her as she spoke, even Chaubenais became sobered. Studying her, his thoughts ran back to when he was a boy watching the film strips of Adolph Hitler addressing the masses. He too had that look. It was the look of people so caught up in their own feeling of power that they are not really speaking to anyone, just reveling in the sound of their own voice, totally engrossed in their own thoughts. Chauvenais half expected her to begin salivating as the near crazed monologue continued.

Breaking into her self-induced trance, Chaubenais asked, "So, Mirriam, you are telling me that our group includes thirteen of the largest banks in this country and seventy-one of the largest corporations? That's incredible!"

Coming back to reality, her eyes refocused, her voice lowered as she confirmed, "That's exactly what I'm telling you....darling." Overcome by her own excitement and the fiery lust that had built up in her, she got up from her chair and, while preventing her skirt from dropping into place, walked over to where he sat. Straddling Jon Paul's legs and slowly lowering herself onto his lap she proceeded to satisfy herself. Controlling every movement, she was making a point of letting him know that she was in control, and that she and she alone had the power. Jon Paul Chaubernais could care less, as long as her lust was satiated and her illegal efforts increased the bank's bottom line. Their lives were now so intertwined that nothing else mattered.

CHAPTER 15

KANSAS CITY, MISSOURI

Bob Lewis had flown to the Midwestern city of Kansas City, Missouri to meet privately with four FBI agents he had worked closely with during his years with the Bureau. He shared deeply the pain of his best friend, David Powers, and sensed there was more going on than either man knew. Lewis had contacted some of his old friends to get a sense of what was transpiring in the international arena of terrorism, drug trafficking and money laundering, but little could be discussed openly on the phone. The four other agents, posted at FBI offices around the country, agreed to fly to Kansas City to meet with him. Anything discussed could never be repeated, and all agreed that once the meeting had ended, for all practical purposes it would have never occurred at all. If nothing else, this was to be a reunion of close friends who had worked tightly together in an atmosphere of mutual respect and shared values. Since the FBI is compartmentalized in its operations, Lewis had invited a couple of agents from the Counter-Intelligence side as well as former associates who were street agents. Having worked as an FBI agent for twenty-five years, Bob Lewis was never quite certain where FBI Counter-Intelligence ended and the CIA's activities began.

Theoretically, the FBI handled both counter-intelligence and counter-terrorist matters within the continental United States, while the CIA's responsibilities started at America's borders. Lewis had heard rumors of overlapping responsibilities and jurisdictional disputes. He had heard increasingly disturbing rumors about mutual distrust and even animosity developing between the two organizations. The relatively new DEA added to the confusion of just who was supposed to be doing what, particularly when it came to the so called "War on Drugs". All of the men checked into the Marriott Hotel at the Kansas City Airport and agreed to meet for dinner in a private room Lewis had reserved at O'Leary's Chop House, located about five miles away in the heart of downtown Kansas City. They were to meet in the bar at 6:00 that evening. Each of the men was from the Vietnam era, veterans who entered the Agency in the late 1960's and early 1970's. Most were near retirement and in their late forty's. Lewis knew that the Bureau would have to add nearly five thousand agents during the coming years as the Vietnam era retirees left the Agency. The Bureau would take on a whole new look as younger agents too young to really remember the impact of Vietnam or the Cold War, provided the new life's blood of the FBI.

Lewis could see three of the men conversing in animated fashion as he entered the crowded bar. The forth had not yet shown up. Lewis nudged his way through the crowd to the far end of the bar and approached the men. He instantly felt the electricity of the kinship of years past.

"How the hell are you guys?!" he inquired as he shook every one's hand.

"Not bad, old buddy, how's it hanging?" responded a tall, well-built man in a tan sports jacket, open collar blue and gray shirt and muted gray plaid pants. Jack Williamson was a twenty-three year FBI veteran presently assigned to the New York City office. He was considered an expert at working white-collar crime, particularly banks and wire fraud cases involving major federal violations committed by federally chartered banks. Trim and well-conditioned, he ran seven miles a day to keep himself more fit than FBI regulations required. The two men shook hands eagerly and greeted each other with the warmth and broad smile of lifetime friends.

Lewis moved to the second man. Ian McAllister stood a little under six feet tall and had the same chunky, square build he had as a star fullback at the University of Colorado in the early 1960s. McAllister, the son of Irish immigrants, had grown up in Chicago. He served two tours as a U.S. Marine officer in Vietnam and entered the FBI after being discharged in 1970. His twenty-two year career had included assignments to six FBI offices prior to his present job as a counter intelligence specialist in San Francisco. He was casually dressed in a red open-collar polo shirt and tan khaki pants. Brown loafers completed the aura of casualness.

Lewis moved to the third man, George Arguelo. Arguelo, the son of Mexican immigrants who came to the United States in the late 1940s grew up in the Barrio in Los Angeles. A star high school baseball player, he had attended USC on a baseball scholarship before entering the United States Army as a Second Lieutenant. He was decorated twice for bravery in Vietnam, having been awarded the Silver Star. He became an FBI agent in 1967 and had spent the last several years working in the counter-intelligence division as an undercover agent heavily involved in counter-drug efforts. He worked out of the Miami, Florida office. Trim, olive skinned, Arguelo, who spoke fluent Spanish, could pass himself off as a willing participant at any level of a drug organization. Many of his experiences had been truly hair-raising. Dressed in a yellow shirt and blue slacks, his bright white teeth gleamed against his dark skin as he smiled to greet his old friend Lewis.

At that moment, Tim Smith, the fourth agent, entered the bar, scanning the crowded room for his friends. The men seemed to spot each other at the same time, and there was a spontaneous outburst of enthusiastic greetings as they shouted and waved. Drawing into a nearly circular group they patted each other on the back, looking like a backfield in an on-field conference at an NFL game.

Each sized his associates up from head to toe, seeking

138

to somehow assure themselves that the world was still okay. Tim Smith was the tallest of the group at 6'3" and the nattiest dresser. He wore an expensive camel hair jacket with the compulsory suede elbow patches over brown plaid slacks. An open collar blue shirt was in plain view under the open jacket. The son of a wealthy Mississippi family, Smith was a star quarterback at the University of Mississippi before passing up a promising NFL career to enter the Air Force as a Second Lieutenant in 1967. He joined the FBI after his discharge in 1971 and had spent the past eleven years also working bank fraud out of the New Orleans, Louisiana office.

The animated conversations continued for about an hour as the men had a few drinks and got caught up on each other's lives. At that point, Lewis looked at his watch and suggested that the group adjourn to the private room in the back of the restaurant. Each had temporarily put aside most thoughts of the past to bask in the warm glow of a temporarily united common agenda.

Lewis paid the bartender and led the group towards the rear of the building. They entered a comfortable, intimate room that had a large round table with five place settings. The agents sat down, exchanging small talk about their families and what they had been doing since they last met. Looking around the table, Lewis realized that these four men were closer to him than any family ever could be. They were truly brothers, having shared some of the most terrifying moments of his life, along with some of the happiest. Flashes of memories of his days at the Bureau ran through his head. He never thought he had missed being at the FBI, but in looking around him he did realize that he truly missed these men. He missed the warm brotherhood, the sincerity and feelings of loyalty they gave him. These feelings had not been experienced by Lewis since he left the bureau, and their rekindling made him feel years younger. They were men of honor and character, the type who always gave Lewis hope when he became the most desperate, the most distraught from working undercover within the darkest lowest pits of our civilization. How many times had each one of them saved his life....?

Lewis' thoughts were interrupted by the waitress entering to take the dinner and drink orders. After she had departed and closed the door behind her, the conversation drifted from catching up on individual lives to the present state of the international underworld. In one way or another, FBI agents Jack Williamson, Ian McAllister, George Arguelo and Tim Smith were all involved in monitoring, pursuing and trying to shut down various dimensions of illicit drug dealing. Lewis spoke,

"So guys, what's new in the game of 'who rules the underworld?' Any new players?" Lewis kept his question light. He knew these men were well aware this meeting wasn't called just to chat, but he did not want to jeopardize their ethics by being obvious in trying to obtain information for his own personal use.

Jack Williamson responded, his Mississippi accent having all but disappeared during the years since his early upbringing in Oxford, Mississippi. "Plenty. They have become extremely sophisticated in doing business. The dark doorway, petty business, sleazy dressed mobster image is long gone. They're now into big business, involved with corporations, governments and even our own banking system. The amount of money being laundered is almost uncountable. It moves around so fast and in such large amounts that it can only be weighed and estimated instead of counted. It is overriding the entire banking system. First Global Bank, which goes by the name FGB, is one major player. The place works like a bookie joint. We wire money to banks all over Latin America, for that matter all over the world, and the activity is many times what it should be for even a bank that large. We also wire funds to a whole list of companies after deducting a few points in fees. In many

140

cases, documentation for these so called loans arrives days, weeks or even months later. Sometimes it never arrives. The counter-intelligence folks are concerned that these might be front companies for terrorist groups who have committed crimes against the United States. Many countries on our terrorist watch list already have agents here and all they need is money and weapons."

Everyone present knew that the "we" reference to FGB meant that Jack Williamson was working undercover inside the bank. It would have been totally inappropriate for any of the other agents or for Bob Lewis to pick up on that fact, so everyone let it pass, as though Williamson were speaking on the basis of outside observation.

Everyone else in the room had grown silent as Williamson spoke, and listened intently to what he said, trying to determine how each of their individual assignments fit into the larger, global issues obviously unfolding. George Arguelo of the Miami office interjected,

"A lot of that money is probably going to the real king-pin, José Ocho Garriana. Our intelligence has him at the top of the roost. You should see his cocaine air force-sometimes we think it's bigger than ours. I've gotten to know one of his pilots pretty well and what he told me blew me away. He's an American who flew for the Air America CIA operation during the Vietnam War. We got drunk one night in Miami and did he have some stories! He used to fly supplies into the hills of Laos to support the fight against the Pathett Lao Communists. On his way back, he'd fly plane loads of heroin out. I asked him why the CIA would be flying heroin around and he said he wasn't sure. Apparently, the same thing might be going on now. About forty percent of the registered pilots who flew for Air America now fly for the drug cartels and have no affiliation with the CIA. This guy admitted to me he now gets a hundred grand per flight. What do you think could be worth that much? This guy also told me that some of his pilot buddies are still working for the Agency."

The room remained silent except for the occasional sound of a glass being picked up, and the ice clinking around and sliding against the glass. Bob Lewis had been away from the inner workings of the bureau since his retirement, and although he read voraciously about world affairs, terrorism and drugs, he was truly astonished at the magnitude of the drug problem and all of its elements. He had been emotionally transformed from a highly paid security director for a large corporation back to a hard working FBI agent. The psychological metamorphosis was now complete. Ian McAllister began to speak,

"We are very concerned in the San Francisco office about what will happen in 1997 when Hong Kong becomes part of Mainland China. The Chinese have been growing opium for centuries and the potential for flooding the United States and the rest of the West with heroin is staggering. Many of the largest and most active banks in the world are located in Hong Kong, and between that and their huge industrial concerns, we could be in for a great deal of trouble. Our preliminary analysis indicates the dollars involved would dwarf anything we have been dealing with in Latin America. The Chinese could flood the global market with heroin of the highest grade derivative from their gigantic opium crop. The Hong Kong banking and industrial infrastructure already in place would provide the mechanism to easily launder several trillion dollars a year. This could seriously impact, on a negative basis, the U.S. balance of payments and will further bankrupt our already drug-infested American society."

The complete silence of all of the participants reflected how startled everyone was to learn the magnitude of what was unfolding and the potential threat it posed to America's economy, and the nation's survival. Latin America, China and other drug growing regions taken together began to add up to an unmeasurable problem. The silence was broken by a knock at the door as the waitress returned to their private room with dinner. Little was said as she went about her tasks, since no-one wanted to say anything in front of an outsider. The silence was deafening, except for the sounds made by the dishes being placed on the table. Each man's thoughts raced to adjust to the seriousness of it all. The realization of the relative insignificance of each agent's role in the battle against the U.S. drug problem when compared to the seemingly infinite size of the whole drug business and the sophistication and success of its big players left each man in a state of somber disbelief. Placing the salads and the main courses down, the waitress left the room. After she had left and closed the door behind her, the fourth man, Tim Smith, provided his perspective,

"You know guys, I'm struck by something. We are also watching a lot of bank activity in New Orleans with money going to Latin American for this Ocho Garriana character. We know he is an active business partner of the Shining Path movement. We also know that the entire upper echelon of Shining Path spent years studying hard line Marxist doctrine under Mao Tse Tung's disciples in China. They are far more hard line than even Mao was. Could you imagine what would happen if Sendero wins in Peru? The Chinese could control 80% of the world's drug trade and probably have quasi control of much of the global economy! They could bury us as Nikita Khrushchev and the other hardliners threatened to do, but never really had the power to follow through."

Lewis had a million questions, and everyone joined in a process of simultaneous conversations that grew increasingly animated. The excited chatter was certainly a way of avoiding having to confront the reality of what had just been discussed. The fact that the CIA was apparently somehow a willing participant in the drug business and that many former CIA operatives were flying for the drug cartels bothered him deeply. He also could not imagine what it would be like trying to deal with a technologically advanced Mainland China that controlled the world's drug dealing and would soon have control over some of the world's largest banks, once Hong Kong reverted back to them in 1997.

Lewis' thoughts returned to his friend David Powers. He needed to learn the answers to a couple of very specific and sensitive questions. Turning to George Arguelo, who was seated next to him, he decided to take a chance and ask a direct question. Lewis knew how careful all agents were about giving out any details on what they are working on or leaking information that they have special access to. After all was said and done, he was no longer in the Bureau and he had less of a right to any sensitive information because of this fact.

"George, do you know anything about the explosion in Little Creek that has been all over the news?"

Looking closely at his friend and seeing the intense look on Lewis' face, Arguelo carefully responded, "Yes, I do. We had someone deep inside the Ocho Garriana organization who was killed in the explosion. Apparently, Ocho Garriana was very pissed off at a U.S. Naval officer stationed at the Little Creek Naval Base and he sent a bunch of his thugs to kill the guy. Our forensic people tell us it was a 500 pound car bomb, detonated with exactly the same M.O. as Ocho Garriana's goons usual trademark. It had the signature of a fat slob hit-man Juan Espinoza."

That answered a couple of Lewis' questions. The next one was somewhat more philosophical, "George, how many governments do we have?" The question was asked innocently in the comfortable atmosphere and camaraderie between old friends reminiscing.

The man looked at Lewis quizzically before he responded, "Probably three or more. One government runs our law enforcement agencies such as the FBI and also commands our Special Forces. I mean military groups like the U.S. Navy SEALs who are sent on special operations such

144

as to kill drug dealers in Peru and elsewhere. A second government is a business partner of the drug cartels, flying their cocaine out and money in. A third decides which governments to destabilize and overthrow. I'm sure there are more."

Lewis continued his provocative questioning, "Which one do you work for, and who exactly did I work for when I was in the Bureau?"

"I guess the one elected within the rules laid out in the constitution of the United States. It's probably the same as the first one I described." Arguelo's voice was soft, reflecting his personal concern as to why and for what reason Lewis was asking *these* specific questions.

With that, Lewis quietly turned to finish his meal. The reality hit him, being with his old friends he had gotten caught up in the emotions of the past, of being "one of the boys....one of the brother agents." He jerked himself back to the present and, although he had enjoyed seeing his friends after all this time, his main purpose for being there was to help his friend, David Powers. He had no idea what he would tell David. Even though he was no longer an agent for the Bureau, he could not break the code of respecting the confidentiality of what his friends had told him. Therefore, he could not possibly divulge everything he had heard. He, himself, was still trying to digest the magnitude of what he had just listened to, and particularly George Arguelo's incredible answer to his question about multiple United States Governments. It was truly becoming frightening.

After everyone had completed their meals, the conversation grew far more philosophical and less specific to federal law enforcement issues. This was due to the combined effects of the pre-dinner drinks, the wine consumed with dinner, and the natural trust and intimacy of being with old friends. It was the type of "high" ultimately reached when you combined these ingredients. Bob Lewis and Ian McAllister became involved in a highly generalized and

145

philosophical conversation about an old case and the war on drugs. Somehow, McAllister had reminded Lewis of a case the retired agent had worked many years before involving an undercover investigation of a vicious motorcycle biker gang. Lewis, undercover as a biker himself, had convinced the top enforcer for the Devils Disciples gang from New Jersey to turn states evidence in return for a suspended sentence. The man had confessed in gruesome detail to being an accomplice in the murders of thirty-nine rival gang members, and federal indictments had been handed down against three of the Devils Disciples' organizers. The three men had all been sent to prison for life.

After a couple of more drinks, Lewis confided to McAllister that he had moral difficulty with the end result of the case for several years. On the one hand, the lenient sentence against the enforcer was okay with him because three top bosses who had given the orders for all but two of the thirty-nine murders had gone to jail. However, the man himself was a monster, the bestiality of one murder often exceeded only by that of the next. He finally put it away emotionally by convincing himself that most of the thirty-nine victims were worse than the enforcer, in essence getting what they deserved. Lewis and McAllister came back to the war on drugs as Lewis asked his friend,

"Ian, tell me about the war on drugs. Is it all bullshit?"

McAllister answered, "Bob, we spend $13 billion dollars a year on a so called war we cannot possibly win. As you heard tonight and I'm sure you are aware of, in some respects we're fighting a war against ourselves, because the CIA is in the drug business with the cartels and that is insane. So are many in the top echelon of this country's so-called legitimate business sector. Those guys rationalize what they do by convincing themselves, and anyone else they feel compelled to discuss it with, that it's for the greater good of our country. They feel that someone will end up doing the money laundering, so why not look the other way

and participate with our U.S. banks and corporations so
we can get at some of the hefty profits for American stock-
holders and taxpayers.

Besides the obvious illegality and lack of ethics, the
major problem with all this is they think they're the only
ones who can decide what the common good really is. The
drug money lets the CIA buy or destabilize governments to
further defend and protect U.S. interests throughout the
world. Only they decide which ones are worth buying and
for how much. What a bunch of crap. No one elected these
guys and they're not really accountable to anyone."

Lewis was feeling a little bit lightheaded, somewhat
intoxicated by not only the alcohol and camaraderie, but by
the intensity of the subject matter.

"Ian, is there any way we could win?"

McAllister paused and thought pensively for several
seconds before responding, "Yes, Bob, there is. Treat all of
this like what it really is, a war to the death against America
and the Free World. Find the bastards organizing, growing
and distributing the crap and kill every one of the drug cartel leaders without pity. Fortunately or unfortunately, to do
the job effectively, you would have to take out some of those
in the middle, the so-called mules, money launderers and
such. Treating American citizens, without due process of
the law is something that may happen if you are fighting a
real war on drugs. Just as during W.W.II, when we fought a
real war against our enemies, we didn't hold up an attack to
read the Nazis on the battlefield their Miranda rights, we
can't hold up today's attacks on the 'drug Nazis' to worry
about everyone of their constitutional rights! In war, certain rights are suspended. We must finally determine that
today's drug situation is so dangerous that it warrants de-
claring a war, and then the U.S. government should declare the war, informing the drug dealers of the world that
the rules of war now apply.

Finally, America's domestic law enforcement agencies

as well as our military could be fully engaged to eradicate the causes and the supporters of this war, for a change enabling the government to take whatever action was deemed necessary to win. That is how the Allied forces won in W.W.II and that is how America and the Free World can win the war today!

Alternatively, we can continue investing our resources in teaching our kids to say 'no,' and it will be years or decades before we even have a clue about whether or not that mild approach will ever work."

Lewis nodded his head in tacit agreement, knowing somehow that, no matter how unpalatable this radical solution really was, McAllister was somehow speaking the truth.

Looking around the room at the friends he felt so honored to have, Lewis realized the endless complexity of the situation they discussed. He found himself actually feeling relief that he was out of that world. No longer having to rationalize against his own morality, dealing within the endless web of deceit that envelopes the dark side of the world these men have to live in. A world that is theirs and theirs alone. A world that they can only share with each other, and no one else, not even with their wives or families. Yet, he couldn't help thinking how he was going to miss these guys, even though he was out of their business....

The conversation continued well past midnight, at which time the men returned to their hotel in preparation for each one's respective departures early the next morning. The flights would return each man from the highly charged philosophical journey of the night before to the cold reality of the world in which each had to live in the present. No matter how unwinnable the war on drugs appeared, each would do his part to rid the world of this evil. The United States Constitution that each man had sworn an oath of allegiance to demanded nothing less, even if it meant fighting, as they were, with both hands tied behind their back.

148

CHAPTER 16

CARDAZANNA, COLOMBIA

José Ocho Garriana was presiding over a meeting of representatives of several governments, organizations and individuals who shared a common interest in strengthening their alliance against all who tried to interfere with their massive operations. Bound together by a common hatred of the West and a preference for the bankruptcy of capitalist ideology, as well as its massive global business interests, the meeting would define the group's agenda for the next several years. Common goals would be established, alliances strengthened, and the financial resources necessary to destroy anyone or any government standing in the way of this onslaught would be provided by Ocho Garriana himself. The meeting would be held in the tightly secured conference hall on the grounds of Ocho Garriana's thirty-eight acre estate. Garriana's megalomania had reached the outer limits, after his facing down of John Nesmuth, the Director of the CIA.

In all, representatives of forty-seven separate governments, nineteen political organizations and two other cartels had been invited. No drug lord on Earth other than Ocho Garriana had the global reach long enough to assemble such a diverse and powerful group of individuals.

Security was unprecedented. Several hundred extra security personnel had been imported from all over the world, and only the best would do. The normal compliment of four helicopters was supplemented by twelve others. All commercial aviation in or out of the country was suspended for forty-eight hours, and no military flights were allowed within seventy-five miles of Ocho Garriana's estate. The outside world was told that all commercial aviation and over flights of Colombia's airspace had been shut down due to a serious malfunction of the country's air control radar system. Nobody could leave or enter the area once the assemblage had gathered on the grounds. Guests were put up in the three hundred room, bomb proof, luxury hotel that Ocho Garriana had constructed on one corner of his grounds.

Prior to the first plenary session, Ocho Garriana was meeting privately with Juan Gabrielle of Shining Path and Jorge Ocholla of the Bolivian FLB. Just as Shining Path sought the overthrow of the Peruvian government with a fanatical Marxist government even more radical than the Khmer Rouge, the FLB sought the overthrow of the Bolivian regime and intended to replace it with a Marxist Government patterned after Mao Tse Tung's China. The two organizations worked hand in hand. Ocho Garriana convinced the two representatives that they should conduct a major act of violence in Caracas, Venezuela to show the world how powerful they had become and to demonstrate that their tentacles could spread in any direction at will. By accomplishing this, Ocho Garriana would demonstrate to the Director of the CIA just how impeccable his intelligence information was, proving that he was certainly worth the increasingly higher price Nesmuth was being forced to pay.

Ocho Garriana entered the cavernous conference hall to a standing ovation from all of the delegates. Surrounded by a cadre of sixteen hand picked bodyguards, the casual observer could discern little difference between these proceedings and what transpired at the United Nations. Ocho Garriana worked the crowd just like any politician, except this man stayed in power by committing an endless string of atrocities, each more hideous than the next. He and Shining Path appeared to revel in the pitiless way they maimed and tortured so many other human beings. Finally reaching the podium, "the magnificent one" spoke after a seventeen minute standing ovation that even he could not quiet, despite signaling the guests to stop on three occasions. The intoxication he felt from the homage paid by the assemblage exceeded any cocaine high.

"Honored guests, you humble me by your reception today—" He was interrupted by a three minute ovation.

"But, our struggle has just begun. The forces of imperialism, of Yankee Fascism are all around—" The applause was deafening. Finally, mesmerized by his words, the group let him continue.

"Our cause is the cause of all oppressed peoples everywhere. The masters want us to be only slaves and dirt farmers, to rub our faces in the ground, to pay constant homage to them and their agents. We will bend no longer to the forces of, racism, expansionism and capitalist debauchery. The decadence of the West has rotted the core of all Western civilizations. Their institutions are bankrupt, their citizens are consumed in the perversion and excess of their daily lives. Their decadence is fatal—they are the living dead. We must double our efforts to hasten the demise of their self serving and morally bankrupt policies—."

In the thirty-seven minutes Ocho Garriana spoke, his henchmen committed eleven murders in his name, nearly a hundred citizens of Western societies died of drug overdoses or related problems, and thirty-nine innocent Colombian civilians died in a terrorist car bombing in a city sixty miles East of Cardazanna. His personal net worth had increased by another several million dollars, and his role as one of a handful of the most powerful men on Earth was further enhanced.

CHAPTER 17

LANGLEY, VIRGINIA

John Nesmuth, General Chaim Ben Lavan and Sir Robert Brethan Chapman had re-assembled to continue the development of a joint strategy for countering the grave threat posed to the institutions of many western countries, including their own, by the growing power of the Narcoterrorists. Each man had personally briefed his respective head of state after the last meeting at CIA headquarters a few months earlier. They had defined the enormous magnitude of the problem for the U.S. President and the prime ministers of Israel and the United Kingdom. With the combined resources of nearly eighty countries providing direct and covert assistance to the terrorist drug trade and its allies, the threat seemed very real indeed. The legal, diplomatic, military and other issues facing the Western countries in their attempts to combat the increasingly serious problem were enormous.

They were no longer dealing merely with conflicting ideologies. These were combined with financial and other resources that were staggering even by Western standards. The Narco-terrorists played by no rules. Violence, murder, mutilation, extortion and intimidation were their weapons. Trying to combat the threat within the strict rules of law governing most Western nations was becoming impossible.

The three intelligence directors realized that the only possible answer resided within a combination of meticulously orchestrated overt and covert strategies. General Ben Lavan and Sir Robert had taken their places in the two blue winged chairs facing the CIA Director's desk, and John

Nesmuth again stood up to speak while standing adjacent to a large, setback lit exhibit. It contained boxes, lines and lettered squares reminiscent of a large corporation's organization chart. The first meeting had defined the general magnitude of the problem and identified many of the countries participating in the terrorist drug assault against Western institutions. This exhibit charted how it all worked and why. Nesmuth began to speak utilizing a large telescoped silver metal pointer,

"Please notice that there is no one ultimate source at the top of this chart. There is not necessarily one Board of Directors as such, although many of the top echelons of these organizations do work together from time to time. For example, the Sicilian Mafia is making enormous investments in the Bekaa Valley drug organizations in Syria and Lebanon. The best we can do is narrow it to four or five major production centers. By doing this, we will be able to pursue the *"Head of the Hydra"* approach to countering this worldwide menace. Once identified and isolated, perhaps we can pursue unified strategies to cut off the heads of these Hydra."

As Nesmuth spoke, both Sir Robert Bretham Chapman and General Chaim Ben Lavan noticed there were four boxes at the top, each at the same level, but none of the four connecting together. Nesmuth continued,

"Notice we have consolidated the large number of individual centers of drug activity into four major ones. While clearly there are others, these four probably provide the greatest immediate threat. They also represent places we might be able to infiltrate and destroy, if we combine our individual intelligence and counter-terrorist assets. The first box on the left is jointly labeled Cardazanna Cartel and Shining Path. José Ocho Garriana controls the Cardazanna, Colombia cartel with an iron hand and Pablo Luis Doval runs Shining Path in Peru. We might as well consider these two as co-chairmen of the board of this combined narco-terrorist/international criminal enterprise."

He pointed to the second box and continued, "Next, we have the Italian Mafia families, the Gioualla, Rico, Salvadori and Bertucci organizations run this heroin trafficking organization from Palermo, Sicily. Obviously, they get help from all over the world."

The lecture continued as he moved the pointer to the third square, "Sayer Ayud runs the heroin trade out of the Bekaa Valley in Syria."

General Chaim Ben Lavan smiled and leaned back in his chair as Nesmuth continued, "We have all known for years that a considerable amount of worldwide drug trafficking from that part of the world has Syria, Lebanon and Jordan as its jumping off points. Beirut is to that part of the world what Cardazanna is to Latin America. Politics, drugs, governments and terrorist organizations all appear interwoven as one."

Nesmuth moved toward the side of the chart showing the fourth box and pointed to it, "This looms as the most serious problem of all, God help us when Hong Kong becomes part of Mainland China in 1997. In the meantime, three groups control the opium trade in the Golden Triangle in Southeast Asia. These are, respectively, the organizations of General Hi Phong in Laos, General Ong Keng in Cambodia, and General Lieu Than in Thailand."

Nesmuth looked away from his board to emphasize one point, "I did not say this was the entire analysis—we also have all of the former Soviet Republics, many of the East European countries and the Indian sub-continent, to contend with as well—but we might be able to do something about this now and deal with the other areas at a later date. Perhaps drastic action against the first four groups will cause the secondary areas and organizations to pause and think about what they will face in the future. Notice, it is almost impossible to separate governments from terrorist organizations, since very often they are one and the same. Any questions so far?"

"No, John, please continue," responded Sir Robert as he mentally computed the enormity of it all, but was uncertain where the path was leading. Nesmuth returned to the exhibit and pointed to numerous lines that seemed to come from the four boxes in all directions. As he did so, he again began to speak.

"Notice, there are almost an infinite number of lines emanating from each box. These represent the almost limitless variety of schemes used to distribute the cocaine, heroin and other drugs—."

Nesmuth then spent nearly an hour describing the latest techniques being used by the "mules," people who smuggled illegal drugs in or money out of a country. He also discussed the latest ways narcotics were hidden on commercial flights or cargo containers of ships anywhere in the world. His briefing included information on the surgical implanting of bags of cocaine into live humans and hundreds of other examples of the often ingenious components of drug distribution networks.

While his visitors were surprised by the creativity that all of this new information represented, their minds were boggled at the thought of trying to even begin to stop as much as they had interdicted in the previous year. The drug dealers were getting richer and richer and had unlimited resources. In contrast, the budgets of the intelligence agencies were being slashed.

Both visitors had heard the nearly endless stories from their own enforcement agencies regarding sporadic and highly publicized illegal drug seizures, but all three men realized law enforcement efforts were only intercepting the tip of the iceberg, probably less than fifteen to twenty percent of the world's illegal drug production.

Both General Ben Lavan and Sir Robert had received information from Mossad and MI5 about the illegal drug trafficking by the CIA's own air force. Neither was quite sure how to broach this most highly classified and most sensitive topic with CIA Director Nesmuth.

The CIA Director then moved to a semi-circular shaped diagram on the chart. It depicted the seemingly endless number of channels used to launder the illegal drug profits back to their sources. Several of the world's largest banks and corporations were shown by name and it sent a visible shudder through the two guests, neither of whom publicly showed any demonstrable reaction to the myriad of terrible and violent events each had seen in his lifetime. It was one thing to deal with the infinite horrors of the Adolph Hitlers of the world, but quite another to have to do something about the illicit activities of the very economic institutions these men were sworn to protect. Nesmuth spent nearly another hour analyzing the last phase in great detail. When he had finished, he folded the telescoping pointer, and returned to the chair behind his desk, somewhat fatigued and nearly breathless from the nearly two and one-half-hour animated lecture he had presented to his guests.

Sir Robert spoke next, "John, while some of this is new to us, we are not sure where you are going with it. Do you have any concrete conclusions, suggestions or recommendations?"

The CIA Director leaned back, cupped his hands together and glanced up at the ceiling for several seconds before speaking,

"Yes, Sir Robert, I do. It's like everything else. Striking at four targets, or fifteen to twenty if we add up each of the four regions' major components, is in many ways easier than trying to intercept tens of thousands of individual "mules" or whatever they're called. That makes it almost like looking for a needle in a haystack."

General Ben Lavan interrupted, "John, are you suggesting we cut off the heads of the Hydra?" This expression, used so often through the years in counter-terrorist and intelligence circles, meant taking out, or killing, those

156

individuals at the head of any particular organization deemed threatening. This became euphemistically known as "cutting off the head of the hydra."

"Yes, General, that's exactly what I'm suggesting. But, there's more. Actually, as historians, both of you should remember what General MacArthur accomplished by undertaking his strategy of island hopping in the Pacific during World War Two. It was brilliant, and it enabled the Allies to save hundreds of thousands of lives and months or years of additional warfare by doing what he did. In much the same way, if we "skip" or "hop over" the mules and immediately move to the launderers, the banks and corporations, the mules will gradually dry up, be starved and wither away. Oh, we'll make it look good by having customs and the DEA chase these characters all over the world, but we can concentrate our best resources on the four organizations and the laundering group."

Nesmuth hesitated briefly for effect and continued....

"So, what do you think?"

While there was no visible reaction to this rather startling confession, the three all realized the inevitability of having to eventually fold-up this world wide rogue operation. The multiple assassinations implied by the strategy were unprecedented, and actually made the two visitors somewhat uncomfortable. Occasionally "taking out" an undesirable through the years was one thing, but simultaneously doing away with so many crime bosses located in dispersed parts of the world was quite another.

Sir Robert spoke first, "I think it's absolutely brilliant, John. While there are a million details to iron out, what would MI5's targets be?"

Nesmuth had carefully thought all of this out in advance, "How about the Italian organized crime families, and the rogue bank, BCCI. Of course, since all of us use BCCI to finance many of our counter intelligence activities, we better hurry and shut down those accounts. You could also

157

help in Southeast Asia with SAS elements."

"And what of Mossad, John?" General Ben Lavan asked.

"I've mentally got you down to cut off the head of the Bekaa Valley Hydra, so to speak, and to help us locate the Hydra heads in Peru and Colombia. Your intelligence network must be very strong in that part of the world since you've successfully tracked down Eichmann, and other Nazi war criminals in Latin America," Nesmuth replied.

Sir Robert spoke again, "And what about yourself, John?" Nesmuth had rehearsed his answer for the entire week preceding the meeting,

"We'll take out the heads of the Colombian and Peruvian Hydra, deal with U.S. corporate and banking elements of the money laundering, and take primary responsibility in Asia." It was somewhat incredulous to the two foreign intelligence heads that a number of U.S. banks and corporations were being discussed in the same manner as the heads of murderous criminal enterprises. But what was the real difference between a Mafia crime boss and the President of a U.S. based global bank whose activities provided the financial underpinnings for the José Ocho Garriana's of the world? It occurred to both men that the answer was, in fact, none.

The three men continued to iron out specific details of operation "Snow Bird" for a couple of hours, while assigning responsibility for final elements of the plan to various components of their respective intelligence services. John Nesmuth told his two friends of his intention to request a signed "finding" (directive to assassinate) from the President of the United States for those aspects of the plan that would involve the U.S. in killing any of the terrorists, and both Sir Robert Betham Chapman and General Chiam Ben Lavan told Nesmuth they would have to obtain similarly signed documents from the Prime Ministers of the United Kingdom and Israel as well. The meeting did not adjourn until well into the evening. The matter of the CIA's drug airforce was left for another day, yet it remained as a torpedo in the magazine of the ship, threatening to detonate and destroy the entire operation.

Although the hour was late, Nesmuth had promised he would call Fred Kimball, the Director of the FBI, to spend some time with him later that evening. Kimball had left a message that the matter he wished to discuss with the CIA Director simply could not wait, even until the next morning. Nesmuth's Secretary dialed Kimball's office, and the FBI Director agreed to be at Nesmuth's office within thirty minutes. Nesmuth used the idle time to grab a very quick bite in the CIA employee dining room. Exactly thirty minutes later, Nesmuth's Secretary, Janet Cummings, announced Kimball's arrival. Frederick Maynard Kimball, forty-nine, had been the FBI's Director for the past two and one-half years. He was an imposing figure at 6'2" tall and had entered the agency in 1967 after a tour in Vietnam as a U.S. Marine officer. Educated at the college of William and Mary in Virginia, he had finished law school and earned a legal degree while in the bureau. He was unerring in both his public and private pronouncements that, while the Director served at the pleasure of the President of the United States, his ultimate arbiter was neither an office or individual, but the Constitution of the United States. Shadow governments, the end justifying the means, and patently illegal plots against alleged enemies of the United States simply were unacceptable to this man and were against everything he stood for.

Director Kimball had spent the better part of his career as a counter-intelligence agent, so the shadowy world of plots and sub-plots was nothing new to him. While the two men professionally respected one another, the somewhat urbane and holier than thou attitude of CIA Director Nesmuth made Kimball highly suspicious of what limits, if any, Nesmuth would place on the CIA's activities. Actually, he couldn't stand the man, although the levels both men were at in the government automatically demanded at least a superficial respect for one another. As Kimball entered Nesmuth's office the two men shook hands and greeted each ther somewhat coolly. After sitting down in one of the winged chairs, Kimball got right to the point,

"John, our undercover operatives keep running into both former and present CIA personnel flying drugs and money for the cartels, particularly out o Latin America. While we realize many of them are there for the money, which is illegal, several others appear to be working for the Agency. It's hard to tell who's working for who."

Kimball, trying to be slightly diplomatic, continued, "I'm sure many of the pilots on the cartel's payroll are providing useful intelligence information to you, but we are stumped that a lot of the drugs seem to end up in a bottomless pit. Can you tell me anything about this?"

Nesmuth did not flinch, although the prospect of getting caught between Ocho Garriana on one side and the FBI on the other was starting to make him extremely uncomfortable. He responded with a question, "You're not saying the CIA is in the drug business, are you Fred?"

The hour was late, both men were tired and Kimball realized that sparring around the issue could continue indefinitely with no resolution. He decided to stop skirting the issue,

"Yes, John, that's exactly what I'm saying. Let me be real careful about this. I didn't say John Nesmuth was in the drug business, or that elements of the CIA are in it for personal profit. Our view is that the drugs are used to pay mercenaries or to influence policies of governments deemed hostile o the interest of the United States. Even in those scenarios, the drugs could ultimately end up on the streets of America to do enormous internal damage to the country. In any event, we believe that the individuals doing this are not under direct control, but represent rogue elements who believe that only they know what is best for the United States."

Kimball had, perhaps deliberately, given the CIA Director a graceful way out. Nesmuth grabbed it,

"I'm not going to be defensive, Fred. I give you my word that I will personally look int this and take any action necessary to deal with it, no matter how unpleasant. Why the Hell would I want to tolerate CIA drug dealing if the Bureau's agents along with elements of our military are putting their lives on the line to stop it?!" While Kimball was impressed by the performance, he was increasingly disgusted by the reality. The meeting was short, but Kimball had made his point.

Business was concluded, so the two men exchanged a few additional pleasantries, shook hands and Kimball departed.

John Nesmuth stood there, shaken. Between the exhortations of José Ocho Garriana and the fact that the FBI had uncovered the CIA's own involvement in drug dealing, he was in the most delicate and tenuous position of his career, not to mention the personally life-threatening dimensions, and he knew it. Never before, in his professional or personal life, had he felt this vulnerable.....he was scared. His mind racing, he realized there was only one thing to do.....survive!

CHAPTER 18

PHOENIX, ARIZONA

It had been several weeks since David and Maggie Powers had returned from Washington and, although their daily lives had almost returned to normal, David had grown increasingly agitated about the lack of answers regarding what had really happened to Jeremy. Fortunately, the boy's condition was steadily improving, although, he was still listed as critical and his actual whereabouts remained one of the most closely guarded secrets in the United States Navy. David Powers had made inquiry through his substantial network of contacts within the United States Government, and having come up empty handed, his suspicions grew. While his normal seventy hour work weeks were at least temporarily diverting, his thoughts never strayed very far from his oldest son. He could not stop the questions constantly running through his mind about what really had happened to him, and this ws reinforced by his feeling that this was nothing short of a major government cover-up.

Maggie had returned at about 10:00 p.m. that evening from a meeting of the Phoenix Board of Education. Extremely civic minded, she donated much of her spare time to the Board and was particularly active at the middle school level. David was watching TV and reading in bed when she arrived. Entering through the bedroom, she began to undress in the sitting room.

Looking up from his book, David saw her slender naked body reflected in the dressing room mirror. The sight never failed to excite him. The intensity with which she undressed, washed her face and went about her other pre-

162

bedtime ritual told her husband that something was wrong. To give her an opening for venting whatever was bothering her, David decided on the simple approach, "How was the meeting honey?" It never failed, just give her an opening and......she took it,

"I don't understand what's going on. Do you remember last year when that sixth grader at the MacArthur Middle School died of a drug overdose?", she asked while continuing to apply her facial cream.

David did remember. The incident had been all over the front pages of the three major Phoenix newspapers. What made it so newsworthy was the fact that the MacArthur Middle School was in the wealthiest suburb of the city. While twelve previous deaths of young, middle school aged Hispanic and Black children had drawn their share of media coverage in the city, the MacArthur School death resulted in outcries from all over Phoenix for the authorities to do something. David was looking in the mirror at his wife as he spoke,

"Yes, Maggie, I do. But, what's that got to do with why you're so upset tonight? By the way, why don't you come to bed now....you can't do anymore to improve perfection."

David watched as she knotted the sash around her floral robe. Even the romantic hint could not blunt the intensity of her emotions concerning the meeting. She finished combing her hair, looked in the mirror from a couple of different angles, turned off the light and began walking towards the bed. Powers switched off the TV and placed the remote control down on the end table next to him. He turned the blanket back on Maggie's side as though to welcome her. She began taking off her robe, revealing the deep lavender night gown she was barely wearing. The color was a startling contrast to her cream colored skin, accenting the lavender specks in her deep green eyes and highlighting her dark hair.

163

She continued, oblivious to how her appearance was affecting David, with her mind intent on the conversation at hand, "Apparently, some of the parents of the MacArthur school kids had enough clout to demand a real investigation. Remember that "sting operation" we read about that the FBI conducted a couple of years ago in San Diego? Well, they did the same thing here in Phoenix. You won't believe this but it turns out that the kid who died at MacArthur purchased the cocaine from his teacher—"

Powers, startled, temporarily forgot his passions. He bellowed out, "His God Damned teacher?"

His wife went on, "Yes his God Damned teacher! Not only that, but three other teachers at MacArthur, the Principal, and....you won't believe this...."

Powers interrupted, "At this point, what won't I believe?"

Maggie continued, "When I got to the meeting tonight, I noticed that the chair usually occupied by Don Carter, the School Board Treasurer was occupied by a very formal, unsmiling man who I never saw before. Would you believe he was an FBI agent? Can you imagine, a goddamned FBI agent at a Phoenix School Board meeting?!"

Maggie was growing increasingly agitated, and was sitting up in bed with the quilt clenched so tightly in her hands her knuckles were turning white. Her husband looked over at her, and tried to soothe her by placing his hand softly on one of her clenched fists. The gentle touch broke her hold on the quilt and her expression softened as she looked over at him. Maggie's tone became softer,

"David, Don Carter, the Treasurer of the School Board, was indicted by the FBI today on multiple counts of possession and sale of illegal drugs, namely cocaine and heroin, and God knows what else. The FBI guy spoke, said very little and only answered questions in a very general way. Apparently, the investigation is not over and God knows who else will get caught up in all this. I can't believe I actu-

164

ally knew someone messed up in drugs....." Her voice trailed off at the end, weighed down by the enormity of what she had said.

The same thought apparently occurred to David and Maggie at the same instant. They each started to speak and nearly simultaneously stopped, not wishing to interrupt the other.

"David....."

"Maggie, do....."

Maggie spoke both their thoughts, "David, our Casey will be a student at MacArthur in three years. In three years it could be Casey who dies of an overdose."

Maggie rolled towards her husband, placing her head on his shoulder she hugged him as tightly as she could. Still sitting up in bed David, continuing to hold Maggie, turned off the bedside lamp. With the room enveloped in total darkness they both quietly lay in each others arms. David slowly began kissing his wife, first gently on her forehead, then, lifting her face to his, he kissed her passionately on the lips. Slowly lowering himself and her onto the silken sheets of their bed, they continued to embrace. David then slid each strap of her night gown down her arms, leaving her breasts bare.

Softly she responded, "David, I love you......"

The country sounds of Phoenix Station WKBC began filling up the bedroom at precisely 6:30 a.m. David slowly slipped his arm from under Maggie, squinting away the sleep in his eyes. Fumbling, he located and turned off the clock radio. Sitting up on his side of the bed, he swung his feet onto the floor. Still rubbing his eyes he picked up the phone from its cradle, and dialed Bob Lewis' number. After the fourth ring, he heard Lewis' sleepy voice at the other end of the line.

"Hello....Lewis here." His twenty-five year career in the FBI had made the formal answer a habit. David spoke, "Hi Bob, David here." (David loved to joke with him early

165

in the morning, and Lewis was so vulnerable it took him at least two cups of coffee to wake up.) David continued, "Please apologize to Janet if I woke you guys up." Janet Lewis was quite a special lady. She had remained married to her husband all these years, through the inevitable roller coaster ride of a Federal Agent's career. Lewis quickly responded,

"We've been up for hours. What can I do for you David?" David's somber tone struck a historical chord. He had heard it many times before, during the incident at Modular Products. While the two often discussed security concerns at the company in very serious tones, Lewis instinctively knew that the early morning call must have something to do with Jeremy.

"What were you doing for dinner tonight, Bob?"

"Nothing. David, but what are we doing now?" Lewis had emphasized the "we." Powers continued, and in so doing, violated one of the few unwritten rules he had with Maggie regarding such matters. The two had agreed years ago that David would never invite a business associate, no matter how close or intimate, to their home for dinner without first conferring with her....

"Bob, why don't you and Janet join us for dinner tonight, say about seven?"

Lewis responded,

"See you tonight, old buddy."

Lewis knew it would serve absolutely no purpose to question Powers further at this point.

Obviously, Dave's conversation had wakened Maggie. Turning towards her and seeing the look on her face, David realized that he had better have a good memory, because, that night may be the last sex he would be getting for a long, long time.

The front doorbell rang at the Powers' home at precisely five minutes to seven. Bob Lewis was fastidiously on time for everything in his life. David answered while Maggie tended to some last minute details in the dining room. Rosa Gomez, their maid, rushed from place to place in the kitchen, talking to herself. David did not understand Spanish but was sure she was cussing over

166

the preparation of dinner. Powers opened the door, and as soon as he saw Janet Lewis on the doorstep, the two spontaneously hugged. She was a stunning tall blonde and, although a mother of three, had kept the body of a *Playboy* centerfold. David backed-up, stepped aside, and after Janet entered, he shook hands with Bob Lewis.

After Lewis had entered, and Powers had closed the door, he asked, "What's to drink?"

"Anything you want. The usual?"

He began pouring a Chivas Regal on the rocks, and a gin and tonic for Janet. Maggie was already sipping a glass of the white wine David had uncorked earlier. After serving his guests, Powers poured himself a Jack Daniels on the rocks. The four close friends enjoyed a graciously served, four course dinner, accompanied by two bottles of fine French wine, and the typical, light dinner conversation. After dessert, Maggie and Janet got up from the dining table and retired to the living room, while Powers motioned for Lewis to follow him into the den.

The wood paneled walls were covered with the mementos of David Power's roller coaster life. They included everything from his laminated college degrees to plaques awarded to him for his substantial civic activities. Even his high school and college athletic photos were there. After entering the den and closing the sliding doors, Powers poured each of them a snifter of brandy. Each man made himself comfortable in one of the two highly stuffed, leather easy-chairs, both removing their shoes. Lewis stretched his legs and placed his feet on the ottoman in front of his chair, knew what was coming, and was mentally preparing himself,

"Bob, have you done any checking on what is going on with Jeremy?" Lewis was in an agonizingly difficult situation. No longer bound by security constraints or his FBI oath, he could not hide behind the mantel of "no comment". He had no idea of what to do or say. He did not wish to watch Powers endure the emotional agony of the Modular Products days, when the inability to tell the man anything concrete almost drove him insane,

167

but what could he do? It was a horribly painful dilemma, and as Powers continued to stare at him, Lewis knew the man was looking right through him. His concern for his friend overrode his long standing oath of silence. Finally, the paralyzing truth came flowing out,

"David, it was drug dealers.....Drug dealers had a hit out on your son."

Powers erupted, "Drug dealers? What fucking drug dealers?!" David Powers leaned forward with such an immediacy that Lewis moved his legs back to the floor and sat up, almost in a defensive position. Keeping his voice as calm as he could, and hoping it would help to calm David down, he gave his friend what he had been waiting for. Something tangible..... a name......a face, something that he could direct all his frustration and anger towards.

"José Ocho Garriana, the head of the Cardazanna Drug Cartel."

There was silence as Lewis studied David's face, trying to read his response to what he had just said. It was several seconds before Powers spoke,

"Why Jeremy?" Lewis' answer was both spontaneous and omitted nothing.

"Because he led a bunch of SEALs on a successful mission against the cartel. His men sank one of Ocho Garriana's boats somewhere in the Amazon River Basin and cost the bastard over two hundred and fifty million dollars."

The men looked at each other for several seconds. Powers' eyes grew misty as he exploded with such a rage that the glass flew out of his hand. He jumped out of his seat and started pacing.

"If you know, our government must know. What have they done about it? Who is this piece of shit José Ocho Garriana?" His voice steadily became a scream.

It was one of those incoherent states that simply had to expend itself, and Lewis knew it. Silence was the best and only support he could give to his closest friend. His eyes had been

168

following the enraged man from one end of the room to the other. Powers' pacing had stopped at the fireplace, and pounding on the mantel, Powers shouted,

"Bob, we went through this type of shit ten years ago at Modular Products. Then it was tied to everybody's rights. Now the government covers up `in the interests of national security'."

Walking back towards his chair, Powers suddenly, and in far more measured tones, blurted out, "Bob, you and I are going to Washington in the morning, and we had better get some answers....." His voice trailed off as he slowly sank into his chair, and covered his face with his hands, as if to close out the entire world. Lewis watched as Powers shoulders rose and fell, and hearing the quiet sobs coming from his friend, he shared in his pain. He also could not help wonder where this all would lead the two of them, now bound together by what seemed like a lifetime of shared values and experience, understood only by those with similar chapters in their lives.

Watching this man, the man he had come to respect and admire not only through the years of working for him, but through the other time....the time when his friend had experienced another lonely hell, Lewis' mind went back to the days at Modular Products in Downey, California. David was working for that company and had inadvertently become deeply embroiled in a potential terrorist nation's plot to acquire a nuclear weapon, possibly to use against the United States. Then too, he was alone in his battle not only directly against the terrorists and the nation behind the plot, but with his own government's "keep silent" policy, all of which nearly cost him his life.

Getting up from his chair and going over to Powers, he placed his hand on his friend's shaking shoulder. Already bound spiritually, the gesture symbolized the deepest possible bond between two human beings. They would see this through together.

CHAPTER 19

WASHINGTON, D.C.

The meeting scheduled to take place this morning would be limited to only three participants and would certainly be among a handful of the most highly classified meetings ever to take place in the White House. President Randolph Eugene Chase would be holding a top secret session with CIA Director, John Nesmuth, and National Security Advisor, Dr. Stuart F. Covington. The only agenda item was to consider Nesmuth's request for President Chase to sign a Presidential Finding, permitting the assassination by the United States of José Ocho Garriana.

While during past decades of U.S. foreign policy, Presidents could disclaim either knowledge or responsibility for the failure of covert actions directed against individuals representing foreign governments or terrorist organizations deemed hostile to the United States, recent evolution of such matters required more direct Presidential involvement, including the signing of what were tantamount to direct orders from the President. "Plausible denial" and other euphemisms for a lack of culpability on the part of the President were becoming a thing of the past. The American people, however, were becoming more vocal in their demands for more clarity and far less duplicity in the tangled web of covert action. This made it necessary to have available the highly classified supporting information to supply the American people with a justifiable explanation for such activities. This often resulted in endangering the lives of participants, but it was becoming a regular part of the conduct of the covert action dimensions of U.S. foreign policy.

The two visitors arrived separately and entered the oval office at staggered times to avoid raising undue suspicion. At precisely 8:30 a.m. the doors to the oval office closed. They sat down in their appointed places across from the President of the United States. President Chase, now fifty-nine, came from an economic background considered to be very middle class. He had grown up in a suburb of Chicago, his father a foreman at a steel fabricating company and his mother a secretary at the local office of the Board of Education. An extremely skilled high school athlete and national merit scholar, President Chase had gone on to set track and field records at the Ohio State University and earned a Masters Degree in Political Science from Dartmouth after six years of service as an Air Force fighter pilot. He entered politics as a State Senator in the Illinois Senate, rose to Governor, and finally went on to represent Illinois in the United States Senate for two terms on the Democratic side before successfully running for the Presidency in 1990. He was no stranger to controversy in the international arena and did not believe in shielding the American people from the harsh realities of the U.S.' leading role in world affairs.

The third participant in this meeting was Dr. Stuart F. Covington, who had set academic records everywhere he went. Having earned a bachelor's, master's and doctoral degree from Stanford University, he was a Professor Emeritus of Political Science at Georgetown before reaching his fortieth birthday. Considered an expert in U.S. foreign and defense policy, he had alternated between academic and government posts and had served in high level defense policy roles with two previous administrations before agreeing to join President Chase's administration as the President's National Security Advisor.

All three men were dressed conservatively in dark business suits, and all realized the serious consequences of what they would jointly decide at this morning's fateful meeting. Once the men had been seated and the formalities concluded, the President addressed his visitors,

"John, I have read the excellent brief prepared by your

staff and have some very specific questions. As I recall from past meetings, you prefer to take them one at a time—isn't that so?"

Nesmuth responded, as Dr. Covington took notes, periodically directing his gaze at the President, then back at Nesmuth, "Yes Mr. President, that would be fine. Fire away."

President Chase lifted his left hand, pointing to his left thumb with his right index finger he started to dramatically count out his questions.

"First, please explain to me why this Ocho Garriana should be the target?"

Nesmuth allowed very little time to elapse before beginning his answer. "I can list several reasons, Sir. First, the man was directly responsible and, in fact, gave the direct order for the car bombing at our Naval Amphibious Base in Little Creek which resulted in the horrible, violent deaths of two hundred and eleven Americans, which included many children...."

The President interrupted, politely but firmly, "John, I would appreciate it if you would avoid using words like horrible. This is a very serious matter at the center of America's Foreign Policy, and our decisions must be made on the most rational analysis of the facts, without emotional influence. There is no need to inflame the situation with that kind of rhetoric. Clearly, most of the things this Ocho Garriana is involved with are horrible. The man is a piece of garbage."

Dr. Covington almost smiled, as his self-imposed image of class and academic superiority caused him to reflect that only someone with as middle class a background as the President would lower himself to call even the world's biggest drug dealer a piece of garbage.

Nesmuth understood completely and realized his answers must be as clinical and analytic as possible and absolutely devoid of anything that would give the President any feeling of being pressured into a decision based on emotion. While not afraid of taking the most sensitive issues head on, he realized that his would be a tough decision and, understandably, it must be made unemotionally and based on the issues of "what is best for the country". The CIA Director continued,

"Second, he has ordered the deaths of at least three hundred other American citizens." The President's expression did not change as Nesmuth continued, not even returning Dr. Covington's occasional glance.

"Third, he is responsible for at least seven hundred other violations of U.S. Federal Law, including illegal drug trafficking, racketeering, prostitution, conspiracy, illegal weapons trafficking and hundreds of violations of Federal Banking Laws."

The President continued to fix his gaze on Nesmuth, with his only visible movement being an occasional sip from his coffee cup. Nesmuth could only guess what the man was thinking as he prepared to wrap-up his answers to the President's first question.

"Fourth, he is directly responsible for the attempted murder of a United States Navy SEAL officer and the attempted murders of the four hundred other people injured in the Little Creek bombing."

Nesmuth continued, "Fifth, Ocho Garriana is aiding and abetting the attempted violent overthrow of the Peruvian Government, a longtime U.S. ally. His activities also pose serious threats to the governments of at least seven other friendly governments including Bolivia, Colombia, Guatemala, Ecuador, Brazil, Argentina, Venezuela, and ultimately, even Mexico itself....."

The President again interrupted, "John, are you telling me he controls this Shining Path movement in Peru? That group is really a bunch of butchers."

Dr. Covington's academic snobbery again took over, as he snickered to himself about how the President of the United States could refer to a Communist organization as people who belonged in the meat section of the supermarket.

Nesmuth paused only briefly, glancing at Dr. Covington as if to see exactly what he was writing down, he then continued,

"No, Sir, I am not. However, as far as we are concerned,

173

the two are indistinguishable. While Ocho Garriana provides Sendero guerrillas with money and weapons, we no longer know where one begins and the other ends."

The President apparently understood, and responded, "Thank you for the clarification, John, is there more?"

Dr. Covington was also wondering how much, in fact, would be enough since his mental running total of José Ocho Garriana's crimes already exceeded a thousand violations of Federal Law, together carrying several hundred life sentences and one hundred and nineteen death sentences according to U.S. Federal Law.

Nesmuth didn't skip a beat, "Sixth, Ocho Garriana provides direct support to several international terrorist organizations that have been directly linked to violent criminal attacks against United States citizens both here and abroad. These groups include The Abu Nidal Organization, the IRA, the PLO and shadow groups carrying out terrorist attacks on behalf of governments included in our list of those that support state sponsored terrorism."

Seeing that Nesmuth had paused, the President asked, "Does that complete the answer to the first question, John?"

"Yes, Mr. President. Would you like to proceed to your next question?"

Nesmuth's tone was flat, and the President showed no visible reaction, positive or negative. He proceeded to his second question.

"John, what exactly would be accomplished by, let us say, neutralizing this man? Aren't there several other criminals just waiting to take his place? How will that affect the Peruvian guerrillas?"

A few seconds elapsed as Nesmuth waited to ensure that the President had completed asking his question,

"I will separate my answer into three parts, Mr. President, to ensure that I precisely respond to everything you asked." Nesmuth tried not to show any visible reaction to the unease he felt at the last questions, as the President seemed to

174

be probing for some possibly hidden agenda. The fears and doubts that Nesmuth had been carrying for all this time came to the surface. Realistically, given the fact that at this moment there was no apparent validity to his fears, the thought that President Chase might have *any* knowledge of his dealings with Ocho Garriana was absolutely frightening. He began to answer with no visible concern in his voice.

"With regard to the first part of your question, Mr. President, I believe there are three answers. First, under existing U.S. law, since acts of terrorism committed against U.S. citizens are now considered acts of war, taking those out who direct, or participate in, these acts is both legal and appropriate within the U.S. judicial system and our Constitution. As you are probably aware, the United States Army's Judge Advocate General's office issued such a ruling within the past year to protect United States military personnel against prosecution if they neutralized foreign terrorists within the guidelines of reacting to terrorist murders of United States citizens. These murders constituted overt acts of war against the United States. Many of our military personnel, particularly members of counter- terrorist units such as SEALs and DELTA Force were concerned that this had remained a gray area for far too long....Second, neutralizing Ocho Garriana would enormously disrupt both the Cardazanna Cartel's activities and those of its allies and partners, primarily the Sendero Revolutionary movement. Third, and perhaps most importantly, such a tough response would signal to others wishing to commit such monstrous crimes against us that they cannot continue to do so with impunity."

Dr. Covington, busily taking notes, looked up to study the President's expression, trying to discern whether Nesmuth's arguments were being effective or not in persuading the man. There was nothing. Dr. Covington could not repress a slight smile as he realized that playing poker with the President could be a very expensive experience. Nesmuth continued.

"Regarding the second part of your question, yes, Mr.

President, there are always others standing in the wings...."
The President abruptly cut Nesmuth off.

"John, please be more precise." Nesmuth immediately returned to absolute specificity,

"José Ocho Garriana's number two is Juan Espinoza, and our intelligence reports indicate that while he is certainly a willing accomplice to all of Ocho Garriana's activities, his power is limited. He does not have the contacts, prestige or following to be accepted as Garriana's replacement. He does not have the charisma to develop the popularity needed to take over. Most of Ocho Garriana's other top Lieutenants look on Espinoza as a fat sweating pig who revels in bestiality and perversion. We are unaware of a specific person who could be considered in the position of Number Three Lieutenant as there is a major drop-off in status after Juan Espinoza. We have generally found that in such matters, where a successor is not clearly apparent, major violence ensues until the last candidate left standing takes power. Certainly Espinoza is ruthless enough to butcher all of the other candidates."

That brought about the first visible response from President Chase, who glanced at his National Security Advisor and nodded his ascent while Nesmuth spoke. The CIA Director was uncertain of exactly what the gesture meant, although he assumed it was significant. Feeling a little unsettled, Nesmuth squirmed in his seat. After adjusting himself in his chair he then addressed the third part of the question.

"With regard to what affect this might have on Shining Path, probably very little, since they are already partners in the cocaine business. Their access to the drugs and money would probably continue."

The President asked for further clarification, "John, are you saying they are a completely separate problem?"

Nesmuth's answer was instantaneous, "Yes, sir, they are." Several moments of silence ensued before Dr. Covington spoke for the first time since the start of the meeting.

"John, over and over we hear confused reports linking

the CIA somehow, even indirectly, to the drug business. You wouldn't know anything about that, now, would you?"

Nesmuth immediately sat upright in his chair. Assuming that bastard, FBI Director Kimball, had passed along more detailed information to the President, he knew his answer would affect the rest of his career. Choosing his words carefully he offered,

"Dr. Covington, I cannot state unequivocally that those rumors are untrue. I can, however, state categorically that I have absolutely no direct knowledge of any such thing, although I will immediately dig farther into it."

Nesmuth was well aware of the look that crossed between the President and the National Security Advisor. Both had been in Washington long enough to realize that the ambiguity of his answer was almost always an indication that the information was at least partially accurate. Nesmuth, however, could not detect any visible suspicion on either man's face. The president was the first to speak.

"John, how could I possibly agree to sign a finding authorizing the elimination of the head of an organization with whom the CIA might be having active business dealings?" The president, growing increasingly more visibly perturbed, was one who normally refrained from cynicism of any kind. At this particular moment, however, he was unable to keep a lid on his emotions,

"Issuing such an order would be reminiscent of something that could only happen at the Mad Hatter's Tea Party! Why, to apply equal justice under the law, we might also have to take you out!"

Nesmuth had no idea of how to respond, so he reverted to the seemingly safe tactic of not acknowledging the last comment and moving on to the next topic. He countered in a highly restrained voice,

"Mr. President, or Dr. Covington, are there any other questions?"

The President got up from behind his desk, abruptly signaling that the meeting had ended. Dr. Covington remained silent as the President addressed Nesmuth, who had taken the signal from the President and had gotten up out of his chair,

"No, John, I don't have any. I will table the request for the finding concerning Ocho Garriana for now, at least until you can shed more light on the CIA's involvement in the drug business. We will expect you to get back to us very quickly on this, certainly within the next three to four days. However, it is obvious that something has to be done about that man."

It was the first time that day the President had given any indication of where he stood on the issue of dealing permanently with Ocho Garriana. Unsmiling, the President walked around his desk and, shaking hands with Nesmuth, he made a point of looking directly into the man's eyes. It was not so much to make a point as to see exactly what reaction he would get, and if any hint of nervousness could be detected.

Nesmuth was very aware of the look from the President. It felt as if he were looking deep, down into his soul. Turning abruptly Nesmuth left the oval office and the White House. At that moment he was more concerned about how much the President knew than whether he would sign the finding or not. However, he was well aware that the failure of getting the President's signature would totally undermine his attempts at a coordinated response to the terrorist drug threat with his friends at Israeli and British Intelligence. He knew he must find an answer, and quickly. He also thought, perhaps incorrectly, that the last remarks directed at him by the President, implied that he wanted the CIA to take action to get rid of Ocho Garriana, but on an independent basis, without his signature. Such misunderstandings had led to a state of paralysis and other serious problems with U.S. covert action in the past. What had been an unnerving situation at best was rapidly threatening to degenerate into a three ring circus that would somehow link the evils of the drug cartels to the CIA. It was the classic case of those choir boys in the top echelons of power not understanding the realities of the world of intelligence. To get

178

the information we need and to secure the extra funding Congress won't allocate to us, we sometimes are put in the position of having to make complex deals with bad guys like Garriana. But those saints in the last meeting think they know everything, and are actually naive enough to imagine that we can suddenly start operating like the Boy Scouts.

We have a lot to lose by not dealing with the Garrianas of the world. This scapegoating of the CIA was, in Nesmuth's opinion, threatening to paralyze America's ability to conduct its foreign policy with the advantages of a world-class intelligence force behind it.

After Nesmuth left, the President privately continued the meeting between himself and the National Security Advisor. The President's remarks were very blunt,

"Stuart, something stinks here and we better get to the bottom of it." Dr. Covington nodded his agreement and left to return to his office. He did not interpret the President's remarks as in any way ambiguous, but privately worried that there might be too many grains of truth within those persistent rumors in the press and in tell-all books by former agents regarding the ugly sides of government covert operations. Continuing to ignore the allegations would only make their ramifications far more serious in the future. It was time to find out the truth, no matter how damaging or dangerous it might be.

CHAPTER 20

Phoenix, Arizona
The Next Day

David Powers woke up with a start and instinctively reached across the bed for his wife, discovering that she was not there. Shielding his eyes, and squinting at the morning light shining through the window, he checked the alarm clock and discovered it was 9:47 in the morning. Bolting upright in bed, he was suddenly stopped by a sharp pain in his head. Holding his head in his hands, slowly the fog began to lift and he relived last evening and everything Lewis had told him. Rocking back and forth not only from the pain of his headache, but from the return of the pain he was feeling for his son, Powers started to slowly get out of bed and grope his way into the bathroom.

After locating the medicine cabinet and taking two aspirins, he splashed cold water on his face and brushed his teeth. Pausing for a moment, David grabbed the sides of the sink and stared into the mirror. Looking at his image David realized the toll all the stress was taking on him. His face had become lined and the skin tone ashen. He felt as if he had aged 15 years in just the past few weeks. Then, with a shake of his head, David symbolically rid himself of any self pity he was starting to feel and decided to take on the day and whatever it brought. Putting on his "comfortable" slippers, which were in fact the tattered remnants of what once was a very nice, soft leather pair of slippers Maggie had given him on one of his birthdays, and an old jogging suit, David went downstairs to the kitchen. As he entered the kitchen, he was greeted by the breakfast tray

Maggie had left for him. It contained cereal, fruit and one single rose, along with a note and the morning paper folded next to it. Pouring himself a cup of coffee still hot from 6:00 a.m., he puckered a little from the bitterness, but knew he desperately needed all the help he could get to start this day. He then sat down to read the note.

"Honey, I called your office and told them you had a 101° fever and they were not to expect you until Monday. Casey is at school, there's cold chicken in the ice box for your lunch and I'll be home by 5:15 tonight, after I pick up Casey from his friend John's house. We'll eat dinner at about 7:00.

Commander Dale Thomas called from the Little Creek, Virginia Naval Amphibious Base and wants you to call (803)-277-2121. Please call me after you read this.

P.S., I love you!! "

Powers smiled to himself and felt a rush of emotion. Opening the newspaper, he scanned through the pages as he picked at his breakfast. Suddenly struck by an article, he sat upright and taking the paper in both hands he read on. The article detailed the drug scandal at the local school. Apparently, six teachers and several students were involved. Profiling a Junior High School student, it detailed how he had started as a $1,000 a week pusher, became addicted and ended up spending nine weeks in a hospital recovering from a vicious beating he received at the hands of a well known local biker gang. From the reports, the gang had acted as enforcers for a local group of teachers and school board members that were involved in the pushing of drugs to students in their own school. The group had reportedly sold several million dollars of cocaine to the students, and the article estimated that at least twenty-two students from the middle school had become hard core addicts, their young lives now shattered. The thirteen-year-old had apparently told his mother, after she discovered his addiction, that he had been pushing cocaine for one of his teachers. The mother, outraged, had called the school and demanded that the Principal take action. From what the police could de-

181

cipher, the information somehow leaked to one of the teachers involved, and the boy was punished for squealing by the biker gang, using clubs and chains.

Powers was enraged by the article. "First my son, then half the school, now this!", he thought. Putting down the paper he dialed the number Maggie had left him for Commander Dale Thomas. He was greeted by a crisply military voice,

"SEAL Team Four quarter-deck, GM3 McSweeney speaking, how may I help you, Sir?"

Powers inquired, "May I speak to Commander Thomas? This is David Powers."

GM3 McSweeney replied, "One moment sir."

The line became silent and a few seconds later the powerful voice of Commander Dale Thomas could be heard,

"Dave, how are you? The doctors tell us that Jeremy's condition is improving daily and that he will be able to return to at least a limited active duty status in about six weeks. There is absolutely no permanent damage, particularly from the head injuries. Of course, had he become deranged, we wouldn't have known what was due to hereditary factors and what was caused by the trauma." Commander Thomas always knew how to gently blunt David Powers' inevitable intensity with a bit of teasing.

Powers had not known and was elated to hear about his son's condition. But the article he read had only further fueled the anger and frustration he was feeling.

"We're doing fine, Dale, but...." Dave hesitated a moment. While not wanting to compromise Bob Lewis by giving away what he had learned last night he could not stop the words from blurting out, "....I understand a piece of shit named Ocho Garriana was behind an attempt to murder my son! I know you can't say anything on the phone," Dave sneered "that may `compromise national security', but I want some answers NOW!"

Commander Thomas was used to having to deflect questions that, if answered, could actually do grave harm to na-

182

tional security. He also knew that every ingoing or outgoing phone call on his line was recorded by NSA, the most secret part of the U.S. Intelligence community. The Commander grew alarmed at the potential ramifications of what David Powers had just blurted out for others to hear. His response could not have been more oblique,

"David, timing in life is always fascinating. I was about to pick up the phone to call you and ask if we could have dinner this evening. I've got some business in San Diego and will be flying through Phoenix and can arrange a lay-over there. In fact my flight leaves in about an hour and should be arriving in Phoenix early this evening."

Realizing the conversation could go no further on the phone, Powers changed his tone and suggested, "Why don't you meet Maggie and I for dinner at the Old Forge Steakhouse on West Mountain in Tempe. Say, about seven thirty. It's around fifteen minutes from the airport. Do you need us to pick you up?"

Thomas replied lightheartedly, "I'm a SEAL, remember? While I might occasionally get lost in exotic countries, I should have no problem finding a steakhouse in Phoenix. Seven-thirty sounds fine. Please tell Maggie I'm looking forward to seeing her again and I'll meet you tonight."

After formalizing the conclusion of the conversation, with Commander Thomas always using the proper military radio protocol of "out here" to sign off, both men hung up simultaneously. David then called his wife at the law firm, using her private line. While David and Maggie agreed that their personal life should be kept away from their respective places of work, the rule was often broken.

Maggie, having a tendency to sound quite officious while at work answered, "Maggie Powers."

David, despite his intense emotions of the past few weeks, and perhaps to lighten what had become a very heavy situation, found his sense of humor and replied in equal tone, "David here."

183

Then Maggie heard that all too familiar seductive tone enter his voice. Bracing herself, she heard him say, "I awoke to visions of your naked body dancing through my head. Take off your clothes and talk dirty to me."

Maggie, who was in the middle of having a conference with one of her VIP clients desperately tried to retain her look of composure. She noticed the client's quizzical look as she could feel the flush work up to the very top of her head. Totally helpless to respond, she cleared her voice and said....

"No, I couldn't possibly do that, at least not until tonight. Are you feeling better?" Her voice was reserved, yet reflected her concern and caring.

"Much better, I took two aspirins and now I'm horny." David, now aware someone was listening to her side of the conversation, was enjoying the vision of her, in her tailored business suit, trying to act professional, and yet squirming, red-faced in her seat. Taking pity on her, he decided to address the reason for his call.

"Honey, Dale Thomas is stopping in Phoenix tonight on his way to San Diego. Since we're all so tired and rung-out from last night, I thought we should take him out for dinner, instead of having him over." David was happy with his decision, remembering well the negative reaction to yesterday's undiscussed dinner party.

Maggie's response reflected her need to get back to her client, "That is fine with me, however, there are some details that will have to be covered later. I will call you back in about an hour."

David unable to resist, had to leave her with a parting thought, "Good, now take your clothes off."

Maggie hardly changed the tone of her voice, "I will call you in about an hour. Good-bye."

Hearing the click of the disconnect, and smiling warmly, David hung up. He had begun to realize the potential seriousness of the mistake he made by talking so overtly about José Ocho Garriana, and became alarmed at how he might have compromised his closest friend, Dale Thomas, by not being able to control himself. He vowed it would never happen again. Looking around the kitchen, and having never been capable of "killing" a day, he placed the first of the many business calls he would make.

At almost 5:00 p.m., while on his last call, David heard the sound of Maggie's car, growing louder as it approached the garage. Powers realized that his wife and son would soon be coming in the house, so he wrapped up his conversation. He heard Maggie and Casey's laughter as they had their usual race to the front door. These sounds reminded him, that despite everything that was happening, he was truly fortunate to have Maggie and Casey in his life. Bursting through the front door, Casey was dressed in a red and white polo shirt that was once tucked into his khaki pants. His Nike sneakers finished the "today" look of an exceptionally active nine-year-old. His mom, close behind, was dressed in a stunning royal blue business suit, with matching purse and shoes (both of which she was carrying). As always, she looked the epitome of professionalism, without losing her wonderful femininity (that is, despite her bare feet). David had to smile watching his immaculately dressed wife running a foot race with a nine year-old, shoes and purse flying.

As soon as Maggie entered the house, jumping from behind the door, David grabbed her in his arms. Fumbling both her purse and shoes, she finally gave up and dropped both, putting her arms around David to return his embrace. Casey had heard the commotion and returned to the foyer. Stretching his arms as far as they would go, he joined the two in the traditional Powers family three-way hug. The group made their way into the family room , when Casey, without waiting to be excused, abruptly turned and, taking two steps at a time, bounded up to his room to busy himself with the electronic games and other affairs of a nine-year-old boy. David and Maggie proceeded towards their room to dress for diner with Commander Thomas attempting to catch-up on what had transpired that day.

Having arranged to meet the Commander at precisely seven-thirty Dave, Maggie and Casey, who had brought the plastic gun he always used to play his own private game of Navy SEAL, pulled up in their deep green Lincoln Town Car to the Valet Parking sign at the steakhouse. Entering the restaurant, David requested his usual outside table for four, which was situated in a private corner of the patio, overlooking the Phoenix skyline. David found this table perfect for the privacy desired for most business dinners, and privacy was mandatory in most conversations with Commander Thomas. The three were escorted by the hostess to the table. It was a clear, warm and dry evening that was so typical of the Southwest. Drinks were ordered and their guest arrived within five minutes, waving to them while the hostess proceeded to escort him to their table.

Commander Thomas, a husky, barrel-chested man with a partially receding hair line, was wearing a blue polo shirt with a white collar that accentuated the massiveness of his arms and upper body. He wore gray slacks and brown leather moccasins. His genuine smile and piercing blue eyes always served as a reminder that this man often had to make almost momentary judgments about those around him. Failure to do so could result in death, primarily Thomas' death, given what he had chosen as a career. His demeanor with friends was less like a radar scan and totally genuine. The four had become like family, and Maggie was as fond of the Commander as her husband was. She had not yet begun to sense that this was not merely a coincidental by-product of a military visit to the West Coast. Why would she? The couple had been with Thomas on a dozen previous occasions as their friendship and mutual respect for each other soared. After a dinner filled with animated conversation and punctuated by Thomas' feigned gunshot wounds from Casey's plastic pistol, the two men excused themselves to go for a short walk. Not only was this not unusual, but the two men did it almost every time the four had been

186

together.

While no classified matters involving national security were ever overtly discussed, the ebb and flow and obliqueness of the subjects often got very close. The issues covered were the sort that could only be understood by private citizens with Powers' military experience, and awareness (due to his constant reading on world affairs and military history). What the two discussed was simply no one else's business. They proceeded along a gravel path that wound along a rocky crag, lit by flickering gas lanterns. Commander Thomas knew that Powers would eventually figure things out, but the danger was that nobody could predict what he would do once he did. Thomas realized that he somehow needed to protect his friend, both from himself and the Ocho Garriana's of the world. He also realized it would be no easy task. He got right to the point,

"David, we ask that you not get involved in this matter. It really has nothing to do with you.....at least directly."

Powers always felt he was being addressed by the United States Government when he heard the terminology "we", particularly since no one else was present. He responded with anger, not at Commander Thomas, but at the implied bureaucracy.

"This piece of shit Ocho Garriana mangles my son, kills hundreds of Americans in the same bombing right on U.S. soil, and poisons my other son's school system, all because of this shit called cocaine, and you're telling me it has nothing to do with me? Come on, Dale!"

Thomas realized there were extremely narrow avenues to go down, because he had become very well acquainted with David Powers' basic philosophy of life. Besides the obvious connection to his son Jeremy, Powers had often explained his views that a common thread existed among large groups in the world, and that a threat to one must be reacted to as a threat to all. If the basic human rights of one were violated, ultimately all would be, if the transgressions were not stopped. The fact that the world had basically stood by while the Khmer Rouge butch-

187

ered more than three million Cambodians, for example, could expose other ethnic groups to similar genocide.

Powers had explained all of this to his own father nearly thirty years before, when he responded to his father's pleadings about why he had volunteered to go to Vietnam as a U.S. Naval Advisor. His logic, sounding somewhat flawed to his father, was that if Powers failed in his obligation to go to the aid of people under attack such as the South Vietnamese or the people of Kuwait under Saddam, why should anyone come to the aid of himself or the Jewish people if another Hitler suddenly appeared on the world stage? Powers' father could not quite make the connection between Hitler and the North Vietnamese, although Commander Thomas could, since these ethical precepts largely mirrored his own. He had most recently participated in military operations against Middle Eastern based terrorist organizations, whose enemy was basically anyone who stood in their way. While return of disputed land or removal of the Great Satan of Western modernity was the alleged motivation for their anger and terrorist acts, these organizations violated the rights of all peoples and the precepts of all religions—but for their own narrow, extremist position.

Only the sound of the two men's shoes on the gravel walkway could be heard until Thomas responded. "No offense, David, but even if it does directly involve you, why don't you leave it to us to deal with Ocho Garriana?"

Commander Thomas incorrectly assumed that a signed finding, permitting the man to be eliminated, would be forthcoming. He did not yet know what had recently transpired at the White House between the President, the Director of the CIA and the National Security Advisor. He also could not get himself to chastise his friend about the security lapse on the telephone, even though the genie might now be out of the bottle. The two men stopped. David incorrectly assumed from this conversation that SEAL Team Four had been ordered to kill Ocho Garriana. He decided to leave it to professionals, and answered lightheartedly, a broad grin appearing across his face.

"I completely understand, Dale. Besides, old farts like myself have no business undertaking commando operations. I'd probably get my ass shot off!"

The two men's conversation grew increasingly animated as they returned to the restaurant, with Casey running out to greet them. CDR. Thomas had followed Admiral Blankenship's orders and felt relieved that he had headed off any possibility of some ill conceived, dangerous and amateurish operation launched against Ocho Garriana by mercenaries hired by his friend David Powers. He grinned broadly as he thought about Powers trying to arrange or perhaps lead such an outrageous operation into the Amazon. As he reached down to pick up Casey, swinging him around and placing him on his shoulders, he looked at his friend and thought how much he admired this man. Powers was a man with simple values and strong beliefs in good and evil, right and wrong and was willing to fight for them. He knew Powers would lay down his life for his beliefs. Thomas also admired the many other strengths of character the man possessed. Most importantly, Thomas trusted this man, something that very few people had earned from him outside of his own select group. It was a mutually held view, rarely, if ever, verbalized, yet stronger than any other bonds that existed in the human condition.

CHAPTER 21

LANGLEY, VIRGINIA

John Nesmuth knew that something had to be done to restore maneuvering room and flexibility to the José Ocho Garriana matter. The President's decision to delay or even refuse to sign the finding placed the CIA Director in an awkward position, to put it mildly. In addition to totally undermining his efforts at coordinating a counter-drug terrorist strategy with British and Israeli intelligence, Ocho Garriana had become a major liability due to his total disregard for any pretext at civilized behavior. Since he had become so uncontrollable and unpredictable, he simply had to go. Perhaps the overriding issue was Ocho Garriana's not so subtle threats to John Nesmuth himself, to compromise the CIA Director to his own government. The implications of this threat were almost beyond Nesmuth's ability to comprehend. Garriana had stepped over the line. Nesmuth had summoned his Chief aid for covert action, Carl Roget. Roget was the consummate "dirty tricks" and "black bag" practitioner within the Central Intelligence Agency. Roget had been called to a top secret meeting with John Nesmuth at 9:00 a.m. that morning at the Directors office.

Carl Longmont Roget, III was a retired Lieutenant Colonel in the Army's famed Green Berets. He had graduated from West Point in 1960 and won eleven combat decorations in Vietnam. After working initially in the highlands with Vietnamese hill people, he led a detachment of Green Beret and Laotian tribesmen against the Communist Pathett Lao soldiers. Practicing every clandestine trick known at the time, he and his men ruthlessly butchered Pathett Lao soldiers in response to similar atrocities carried out against the Laotian fighters by the Communists. While never confirmed or acknowledged publicly, rumor had it that Roget was one of the U.S.'s chief assassins during operation Phoenix, the infamous CIA program aimed at destroying the Viet Cong's infrastructure in South Vietnam. After retiring from the Army in 1978, Roget had joined the Agency as an undercover operative where his skills were extremely useful. He had been an active participant in virtually every major secret covert action program during the past thirteen years and had been particularly active while fighting with the Nicaraguan Contras. Fluent in four languages, he was trusted by the CIA Director to successfully carry out the Agency's most sensitive and secret operations and particularly those that, if failed, carried the most risk to the U.S.' prestige. Roget entered through a secret underground entrance at CIA Headquarters in Langley, Virginia, precisely five minutes before the scheduled meeting and entered the Director's office via a secret elevator at exactly the scheduled time.

The square jawed 6'2" Roget, still maintaining the same rock hard physique and weighing the same 197 pounds he had as a West Point Cadet, seemed to be gazing straight ahead through his steely light blue eyes, which always seemed to unnerve those around him. That same gaze was the last thing seen by many of those he had killed, particularly during the assassinations he had performed at extremely close range. Attired in a dark gray pinstripe Brooks Brothers suit, he was ushered in by Nesmuth's secretary, Joan Waters, to one of the chairs facing the couch which was occupied by Nesmuth. After turning down Ms. Waters' offer of coffee he made himself comfortable. There was a level of trust between these two men that would remain unbroken, always transcending the mundane issues that inevitably seemed to come between even the closest friends, no matter what the consequences might be to the contrary of anything they did within the CIA's covert action program. Roget sensed that this particular meeting was perhaps the most important to ever occur between the two men. He

191

also sensed a very high degree of anxiety on Nesmuth's part and intuitively realized that the matter must have something to do directly with the CIA Director himself.

Nesmuth leaned forward, his elbows on his knees for support and his hands cupped against his face as though someone might be listening. Carl Roget sat upright, both hands pressing down on the two arms of his chair. After extremely brief pleasantries, John Nesmuth spoke, "Carl, I have a problem and badly need your help."

As fond and respectful of the man as Roget was, he couldn't help but reflect to himself that this seemed to be the way every request for some covert action kept, "off the books" always seemed to start. Of course, someone had a problem, or Roget wouldn't be there to begin with. Feeling the slightest trace of uncharacteristic anxiety, and looking intensely at Nesmuth, he spoke almost cavalierly, "I sense it's unusually serious John, of course I'll help. What's up?"

Nesmuth always knew he could rely on this man, and continued, "How much do you know about José Ocho Garriana, Carl?" The Director slid a thick, gray folder across the table that separated the two men.

Roget, looking down, saw the familiar red stamp "Top Secret" boldly printed on the cover of the folder. Picking it up, he acknowledged his familiarity with the name, "Probably a great deal, John, but what specifically are we talking about here?"

Nesmuth realized it was time to cut through the rhetoric, and he spoke while Roget opened the folder and began leafing through it.

"José Ocho Garriana is the most powerful, wealthy and ruthless leader in the drug world. He has become a serious threat to the security of the United States and has direct links with some of the most violent and dangerous terrorist organizations arrayed against us in the world, including Shining Path, the IRA, PLO and several others. As you may already know, he was responsible for detonating the car bomb in Little Creek and for trying to assassinate a United States Naval officer at the Little Creek base. It's all in that folder, Carl."

Roget had already concluded, through all his years of being in this exact position, either in Nesmuth's office or elsewhere, that he was being ordered to have the man assassinated, or quite possibly do it himself. After all, that was his job. He knew that for security reasons the fewer words that passed between Nesmuth and himself, the better. He did, however, have to cover the basics.

"John, is there is a Presidential Finding on this or do we need a cover story and plausible denial for the President?"

Nesmuth had carefully rehearsed his answers to provide as much ambiguity as possible, even to his most trusted operative, and close friend,

"The President is seriously considering signing a finding and is evaluating all of his other options. Since time is of the essence we must act now, and he must never be either directly or indirectly associated with this. It should not even be traceable to the United States Government—perhaps his rivals within the Cardazanna Cartel itself could eliminate Ocho Garriana."

The deliberate ambiguity had the desired effect, and Roget incorrectly concluded that this covert action, as many others in the past, was directly sanctioned by the President himself, even without a finding. Roget had closed the file and placed it carefully down on the table before speaking,

"John, I understand. Are there any other dimensions to this and what is the desired timing?"

Nesmuth was already feeling a tremendous sense of relief as he realized Carl Roget would never let him down. He reflected for a few moments before carefully framing his answer. He knew that Roget had to feel totally comfortable with the assignment in order to properly carry it out and to avoid even the most remote possibility of any backlash or resistance on his part. Nesmuth continued,

"Yes, Carl, there are certain aspects of this that I cannot reveal even to you, but they would have no impact on you or your mission. I will say, however, that Ocho Garriana poses a direct and serious threat to me, personally."

"My God," Roget thought to himself, "Ocho Garriana must be trying to kill the Director." Nesmuth's vagueness had worked just as it was intended. There could be no more serious or personal motivation to Carl Roget than the thought that by acting pre-emptively against Ocho Garriana he would be protecting the CIA Director, his family, or both against assassination.

Nesmuth continued, fully aware that he had succeeded in motivating Roget to kill Ocho Garriana, through his personal loyalties to the director. Further discussion could only detract from the initial impact of what he had said. He quickly switched to the second issue....

"As for timing, allowing for the minimum number of days necessary to plan such a major operation, I would say anytime you are ready, beginning three or four months from now."

Having conveyed the necessary clarity of the mission, it was time to end the meeting. Nesmuth stood up, warmly and vigorously shook hands with his guest, ending the meeting. Turning away from Roget, he returned to his desk to address a large stack of papers requiring his immediate attention.

As Carl Roget left, he could not avoid asking himself why the President of the United States, who certainly must be aware of the fact that José Ocho Garriana was one of the primary sources of intelligence to the CIA in Latin America, would suddenly want the man dead. Having mentally raised the question, Roget reminded himself of something he had learned years before, that only endless questions resided within the answers to such sensitive matters. More to the point, there never seemed to be ultimate answers anyway, only more questions. And, in the end, it never seemed relevant, since for every apparent absolute truth there was always the inevitable contradiction. His mind quickly moved from philosophy to the stone cold reality facing him. How should he go about trying to eliminate Ocho Garriana?

CHAPTER 22

CARDAZANNA, COLOMBIA

Roberto Felipé, Vice President of Latin America for First Global Bank, had recently expanded the bank's geographic operations considerably. This was largely due to the greatly increased commercial relationship with the most powerful industrialist in the region, José Ocho Garriana, the Cardazanna, Colombia based businessman. How or at what cost, human or otherwise, the man made his money was of no concern either to Roberto Felipé or FGB. All that mattered to himself and the bank's other senior officers was immediate improvement in the bank's dismal operating results.

The bank was handling a greatly increased number of wire transfers from New York headquarters to individual banks located throughout every major city and country in Latin America. The transfers were being sent to hundreds of individual accounts controlled by Ocho Garriana. In addition to Latin America, transfers were being sent to banks for Ocho Garriana's accounts in forty-six other countries of the world, throughout Europe, Asia and Southeast Asia. Particularly large deposits were being made in Switzerland, Panama, Tokyo, Hong Kong and Jakarta. The increased activity was now generating six times the normal amount of banking fees to FGB. Roberto Felipé had done his job so well that he believed FGB would achieve the desired turn-around in its operating results well within the deadline set by the Directors at the highly charged meeting in New York.

Roberto Felipé had come to Cardazanna to meet with Ocho Garriana, Garriana's legal advisors, and representatives of the National Banking Bureau (NBB). This organization, within the Government of Colombia, was responsible for chartering new banks at the federal level and for writing and administering the country's national banking laws. The meeting was being held for two reasons. Primarily, First Global Bank (FGB) was providing a substantial amount of the seed capital required to start a new bank in Colombia, in partnership with Ocho Garriana and other Garriana business associates. Secondly, the National Banking Bureau had agreed to rewrite Colombia's banking laws to insure that Ocho Garriana and his associates could function with the minimum amount of interference, or preferably none at all: Anything to keep the most prominent businessman in the hemisphere happy. The meeting was the direct result of a phone call placed by Ocho Garriana to the President of Colombia, Ralph Eduardo Garza. Garza, in turn, contacted the Chairman of NBB and directed him to cooperate in any way possible. Roberto Felipé had also established a close working relationship with both Colombia's President and the Chairman of the NBB. In fact, FGB had made a five-million-dollar contribution to the last reelection campaign of President Garza. While seemingly trivial compared to the fifty-million-dollar campaign contribution made by Ocho Garriana, it was appreciated nonetheless, particularly since it had been made by a U.S. bank.

By rewriting Colombia's federal banking laws, many acts considered illegal under existing Colombian banking laws would no longer be considered improper, rendering attempts at cooperation between U.S. and Colombian Federal Law Enforcement practically useless. Ocho Garriana's approach was extremely simple and direct: If his actions were illegal and made him in any way vulnerable to prosecution, simply buy the country's politicians and change the laws. This, of course, always came after more violent and far less suitable methods had been tried. Murder, torture, threats and intimidation were all on the approved list of acceptable business practices.

The nightmare that this would create for U.S. and other

Western law enforcement agencies in the future in terms of their attempts to go after the Ocho Garriana's of the world had yet to be understood. If money laundering activities within Colombia were no longer illegal due to new banking laws, how could any Western governments exchange evidence or pressure Colombian authorities to prosecute those committing the crimes? In fact, they could not.

With normal judicial channels eliminated, the only alternatives left for the United States or other governments trying to defend against the drug traffickers would be overt or covert acts of war. It was already rumored within U.S. intelligence circles that the drug cartels were exercising so much control over the Colombian government that the nation's entire judicial code and constitution were soon to be completely rewritten by drug cartel lawyers. This would create an unprecedented situation whereby a supposedly legitimately constituted government had, in fact, become one vast criminal enterprise and where the drug traffickers themselves were indistinguishable from the government (this type of situation to an extreme would become apparent in Mexico five years later, where the country's top anti-drug official, General Jesus Gutiérrz Rebollo, who functioned as the equivalent of the U.S.'s Drug Czar, would be indicted on several counts of illegal drug trafficking. General Rebollo would mastermind the shipment of 10 tons of cocaine per week, worth several hundred million dollars, into the U.S. So many other individuals at the top eschelons of power in Mexico would be rumored to be involved that the matter would be referred to as a "Narco-Scandal".)

It was no longer an issue of merely exerting influence. Facing governments that posed a direct threat to U.S. and Western institutions due to the terrorist drug assault directed against them could not have been imagined only a decade ago. The new element was neither ideology nor raw political power. It was both, coupled with a nearly infinite supply of money and the absolute corruption of entire governments which inevitably followed. This unprecedented combination of weap-

197

ons was lethal to any governments or countries that tried to resist.

The group had gathered in the spacious conference room located on the top floor of the Colombian Federal Office Building in the heart of downtown Cardazanna. Present were Fernando Rios, Chairman of the Colombian National Banking Bureau; his attorney, Orlando Ruiz; José Ocho Garriana and his attorney; Carlos Rodriguez, and completing the group were Roberto Felipé and FGB's Senior Legal Counsel, John Swanson. As Roberto Felipé looked around, he reflected on how the opulence of the conference room made the grandeur of FGB's New York conference room look like a boot camp barrack. Felipé mentally calculated that the marble table, rich leather chairs, original antique Persian carpets and Colombian period artifacts dating back hundreds of years, must have been assembled at a cost exceeding several million dollars. He was awestruck, but did not wish to appear to the others as being a peasant or as little more than a gawking low class tourist. So, being the aristocrat that he was, he carried the mannerisms of one who lived in such opulence on a daily basis, and who therefore was not overly impressed by it.

Felipé, in fact, was not aware that most of the artifacts had been donated to NBB by José Ocho Garriana from his personal collection. While Felipé had never met Ocho Garriana before and had only dealt with his appointed legal and business representatives, he was struck by the man's commanding presence and by the deference of everyone else in the room. He could not fathom how such a polished, sophisticated individual, with such a complete grasp of even the most minute business detail, could possibly be depicted by the press as one of the world's most violent and ruthless criminals. Because of all the media propaganda, he had simply expected something quite different. The presence outside the door, on each floor and all around the building of more than one hundred heavily armed security personnel seemed somewhat incongruous for only a local businessman, but Felipé convinced himself that there must be some valid explanation. With Felipé's having been raised in a very protected, aristocratic family himself, he was quite surprised at how personally secure he felt in this violent atmosphere with machine guns carried by almost every guard, Obviously, there were good reasons for having so much artillery around.

Despite the fact that the meeting had been convened by the Director of NBB, Ocho Garriana was the one who opened the meeting with a speech that mesmerized everyone present,

"Gentlemen, welcome to Cardazanna. It makes me truly exhilarated to know that our country's greatly enhanced standing in the international world of global finance will be expanded even further by the creation of the new bank we are proposing, International Bank of Trade, to be known as IBT. With the proposed capitalization of three hundred billion dollars, the IBT will be the first Colombian chartered bank to break into the International Top Ten Banks and will bring great honor and prestige to our beloved country...." Garriana paused to allow the audience to show their admiration.

On cue, they rose to pay homage to the genius of Garriana. Applauding and cheering they chanted, "Viva José!!, Viva Garriana!!" As they shouted, each thought of how he fit into this big picture and, of course, what and how much he might expect to get as his share.

Garriana, who remained seated while nodding his head in acknowledgment of the cheers of his "followers," raised his hand in a polite gesture requesting silence. As if the applause sign had gone out, the other participants immediately responded on cue and simultaneously returned to their seats. Garriana continued.

"Gentlemen, thank you. You honor me by your response. And now, to demonstrate my own commitment to the future of our great country, I have a little something to show you." With that, Ocho Garriana moved his chair back, and gestured towards one of the guards standing at the conference room entrance. Within moments the lights dimmed and to everyone's amazement, a multi-media presentation enveloped the conference room, complete with flashing strobe lights, blaring music and rhythmic Latin drums. The double-door entrance to the room opened and, two by two, two dozen Latin dancing girls whirled in, each more beautiful than the last. Their costume was typical of that worn by exotic dancers. In they came, gyrating ever so sensually as if hypnotized by the music. Each young woman passed by Garriana, lightly touching his cheek. Garriana leaned back in his chair and acknowledged each girl as they passed with either a light pat on their butt, or a little grab at their breasts. After paying homage to Garriana, the girls proceeded around the room individually greeting the men in their own way, some with a light kiss on the cheek and some with a little more abandonment.

Roberto Felipé sat frozen, his eyes transfixed on the table in front of him. Staring in horror as the first girl approached, Felipé concentrated as hard as he could on anything and everything he could that would take his mind off the scent of jasmine that floated towards him as she got closer. Almost forcing herself onto his lap, he found her face and her lips inches from his. He could no longer ignore her and the evidence of his attraction became obvious. Adding to his humiliation, she pinched his cheek, and making her observation obvious to all, giggled as she rose from his lap to proceed to the next, her hand passing lightly against his groin, turning his face deep red.

As the men were greeted by the girls they were given a slip of paper. The girls then returned to gather around Garriana. Standing up from his chair and placing his arms around the nearest girl to the right and the left of him, Garriana called for silence.

"Gentlemen there are many surprises in store for you today. First, please note the slips of paper that were handed to you by our beautiful girls. Each slip contains the name of one of these lovely ladies. You are to choose two names from all the slips given to you. After the meeting has been concluded, the ladies of your choice will escort you to my estate where you will be my guests for the next three days. During your stay these two young dancers will be available to you for as long as you can tolerate them. There will be an open house to start the festivities, then you are free to enjoy the remainder of your stay as you wish. Please hand your choices to the man coming around the room now. If the same name is chosen by more than one of you, you will all choose a new name. I hope they please you."

By this time Roberto Felipé could hardly keep from sliding off his chair under the table to remain there for the rest of the meeting. He knew he was still blushing as this unbelievable behavior was totally beyond him. While not intimidated by the girls, and despite being a little titillated by them, this open gift of sex was something he never expected while attempting to conduct serious international banking business. This was not the way he had ever seen bankers do business anywhere else.

Motioning for silence, Garriana nodded to one of the young women who then handed him a poster size envelope measuring approximately a foot and a half high and three feet across. Garriana grinned broadly as he addressed his guests.

"Ah, gentlemen, if we could return to the business at hand for just a moment." He paused to open the envelope while everyone nodded in anticipation. He then placed the open envelope on the table in front of him, while removing a much smaller piece of paper and holding it in his hand, held up high for all to see.

"My friends, I have a cashier's check in my hand from BCCI Bank, where my company maintains several of its operating business accounts, made out to the order of International Bank of Trade, our new Colombian bank, for the sum of fifty billion dollars."

Everyone in the room visibly gasped. Every man's attention had been drawn away from the nearly naked young women to the piece of paper in Garriana's hand. Unknown to Felipé, Garriana was staring at him with a visible glare in his eyes. Poor Felipé was struggling to remove his fixed stare at a particular young lady's exposed breasts. Awkwardly getting to his feet and fumbling with something in his pocket, he finally produced an envelope and, as though to offer a toast to his host, started to speak, but the only audible sound that could be heard was a slight squeak. Clearing his throat he made a second attempt. "Thank you for that magnificent, generous contribution to IBT's capital base, Señor Garriana. In order to show FGB's confidence in the global future of our new partnership, I have been authorized to also present a cashier's check from FGB made payable to IBT in the equal amount of fifty billion dollars!"

The gasps were repeated. A low mumbling sound could be heard as each man exchanged a comment with the man next to him. A slight grin could be seen on Garriana's face as he looked around at the men. He knew that they had no idea that this one hundred billion dollars that had just been invested was money earned from illicit drug profits and had just now been laundered into the capital base of a new worldwide banking powerhouse. Also, Garriana realized that, even if they did know, they probably wouldn't care. A couple of dozen young women was certainly a cheap price to pay for entertaining, relaxing and pleasing the power elite controlling Colombia's commercial banking infrastructure.

Having paused long enough to give the proper effect, Garriana motioned a dismissal to the dancers. Twirling as they departed, they filed out two by two. The rhythmic music, which had been turned off during the exchange of pleasantries, toasts and cheers, was again turned up to provide the background sounds for the girls' departure.

Felipé, having watched the girls' every move, now cleared his throat and blinked his eyes, returning his attention to the other men at the meeting. The pulsating, erotic music had ended. He could not entirely clear his mind, however, of his visions of the evening to come.

Garriana called for order, and the men returned to the

business at hand. Not discussed were the actual details on the structure of the percentage of interests held, and who held them, for the new bank. These details would be left to the phalanx of high priced lawyers on Ocho Garriana's payroll, and would be finalized prior to the departure from Colombia of Roberto Felipé and the others. While the new bank was incorporated under the Colombian Commercial Code, Ocho Garriana's sixty-eight percent interest was hidden under three dozen layers of holding companies, aliases, dummy corporations, loans to affiliates and dozens of other schemes. FGB's thirty-two percent interest was merely carried on the bank's books as an investment in an affiliated enterprise, along with similar investments in a dozen or more comparable foreign banks.

Once the documents finalizing the incorporation of the new enterprise were completed, the men turned to the next major item on the agenda, redrafting the country's banking laws. While these had already been preliminarily drawn-up in advance by Ocho Garriana's attorneys, copies were distributed to the other participants, who approved them without comment or criticism, after cursory perusal. Felipé, following the instructions he received before leaving New York and the FGB Bank, also quickly gave its approval. He did, however, recognize the total lack of regulations involving the movement of capital which made him extremely uncomfortable. But, remembering how he had been cautioned by his superiors not to think independently and not to rock the boat, Felipé closed his mind to any far reaching or dangerous implications of the new banking laws.

Among other things, margin requirements were removed, documentation was all but eliminated, deposits and withdrawals could be made with no holding periods, all limitations on either the amounts or nature of investments made by local banks in outside enterprises were removed, and no information could be provided to any outside parties or investigative bodies on the bank's transactions even if there were subpoenas. The

203

Cardazanna cartel and its allies such as the FGB were now able to conduct totally unobstructed money laundering activities. Certainly there were no apparent opportunities for law enforcement agencies to monitor these currency movements.

Deprived of legal and judicial means with which to withstand the onslaught of countries controlled by drug cartels, several democratic nations, perhaps unknowingly, were being pushed ever so brutally towards a global conflagration. How else could the narco-terrorists, no longer organizations outside of governments and rapidly becoming one-in-the-same as these governments, be stopped—short of direct military action against them? And how could such powerful foes be taken on without running the risk of a full scale regional war?

Garriana concluded the meeting, at which time his guests were directed to the waiting limousines that would take them to the man's palatial estate. There they were "expected" to enjoy three days of partying, accompanied by the young ladies of their choice.

CHAPTER 23

WASHINGTON, D.C.

President Chase had never been so enraged during his entire political career. Normally unflappable, he ranted and raved, gesturing wildly as he paced back and forth across the Oval Office. Dr. Covington, trying to avoid being run-over by the enraged President, remained silent during his demonstration of total disbelief and frustration. He had just had the unfortunate obligation of delivering information that he, himself, could not totally comprehend. It was against everything he had believed his democratic government stood for and the values he thought it represented.

The President ranted, almost inaudibly, in incomplete sentences.

"How could!!......"

"What?........"

"Who could have?........."

"Goddam it, Stu, do they realize what they have......?"

Dr. Covington could only continue holding his hands open in repeated sympathetic gestures, mirrored by the slow and steady nodding of his head in response to each partial question. He too could not understand how this could happen. The thought of this country's supposedly, finest representatives of the United States and guardians of everything it stands for, our CIA, being directly involved in the drug business for nearly forty years was unthinkable. The thought of the CIA being accomplices in the early opium trading days in the Laotian Highlands was still sticking in Dr. Covington's mind and in his throat.

Suddenly, the President wheeled around, walked disjointedly behind his desk and dropped exhaustedly into the over-stuffed leather chair. Motioning for his advisor to take a seat, he leaned back and cradling the back of his head with his hands, stared at the ceiling. After what might be best described as a "pregnant pause" he addressed Dr. Covington.

"Stu, this is one of those unfortunate moments in American history when our very existence and worldwide reputation, along with those in charge of caring for our ideals, must sustain a black eye. While CIA drug running has been going on since the Vietnam War era, it sounds like we can no longer deny it or pretend it doesn't exist. How did it get this serious?" Sitting-up straight in his chair and turning his gaze directly into Covington's eyes, the President waited for an answer.

"Mr. President, based on the information provided in the FBI report, all of this started with the Air America operation that the CIA started throughout Southeast Asia early in the Vietnam Conflict, around 1962 or so, possibly a couple of years earlier. Apparently, opium and heroin were used to pay the various indigenous groups such as the Laotian Hill People who the Agency recruited to be our allies and fight with us during that conflict. Frankly, nobody seems to know who authorized this payment in drug money or why drugs were used as payment in lieu of cash."

The president interrupted, "Stu wouldn't a decision like this have to be made by someone holding a position fairly high up in our government's hierarchy?"

Dr. Covington responded immediately, "Mr. President, it's probably one of those questions that will never be answered. After thirty years, memories fade, directives that were clear at the time become hazy, records tend to be misplaced or disappear, and it is doubtful that any one individual would ever step forward and take the responsibility for something of this magnitude. While I find it inconceivable that an entire CIA Air Force could have been flying drugs all over Southeast Asia for all this time without anyone knowing, I think our chances of finding out all the details are extremely remote."

Both men realized what was at stake. With U.S. foreign policy linked to the so-called "War on Drugs" and with the Chase administration's unyielding stand on the subject, any leak regarding the CIA's involvement in the drug trade could damage not only the United States' credibility in the eyes of the world, but also the credibility of his administration. The potential impact of this information getting out to the public was frightening. It would totally destroy any moral or even legal basis the United States might have as its basis for the "War on Drugs". Logically, it would mean that the United States would to a degree have to go to war with itself and its own dirty agencies!

As experienced as the President was in the world of politics, this was even beyond his grasp of the nuances of both domestic and foreign policy as these revelations were unprecedented in U.S. history. How could a government agency acknowledge a 40 year track record of breaking and disregarding the laws of this nation? Desperately, he posed the question to Covington.

"Stu, exactly where have the CIA's drug activities occurred, have they broadened from the Laotian region, and what can be done about it now? What specific activities are occurring at the present time, and where? More specifically, what in God's name do we tell our allies, particularly the British and Israelis, about our ability to pursue a joint strategy in the fight against the drug cartels?"

Trying to keep a positive note in his voice, the National Security Advisor replied, "Well, Mr. President, I can answer the first part of your question. It seems the CIA's drug activities have spread from what might have started out as an isolated, single operation into one that covers Southeast Asia as well as Central America and Latin America. The reasons, as I have been told, have something to do with the CIA's ability to influence policies in a number of governments around the world. As far as what it does to our ability to help orchestrate a coordinated counter-drug strategy, I have some very bad news.

207

One of our closest allies, the British, possibly somewhat meta-phorically, asked whether they should shoot down aircraft loaded with heroin if their intelligence agencies had determined that the planes were piloted by the CIA? Their representative in Washington could hardly keep a straight face when he asked the question."

(Actually, the same diplomat had been trying to con-vince the U.S. Government for years that the real War was the one being fought against the United States and many of its allies by more than 60 hostile governments connected with ter-rorist organizations and drug cartels: The so called "narco-terrorists", so far without much effective resistance. The Ameri-can version of a domestic "War on Drugs" fought through Edu-cational programs and Law Enforcement agencies on Local, State and Federal levels—stood absolutely no chance of suc-ceeding against the massively well financed and determined external and internal forces allied against the U.S.)

The President, perceptibly stunned, returned to his pre-vious posture of staring at the ceiling. His effort to conceal his frustration was unsuccessful. His voice took on an iciness, "Dr. Covington, this is intolerable. We need a major damage con-trol program. Write a Presidential Directive for my review or-dering the CIA Director to instantly terminate any Agency in-volvement in the Drug Business. Also order him to cancel this asinine program with that fellow Carl Roget to assassinate Ocho Garriana. That one would, without a doubt, obviously get hung on us...."

The President paused momentarily as he noticed Dr. Covington feverishly trying to keep up with him by scribbling notes. He realized it was becoming impossible for the Doctor to keep up with the rapid fire delivery of his directives. As the President paused to allow Dr. Covington to catch up, he did not look up from his pad, but merely nodded his appreciation for the temporary respite. The President continued his pause for several more seconds, then continued,

"Also, write a second Presidential Directive to FBI Director Kimball, congratulating him on the Bureau's successful penetration of the CIA's drug operations. Remind him, however, to be ever vigilant in the future. Once these things start with shadow governments and the like, they have a tendency to keep perpetuating themselves."

The National Security Advisor, knowing the President for so many years, realized the comments about shadow governments were strictly editorial and did not include them in the Presidential communiqué to Kimball. He also privately considered the complexity of the relationship between the two competing entities, the CIA and the FBI, both of whose existence was supposedly to protect the integrity and security of the United States. Yet one ends up spying on the other, with the CIA unfortunately, directly participating in and assisting those involved in the single most serious threat to the security of the United States: drugs.

The President, who apparently was thinking along the same lines, asked, "God damned it, Stu, what have things come to when we have to spy on ourselves?"

The irony had apparently not been lost on either man as they set about developing a damage control plan that, among other things, would force them to come clean with the United States' allies. It would not be an easy task, and the long term cost to the country's overt and covert intelligence operations could be incalculable.

The President and his National Security Advisor looked at each other with expressions indicating both individuals knew who would say what next.

"Mr. President, why don't we finally declare an aggressive, open war on drugs as millions of American citizens, law enforcement agencies at all levels, and a significant number of our political colleagues, as well as our allies everywhere, would certainly welcome? You know that with the capabilities of our tier one forces of SEAL Team Six and Delta Force, we could go right into the waterways of the Andean Ridge countries such as Peru and Bolivia—where 70% of the coca leaf is grown—

209

and into Colombia from where it's refined into cocaine and shipped—and blow the stuff right out of the water!"

The answer to this obvious question comprised a mixture of the same old political excuses and the usual reluctance to use the country's military capabilities to solve what, in essence, had become a military problem.

"Stu, I'm not going over that same ground again, no matter how tempted I am personally feeling to do in this Garriana character. The State Department would have a fit over our interference with the internal affairs of sovereign nations, and the DEA and other Federal agencies still believe we can be successful by throwing more resources at crop eradication, border seizures, education and all that stuff."

Both realized this was the biggest self delusion in the history of our nation, since the United States was literally awash in cocaine, crack and other illegal drugs. In fact, daily reports were reaching the President about law enforcement agencies being overwhelmed and spending more than 60% of their resources and time on illegal drugs and drug related crime, about emergency rooms overflowing with more than 500,000 Americans requiring ER treatment a year due to drug overdoses, and perhaps another 500,000-1,000,000 either receiving private medical treatment or not reporting their medical problems. In addition, the reports included information about an alarming increase in drug addiction among the nation's 12 to 18 year-olds, about the levels of drug-related deaths now exceeding casualty levels during the Vietnam War, and about prisons overflowing with drug users.

Law enforcement is now so involved with drug crime that they haven't the resources for the far more violent street criminals out there, leaving the populace more and more vulnerable.

CHAPTER 24

WASHINGTON, D.C.

The phone call placed by President Chase to Admiral William Blankenship in the Pentagon seemed highly unusual. Yeoman Farraro, who was used to receiving phone calls from senior intelligence officials from all over the world, as well as both U.S. and allied senior military officers, could not recall the last time the President of the United States had phoned directly. She was astonished at the direct contact, as routine communication was normally reserved for government officials and advisors who surrounded the President. While the two men had first met personally nearly fifteen years ago, while working together on the National Security Council (NSC) under then President James Washburn, the two had not spoken in more than ten years. President Chase, alone in the oval office, had asked the White House Switchboard to place the call on a totally secure line. Yeoman Farraro was visibly taken aback as she finished her normal response to the ringing of the red phone.

"Admiral Blankenship's office, Yeoman Farraro speaking, may I help you Sir or M'am?" The White House Switchboard Operator, responded somewhat dryly, "Please tell Admiral Blankenship that the President of the United States is calling,"

"One moment....M'am." Yeoman Farraro responded as she pressed the intercom button, ringing the Admiral's office,

"Admiral Blankenship, President Chase is calling, Sir." It took even the top Navy SEAL a few seconds to connect the name, at which time he immediately picked up the red phone and responded,

"Good morning, Mr. President, what can I do for you, Sir?"

The President, not quite used to the directness of military protocol, was quite aware that this conversation had to incorporate all the political strategy he had learned in his career. Direct was not the approach he could allow in this conversation.

"I'm fine, Bill. By the way, how is that boy of yours, Andy?" President Chase always did his homework before having personal conversations where intimacy was important in order to draw the other party onto his side and into his way of thinking.

"Fine, Sir. Andy is now in his Junior year at William and Mary. He's an NROTC Regular and wants to become a SEAL." The President could not have hit on a subject closer to the Admiral's heart and pride. It took the Admiral several seconds, unusual for him, before his instincts kicked in and with them his suspicions. He was sure the President did not place a call to chat about his son, or the weather.

The President pursued the personal dimensions of the conversation, "Well, Bill, that's no big surprise. As they say, acorns never fall far from the tree."

Not responding, the Admiral waited for the bomb to drop....and it did.

"Bill, what do you know about that José Ocho Garriana?"

"Only what I read in the intelligence reports. Apparently, he's the head of the Latin American Drug Cartel and has substantial influence all the way to the top of the Colombian Government. He also was responsible for giving the direct order to assassinate one of our officers in SEAL Team Four," the Admiral responded. He hesitated, not quite sure what the President was leading up to.

The President, offering a little more about the purpose of his call, if not directly getting to the point, responded, "Admiral, the United States has a very serious problem. This Garriana character is using his power to the point where he has now become a serious threat to the security of our nation. His acts of terrorism are now being specifically directed against the United States, and, as you have pointed out, he is not only attacking the United States but members of your SEAL Team."

The President stopped and intentionally let the impact of Garriana's attack on one of "his own" fully register. He continued, "I have been advised that we probably have the constitutional authority to eliminate him and therein lies the problem. As you are probably aware, the Judge Advocate General's office recently ruled that it is permissible under the U.S. Constitution to kill terrorists, since their actions constitute acts of war against this country. This Garriana is certainly a terrorist and has committed numerous acts of war against us."

The Admiral was uncertain about the point the President was making by personalizing Garriana's actions as a direct threat to "his men", and not just the United States as a whole. He wasn't sure where this was going, but with the last remark, he was sure that somehow the President's intentions were to get him, as an individual, involved, or perhaps the SEAL Team itself. The Admiral was well aware that normally the President would have gone through the chain of command, including the Joint Chiefs of Staff, who would then pass any directive on to him. He was starting to feel a little uneasy. While José Ocho Garriana might in fact be committing acts of war against the United States, the Admiral realized that President Chase coming directly to him was a violation of every normal procedure within the United States military. It was possibly illegal if a direct order were issued by the Commander in Chief authorizing military action against Ocho Garriana. He again tried to get to the point.

"Mr. President, are you asking my opinion or is there a direct order you wish to issue?"

The President knew from the Admiral's directness that he was not going to be cooperative with any plan that would hint of unlawful orders or shadow governments. But, with the situation being so desperate, it called for risky actions and therefore he felt it necessary, in order to keep him and his administration as "clean" as possible, to get this problem off his back at any cost. The only desired exclusions were the continuation of both his administration and his personal political future. He decided to give it his best shot, and continued,

"Well, Bill, you could say I am seeking your advice, since internal political considerations of the worst kind are preventing me from signing what you would recognize as a 'finding' to get rid of this son-of-a-bitch."

The Admiral took a deep breath, and thought to himself, "there, it was out, the President was on a fishing expedition." The workings of the political mind never ceased to amaze him. What the President obviously was getting at was for the Admiral to go against all ethics and well beyond his authority, to bypass all channels and commit an illegal act by assassinating Ocho Garriana on his possibly illegal presidential orders. As much as he too wanted to get rid of the "son-of-a-bitch" Garriana, he would not ignore the standards that had been instilled in him from birth and throughout his career in the military. Ending the mind game, he spoke,

"Mr. President, in terms of general advice, there are many ways we could handle eliminating our problem with Garriana. However, without a signed Finding I can't see any way of considering any one of those options."

The Admiral was hoping that the conversation would not turn into a full fledged confrontation. He knew the President had a very serious problem, and while his sympathy was definitely with him, it was clear to him there was no way he, or his Navy SEAL Team could involve themselves without properly signed orders issued through the proper chain of command.

The President took note of the finality of the Admiral's comment and, backing-off, quickly closed the conversation. "Bill, I guess I'm just looking for a good listener, and you've certainly been that. Don't worry, we'll find an acceptable way to get rid of this problem. Meanwhile, send your son, Andy, my personal best, and keep up the great work. We'll be speaking again soon!"

The phone clicked and the Admiral, realizing the President had terminated the conversation, stared at the receiver for a few moments, then slowly placed it on its cradle. He sat frozen in his chair. The impact of what was obviously an attempt by the President to get him and his men involved in an "off the record" assassination plan had left him visibly shaken. During his entire career, through all the conflicts, the barbaric dimensions of brush fighting in jungles, incomprehensible to most human kind, and dealing with assorted guerrillas and terrorists who's humanity was non-existent, he had never run-up against anything that was more perplexing than this conversation with his Commander in Chief. It was more frightening than any combat situation the Admiral had ever been in.

He sat there, his mind wandering from disbelief to fantasy. He did hate this man, Garriana, for what he did, and tried to do, to one of his men and to all of the innocent civilians who were murdered. He despised everything his kind stood for, and realized only killing him would stop his brutal assault against the country he so deeply cared about. He would love to have personally had the opportunity to shoot him, however, his absolute belief in the Constitution of the United States, and his sworn oath to uphold and defend it and all that it stands for, made it absolutely impossible for him to have that opportunity other than through the receipt of a lawful order. But, being human, as well as a soldier, he allowed himself to indulge in a little fantasy. He started to put together various plans that could be pursued, how they would be synchronized and how many men they would take, to be successful. It really wouldn't be that difficult. Unknown to most people, the very arrogance so deeply ingrained within the Ocho Garriana's of the world made them vulnerable due to their almost total disconnect with reality. They believed they were above all humanity, invulnerable, immortal. Bullets and bombs were meant for lower class "others", not them. Their self importance was

215

blown totally out of proportion. Their invulnerability to anything human was even above God's, or so they thought.

All of a sudden the Admiral jolted upright.....He became consciously aware of the fact that Dale Thomas commanded the SEAL Team with operational authority in Latin America. He instantly reached for the red phone and speed dialed the direct number to SEAL Team Four's headquarters and Commander Thomas' office in Little Creek, Virginia.

Commander Thomas was in the process of doing the one part of his job he hated....administrative paperwork. When he was not on a mission, or in the midst of planning one, or had just run out of excuses, he was forced to face the tediousness of the inevitable paperwork which included reports, evaluation forms, orders, etc. It was always there, cluttering up his desk as a constant reminder. His mood became sullen when he was faced with this drudgery. As he sat and concentrated on a particularly boring and lengthy report, a welcoming sound broke the silence. He quickly reached for the private phone and answered in his most commanding voice, the anticipation of something that would allow him to deviate from the task at hand highly visible in his tone....

"Commander Thomas."

A familiar voice came from the other end, "Commander Thomas, Admiral Blankenship here. How are you, Dale?"

Relaxing his professional posture and returning the familiar greeting he said,

"Admiral.....partly cloudy." (This was a typical greeting between members of the SEALs which meant that everything was okay at the moment, but the future was uncertain.) "What can I do for you?"

The Commander, being only a few months from retirement, momentarily reflected on how he would miss these energizing moments shared so intimately and spontaneously with fellow SEALs. He was facing his entry into the "Civilian World" with mixed emotions.

The Admiral, not only appreciating the discretion and

professionalism of Commander Thomas, was at this moment counting on it.

"Dale, I just received a very interesting phone call from President Chase. Wading through the typical political word games, I deciphered that he was calling to test the waters on getting us to "unofficially" eliminate Ocho Garriana. He did state that due to political pressure he couldn't sign a "Finding", therefore, he did not give a direct order. But the intent was sure there."

The Commander reacted in much the same manner as did the Admiral at the time of his conversation with the President. "What the hell, if he does want to get rid of that son-of-a-bitch, why doesn't he just sign?"

The reason given by the President to him was just as foggy to the Admiral as it would be to the Commander. The only answer the Admiral could give the Commander was to quote the President. "Dale, all he said was that he had a problem with `internal domestic political considerations'.....whatever that means?"

The two continued a thirty minute conversation, during which they reviewed the highly classified SEAL Team operations against Ocho Garriana's fleet of riverboats being used to transport the cocoa base. Both realized it would take very little extrapolation to elevate the operations from Ocho Garriana's fleet of boats to killing the man himself, but it would still require properly signed orders. For their own integrity and security, and even as a basis for any future action that might be ordered against the man, the two covered everything that was known about him, his network, contacts and activities. They both expressed their individual curiosity about how Garriana continued to go about his business with, what seemed to be, impunity. It seemed to both men to be tantamount to diplomatic immunity. Due to instincts about such matters honed to a fine edge through years of being involved with such convoluted affairs, both began to sense that there had to be some link, directly or indirectly, at some level, between José Ocho

217

Garriana and some elements in the United States Government. The thought that this might even be a remote possibility made each man feel queasy, almost sick to their stomachs.

During the conversation, Commander Thomas sensed an addition to the agenda as the Admiral's reason for covering all known information on Garriana. While the Commander was uncertain regarding the precise nature of the unknown agenda item, he did know that the Admiral shared his desire to get rid of this man, who had become such a threat to the safety not only to the United States, but to his men working in Latin America as well.

Suddenly, toward the end of their conversation, the Commander realized where the Admiral was leading. Despite Admiral Blankenship's protestations in response to the possibility that the President was asking him to act "unofficially", he himself, was subconsciously asking Commander Thomas to do the exact same thing. While neither man made any direct statement acknowledging this thought as they ended their conversation, it was very obviously left hanging and clearly mutually understood that it would be discussed later.

Tactfully changing the subject, the two men ended the conversation by discussing the details of the SEAL Team Four Change of Command ceremony to be held at the Little Creek Naval Amphibious Base two weeks hence. At that time, Commander Thomas would be relieved of command of his unit by Commander Jason Williams, and commence a thirty-day separation leave prior to his retirement from the Navy. The plans they agreed on were: Admiral Blankenship would be the keynote speaker; there would be a list of dignitaries along with representatives from several Western counter terrorist units, including the British SAS, Germany's Einzgruppen 9, Israel's Golani Brigade, Norway's Para Commandos and the French Foreign Legion. With the large list of requests to attend due to Commander Thomas' outstanding career, the planning took far more effort and coordination than usual. Being a traditionally formal ceremony, the logistics were crucial to keep the dignified atmosphere that an occasion like this demanded. After exchanging final pleasantries, the conversation ended.

As in the domino theory, now it was Commander Thomas who sat in thoughtful silence, staring out the window behind his desk....After several minutes he couldn't refrain from laughing out loud, "So you thought you were going to retire to the nice quiet life of a civilian! HA!" Swinging his chair around and in the same motion, with one swipe of his arm he cleared the paper from his desk, and took on the look of one who had been reborn. At that moment, Yeoman Farrarra announced that a David Powers was on the line for him.

Pausing for a moment, the Commander was so energized by his conversation with Admiral Blankenship that he thought his heart would pound out of his chest. The queasiness he had begun to feel in his stomach now gave way to the euphoria of possibly doing away with this predator. He had to call upon the self control and total internal dominance over one's very being that is taught to every SEAL. David Powers would sense none of that at the other end of the phone. The Commander quickly picked up the phone.

"Dave, I'm so glad you called. I was anxious to tell you about Jeremy. He's doing great." The calmness with which Commander Thomas spoke belied the inner turmoil born of a mixture of excitement and anticipation.

The Commander filled in Powers on Jeremy's still being in severe pain and under heavy guard, although he had returned to the Little Creek base under limited duty status. Powers, of course, found it highly unusual that the Commander kept rambling on about the well-being of one of his own men, particularly since his son's condition was well known to both men. He realized that the Commander must be covering something up, but decided to let the matter pass. Powers then asked Thomas whether Casey could do a small reading at his Change of Command Ceremony.

The Commander expressed his joy at Jeremy's progress and his delight at Casey's participation in one of the most im-

219

portant days of his life. As the conversation drifted from one subject to another, Powers finally brought up José Ocho Garriana. Thomas responded obliquely to a general question about whether there had been any resolution to the Garriana problem.

"No, Dave, there seems to be a hang-up somewhere up the line within the political system. I really don't know what all of the issues are, and unfortunately, the days of unauthorized action by military units such as the Green Berets, or the CIA, seem to be a thing of the past."

Powers could begin to feel the rage building from somewhere deep inside until he could feel it reaching the nape of his neck. Thomas heard him cup the speaker to the phone to politely answer a question being directed at him from his secretary in the background, then he asked her to please close the door. As Powers returned to their conversation, Thomas was somewhat taken aback by both the directness and explosiveness of Powers' response. He had seen traces of this side of his friend before, but not to this degree.

"Dale, who is protecting this son-of-a-bitch? It wouldn't be our own government would it?! What the fuck is going on here!?" Having had some, quite literally painful past experience with the inner workings of his government, Powers had learned not to believe in, trust in, nor count on completely, anything that involves the vague concept of "the Government".

At this point in his life, Powers was uncertain as to whether, in fact, he could even define what "the Government" was. It was excruciatingly painful and complicated for someone who had grown-up believing in the absoluteness of the United States and its ideals. Perhaps during his formative years there had, in fact, been only one government. As the world grew more complicated and dangerous, with threats coming from many far off corners of the world, the U.S. response had itself grown far more complicated. Perhaps it was during these more recent years that the concepts of shadow governments, and rogue elements of organizations such as the CIA acting on their own, were born.

The question of the United States' government complicity in the protection of José Ocho Garriana had only very recently occurred to Thomas. He was quite used to all sorts of government secrecy, contradictory behavior, and duplicity of every kind. Thomas' voice maintained the equilibrium of what Powers liked to refer to as his "command presence".

"Dave, I can understand how you feel, but you of all people certainly know that we cannot unilaterally and randomly take people out. You don't want us to start acting like the Gestapo, do you?"

Powers had heard the Gestapo lecture before from former FBI agent Bob Lewis during the Modular Products intrigue. While it always seemed to blunt his rage, he had a much harder time swallowing the logic this time. The basic question as he saw it and one that had kept repeating itself over and over in his mind was, "No, Dale, God damn it. I don't want a fucking Gestapo. But, how long should someone who commits acts of what I would consider as "war" against the United States on what I have heard he does on a daily basis, be allowed to stay alive? This bastard has murdered hundreds of Americans, corrupted our banking system, polluted our schools, eroded the fabric of our society, not to mention trying to murder my son. Yes, Dale, I've done my homework. I don't give a rat's ass what the political issues are, they can't possibly override the need to get rid of this piece of shit. I don't believe in vigilante justice, but...."

Commander Thomas didn't need to hear any more. After the conversation he had just had with the Admiral, his mind had been made up, although, in looking back, he had to admit there was a slight chance it had been made up, even before his conversation.

"Dave, calm down. Now listen to me. After the Change of Command ceremony in two weeks, I go on thirty days of separation leave before retiring from the Navy. An awful lot could be done during that time. Why don't you and I take a vacation together during the month so we can finally spend some uninterrupted time going over the various subjects we never get a chance to fully discuss. Let's pick some exotic far off place where we both can get away from civilization, 'stand down', and relax."

The Commander's highly-trained mind had already entered the operational planning phase, "Why don't you come and visit me at the base in Little Creek a day or so before the ceremony. Since you're attending anyway, you won't have to make two trips. It will give me time to get some logistics together, since this will be a vacation taken by civilians. It should commence the minute after I begin my separation leave, which is 30 days before my final retirement from the Navy and Dave, could your friend the FBI agent you're always talking about, Bob Lewis, join us? After what you two did to stop those nuclear terrorists at Modular Products, I really would like to spend some time with him and hear the whole story."

Powers' heart jumped. If Commander Thomas was disposed to do what Powers prayed with all his heart he would consider doing....Well that might just be too much to hope for. He knew the responsibility he was taking by committing his best friend to something that would be very dangerous, possibly even fatal.

Powers answered without hesitation, "absolutely!"

Knowing it was unnecessary, but making sure to avoid all possibilities of complications, the Commander cautioned, "Dave, the plans of this vacation as to where, when and why, are to be strictly between us vacationers. Do you understand?"

Exposing his mixture of excitement, anticipation, and a little fear, Powers spoke in his own command voice, mixed with remnants of what he could recall about military communications protocol,

"Roger that, Commander. We'll see you at the Little Creek HQ at zero eight hundred, Thursday, twenty-one May. I'll slap a top secret, crypto lid on this, and tell Bob to do the same."

Smiling in response to the top-secret crypto reference, the

classification reserved for the most highly-secret national security matters such as a pre-planned date for United States offensive military action, Commander Thomas concluded the conversation with the usual, "Roger that....out here."

After hanging up, the Commander mused to himself how the overriding concept of "Plausible Denial" was omnipresent in such matters. The President could always claim he knew nothing of what happened, Admiral Blankenship would recall no direct or indirect orders to do anything, Commander Thomas would be retiring and leaving the Navy altogether, and David Powers and Bob Lewis would both be on a vacation. What could any of these people have to do with any direct order to eliminate José Ocho Garriana? Nothing!

In addition to " Plausible Denial", Commander Thomas realized just how serious such matters were. While many civilians incorrectly looked upon the military as a place for individuals who could not handle the so called "Responsibility" of civilian life, that was simply untrue within the SEAL Team. Given the catastrophic impact on U.S. Foreign Policy resulting from a failed mission, SEAL Team Commanders only had three choices. One was to succeed, the second was to die, and the third was to voluntarily resign from the military if neither of the first two situations occurred. There was absolutely no in between.

Hanging up from Commander Thomas, Powers immediately dialed his wife at the law firm. Asking her to join him for dinner, they agreed to meet at their favorite Phoenix restaurant, Le Trois Rouge, at 7:00 p.m. While David gave little inkling of what this special occasion was, Maggie intuitively knew something was up. Powers' heart raced and he began to plan his own dimensions of the military action against José Ocho Garriana. He silently admitted to himself that he had last experienced this inexplicable combination of emotions during the Modular Products episode.

After the two were seated by Jacques Barzin, the Maitre D', at their favorite private corner table, Maggie studied her husband's every physical movement and facial expression. After the waiter had uncorked their favorite French wine, David completed the tasting, and the wine was served. Maggie waited for the ceremony to be over before asking,

"So, David, lay it on me. Is it your job? Jeremy, or what?"

David tried to look puzzled and responded with the normal "husband's" answer, "Why nothing dear! I thought we just deserved a romantic, pleasant dinner out. Besides, I don't think I've told you I love you enough this week."

That did it. Maggie knew something was up. "David, if you don't tell me now I can guarantee this evening will not end on a romantic note!"

David, knowing his wife, quickly reflected on what he could say and how he was going to explain his absence for the length of time it would take for Commander Thomas, Bob Lewis and himself to complete what he believed they could all agree had to be done. Suddenly one word jumped into his mind. A word Dale had used during their conversation, "vacation". Taking a deep breath, he quickly prepared himself for the first lie he had ever told his wife, and definitely the biggest he had ever told anyone in his entire life.

"Well....Dale and I were talking today and he asked if Bob Lewis and I would be interested in going on an 'all men' vacation after he is officially out of the service. It will be a sort of celebration. Of course I told him I would have to discuss it with you first, but as I told him, knowing you, I can't imagine why you would object to me having this time with my friends. Especially with what has been going on in my life lately. I'm not quite sure the exact date we would leave, or how long we will be gone. Dale will be filling me in on the final plans while we're there at his Change of Command ceremony. We shouldn't be away for long. You know....the business here can't do without me."

Powers had to cringe at his obviously insincere, flippant approach to this. His only hope was that the wine was getting to Maggie and she wouldn't notice. The fact that he kept refilling her glass after every sip was her next big clue.

No such luck. Maggie was well aware that she had just heard the biggest piece of garbage since one of her clients pleaded innocent to embezzlement, while she was holding his Swiss Bank account book in her hand. However, David had never lied to her before, and she knew he would have to have a good reason to be doing so now. Maggie did have a suspicion it had to have something to do with Jeremy's attack. Putting together the three men involved: Commander Thomas, Bob Lewis, and Dave, not to mention the last little venture Dave himself had with that foreign intelligence service, she could conclude nothing else. Along with all the security and mystery surrounding Jeremy now, she could only guess it had to be something very dangerous, and probably highly classified.

Since the attack on his son and knowing her husband, his values and how he reacted when those values were threatened, she had been waiting to see what kind of action he would take. All she could hope for was that it not be too radical, or life threatening. David had a way of not letting something go when he felt a wrong had to be righted. He had told her the story of what had happened 10 years ago when he was working for Modular Products and stumbled upon the nuclear terrorist plot. He told her what he had gone through, having only Bob Lewis, who to this day remained one of his best friends, in his corner. What developed was a type of friendship that could only be forged by the two sharing such a deadly experience. All the obstacles thrown at Powers did not stop him, nor could countless warnings and threats from both sides prevent him from fighting for the security of both his country and family. And, despite almost losing his life on several occasions, he waged his private battle until the conspiracy to steal our nuclear technology was abandoned by those involved. It had left him emotionally and physically spent, and while those who truly cared for him pleaded for him to abandon the fight, his values and patriotism were too strong to deter him.

Maggie felt a tightness starting to develop in the pit of

225

her stomach. She knew it would be best if she just let it pass and trust him to tell her what this was all about at some later date. Right now all she could do was to be supportive and, if necessary, pretend to buy his story, and most of all send her prayers, support and love with him.

Maggie looked across the table into her husband's eyes. In them she saw his love reflecting back at her and quietly gave thanks for all the strength he gave to her. Raising up her wine glass she offered her husband the following,

"Dave, may all you wish for come true. May God be with you in all your endeavors and may you always be in my life."

Startled, Dave returned her toast, "And to you dear, may I always be worthy of the woman I am honored to call my wife."

CHAPTER 25

LITTLE CREEK, VIRGINIA

I n a secluded back corner of the Officers Club, at the Little Creek, Virginia Naval Amphibious Base, sat two men dressed in casual civilian clothes. The men had managed to break away from their wives and all the excitement of the celebration parties which followed the Change of Command Ceremony. The ceremony had gone well. Commander Thomas was truly embarrassed and touched by not only the contents of the speeches made in his honor, but the quality and quantity of the officials and representatives giving those speeches. He was truly honored that men of that caliber would take time out to not only attend, but to recognize all he had done during his career in the Navy.

The Commander was leaning back in his chair, and was thinking how good it felt to get out of his rigid formal uniform and into his casual, civilian clothes. As Powers approached the table he saw that Bob Lewis had already joined Dale Thomas and noted that both men had seated themselves in a position to have a direct view of the front door with their backs to the wall. Seating himself to the Commander's immediate right, Powers quipped,

"Jeez, guys, do we even have to be paranoid on a United States Naval base!!"

Thomas grinned and slightly parted his blue sports jacket, exposing an HK P9 M13 9mm automatic. This particular weapon was favored by SEALs because the safety was located on the front of the weapon's handle, so when carried concealed, as the pistol was drawn, the act of wrapping an individual's hand around the grip also took the safety

227

off. The shooter did not have to fumble with his thumb on the safety as with most other automatic pistols.

"Well, maybe not paranoid, but the drug lords must have paid a lot of money to try to set up your son. Who knows how much they might pay to take us out."

The irony and seriousness of that remark was not lost on either Lewis or Powers. Both men realized that many other governments in the world had already demonstrated that the price was, in fact, not all that expensive if a drug lord wanted to buy control of a sovereign government or to buy the necessary information to have any enemy assassinated. Each one of them at one time or another had done something to put them on a terrorist's "most popular" hit list. Commander Thomas had once shot a high ranking member of a drug cartel through the head for offering him a $10,000,000 bribe to have his SEALs look the other way while a boatload of cocoa base made its way out of the Amazon River Basin.

After exchanging comments on their respective impressions of the ceremony and the various guests and speakers who attended, Powers attempted to firmly focus the conversation to what he hoped would be the business at hand.

"So, Commander, what's the plan? Where and when are we taking that 'vacation'?"

The Commander responded, as he got up from the table, "I've arranged for us to use a spare office over at SEAL Team Four. Why don't we go over there?"

Both Lewis and Powers realized it was best to drop the conversation until they were in a more secure area. Following the Commander, they found themselves at a relatively nondescript brick building, about a hundred yards from the Officer's Club. They said very little as they walked, just occasionally gesturing at something of particular interest, such as the obstacle course next to the building they were entering. Like Lewis, during his reunion meeting of his fellow former agents, Powers mentally joined the present environment and somehow felt he was taking a journey back in time to the 1960s. Little had changed since his time in the military and, as most other Navy veterans, he always felt a little part of him had remained behind in the Navy. Powers' kinship with the military had remained intact for the three decades that had passed so rapidly since he left the service nearly thirty years before. He had remained a strong proponent of the Navy SEAL Team and had supported them in a variety of ways.

Suddenly, the men entered the barbed-wire compound that separated the building from the rest of the base. As they approached the front door quarter-deck area, Powers was struck that he could not detect any overt means of security other than the group of Naval personnel immediately inside the front entrance. Somehow, he sensed that he was under the watchful gaze of something akin to big brother. A sudden chill ran up his spine as he realized the world he was entering had always represented an almost sacred place to him and something that he had himself aspired to. As Commander Thomas entered the quarter-deck area, the three armed SEALs snapped to attention, one of them issuing the order, "Attention on the quarter-deck!" The three sentries remained at attention as Commander Thomas stopped to register his two guests and issued them temporary visitors' passes. They remained at attention as the Commander and his group filed past. The Commander walked about fifteen paces past two doors, came to a third, and entered using a security card he had taken out of his jacket. The door was identified by a simple white "XO" in block letters that had been painted on. It was the office normally reserved for Lt. (Cdr.) Ernest R. Guarido, the Executive Officer or number two of SEAL Team Four.

A slight buzzing sound emanated from the door as it automatically opened to a distance of approximately two inches. Thomas pushed the door open, motioned his two guests to follow, and locked the door behind them. Inside, the sparsely decorated room contained a bare conference table, six chairs and a silver pot of coffee surrounded by three cups. A gray metal table on which rested a red phone was located against the wall at one end of the room. The walls were covered with pictures of graduating students from previous training classes going all the way back to 1967, the year the unit was first commissioned. Powers scanned the walls and instantly picked out the picture of his son, kneeling in front of the twenty-eight officers and men who had graduated with him in Class 47. He welled up with pride and smiled to himself as he realized that Jeremy's entering class had twenty officers and ninety enlisted men. His son had been one of only three other officers who graduated and entered SEAL Team Four on a probationary basis after the initial thirty-six weeks of grueling, non-stop physical and mental duress.

Powers realized this was the moment of truth. The Commander was either going to let him in on something highly confidential or even possibly involve him in some way in the mission—why else would he have set this meeting on a secure military base where there was no risk of being overheard?

The Commander, taking a large map out of his inside coat pocket, then hanging it on the back of a chair, stood by the conference table and motioned for the other two men to seat themselves. Spreading the map in front of them on the table, the Commander removed the 9mm automatic from its holster and placed it atop the map as a paperweight. Powers noticed that the weapon contained a fully loaded clip. Security was omnipresent.

Lewis thought to himself that it had taken nearly three years after he left the FBI to stop reaching inside his shoulder holster to remove his weapon whenever he had been in similar circumstances. Leaning over the table with his hands braced on either side of the map, the Commander finally spoke,

"As you guys can see, we're looking at Latin America." Then pointing to a specific location, with Lewis and Powers leaning forward to get a good look at exactly where that was, he continued.

"Over here is Cardazanna, the headquarters of Ocho Garriana. That's not where we want to go, because the security at the headquarters location is extremely tight and it would take major air strikes or a frontal assault with many more men than we have to get to him. We pretty much know from highly classified intelligence reports when this guy comes and goes, when he travels, etc."

Powers realized that certain things were none of his business, and while dying to know, he didn't dare ask how someone surrounded by his own private army could be monitored so closely. It suddenly occurred to him that such information could only be known from the inside. But Powers was still not sure why Commander Thomas was bringing him into his confidence this way, revealing secret maps and other classified information. He knew the answer would be forthcoming.

"Our best opportunity, " Thomas continued, " will be to get him when he has traveled somewhere near an inland waterway, such as the Rio Fuego, or Magadena, when his security is both lax and at its lowest level in terms of personnel. The Amazon Basin inside Peru, for example, would be perfect and we know that Garriana meets there with Shining Path representatives on a regular basis. He also travels along the rivers in his private yacht to meet with other friendly cartel heads who then take cruises together to discuss business."

Bob Lewis was already mentally ahead of Powers in terms of understanding the unfolding scenario due to his more recent experience as an FBI Agent. He was uncertain, however, as to why he was getting such a high level briefing and where it would ultimately lead them.

Commander Thomas moved the pointer towards the blue, water colored area on the Pacific Ocean side of the map. Retrieving a miniaturized replica, of what looked like a boat, from a small end table, the Commander placed it on the map and announced....

"Gentlemen, meet the *Vindicator* Boat!"

The two men stood up and studied the little boat very closely. Somehow they felt from the way the Commander presented it, it was critically important to whatever they were about to learn. Lewis and Powers looked at each other, both showing no comprehension whatsoever regarding the vessel. Powers put it best by exclaiming,

"What in the hell is a *Vindicator* Boat?"

The answer should have been apparent,

"It's just like it sounds. It's our ticket in and out of where we have to go. It's difficult to detect even with radar, totally silent, travels at a high rate of speed and can carry a shit load of armament. Essentially, it's the SEAL Team attack boat."

What was everyday business to most of today's SEAL Team members was the stuff of James Bond movies to Bob Lewis and David Powers. Both men kept staring down at the little miniature boat and obviously didn't know what to say or ask next. Neither man wanted to appear uninformed, nor did they wish to probe too deeply into the SEAL Team's obviously highly classified technology, although both men had heard of the United States Air Forces' fleet of nearly invisible Stealth bombers, and other creations of the government's famous and most top secret "Skunk Works".

Looking from Lewis to Powers, the Commander continued, "Let me make it real simple for you guys and tell you exactly what I have in mind. We're going to find this guy in a highly vulnerable situation, come in fast, pop the son-of-a-bitch and then get out. Piece of Cake."

With that, the Commander sat down and obviously was quite pleased with what he had come up with. He then began to lay-out his highly complex plan, trying to communicate in words and gestures that would be understandable to his civilian friends. Although he spoke very deliberately, what was so apparent to him was virtually incomprehensible to his visitors. Both Powers and Lewis looked at one another, wondering why the hell Thomas was giving them so many details of the operation. The Commander continued to explain how the participants in this mission would board a new special operations craft known as the Serpentine Class that would transport the men from the Jacksonville, Florida Naval base, more than two thousand nautical miles to a point just off the coast of Colombia. There, they would change to a *Vindicator* Boat, travel at a high rate of speed undetected to the point where the Atlantic met the appropriate inland river, proceed upriver to a designated point in Ayachuco Province, and eliminate Garriana when CIA intelligence identified his location in the Andean Basin.

At that location he would be having his regular meeting with the representatives of the Shining Path, or be cruising along the river with one of his many "business associates." The attack team would make their getaway the same way, leaving virtually undetected. Commander Thomas mentioned in passing that the final assault might consist of a seaborne attack by the *Vindicator* Boat against Ocho Garriana's yacht and any accompanying patrol craft. Neither of the outsiders could possibly realize that a couple of noteworthy omissions from the presentation of the plan placed it in the ozone layer of techno-military lethal capability. Even if they did know the missing elements, these details would be unbelievable to the uninitiated.

At this point in the presentation, the Commander looked at both men and dropped the bombshell. "So, gentlemen, if you like the plan so far, how would you two like to join me on my last mission before my retirement becomes official?"

Powers and Lewis were speechless. This was beyond Powers' wildest dreams. He hoped that the U.S. government would seek revenge for Garriana's senseless slaughter, but he never expected the privilege of participating with the SEAL Team. Well, maybe "participating" was too strong a word as he still didn't know what he'd be doing with the SEALs. This was all so unthinkable—yet it was happening.

"Commander," Powers finally blurted out, "I'm not going to ask how you managed to get me included, but you know I'd give anything to serve with you on this mission. You know how badly I want this, to settle a score for my son and for my country. But I'm a crazy son of a bitch. I don't think Bob here needs to risk his life on this mission."

Bob had heard enough. "Now hold on just a minute! I'm in, and I'm in deep. There's nothing that would keep me away, and Powers doesn't have the authority to stop me. This is my fight too."

Powers gave up trying to cut Bob out of the mission, and the two men paused, then solemnly shook hands.

"OK then, gentlemen," said Thomas with the tone of a pre-fight referee, "it's settled. The three of us will be working together to achieve our stated objective. I am taking you both along as civilian advisors on a top secret drug eradication mission. But we will be eradicating a lot more than just the drugs. Now listen up and get familiar with the rest of the plan."

Bob Lewis, David Powers and Commander Thomas continued into the early hours of the morning, consuming endless cups of coffee, ironing out details of what would be the toughest and longest journey of their lives. Each of them felt apprehensive, fearful and exhilarated, all at the same time. Somehow, Powers knew that Thomas would get the mission accomplished and return them to the relative sanity of their present lives, alive and in one piece. In many ways, such a mission represented a secret wish he had harbored ever since he had left the Navy so many years before. It would also represent justice against the man who had so ruthlessly and pitilessly mangled his son while trying to kill him, and obviously still had contracts out to finish the job. It would serve as a warning to everyone around José Ocho Garriana to leave Jeremy Powers alone forever, since the group would somehow deliver a still to be defined message of why this man had been killed. Normally, no trail would be left, but since this was intended as a deterrent against further attempts at killing the younger Powers or anyone else in a U.S. military uniform, a message would simply have to be delivered that went beyond the killing itself.

For Lewis, participating in this venture represented the unyielding loyalty that his values demanded to such a close

234

personal friend. It also represented the opportunity to take the type of action against such a hideous wrong that had not been possible so many years before at Modular Products, or, for that matter, during Lewis' entire career with the FBI.

For Thomas this was yet another chance to simply do what was right within the confines of his official responsibilities and his discretionary responsibilities.

He was going to be officially retired in a month anyway, so there could be no effective repercussions. Exactly what would the powers that be do about it if they found out, take away his soon-to-be-relinquished command? Besides, the orders for this mission came indirectly from the Commander in Chief himself. Of course, no one would take responsibility for the mission if it failed, just as no one could take credit if it succeeded. It would be a lose-lose situation for the person commanding this mission. Still, it was the right thing to do. He was determined to go for it.

For Thomas, it was yet another chance to strike a blow for what was right in a world that had grown all too contradictory and complex.

The three men did not leave SEAL Team Four's headquarters until nearly 3:00 a.m. After returning the visitors passes, they went back to their hotel and agreed to reconvene at 1:00 p.m. the same day to begin their arduous preparation for the journey ahead. One of the main concerns of everyone, including Powers himself, was that while Thomas and Lewis were in excellent physical and mental condition for what lay ahead, Powers had many mountains to climb, due to the relatively sedentary life he had been living for many years and only two weeks remained before they entered what could be the jaws of hell. The two outsiders each harbored a nagging feeling that these jaws would actually open to them even before landing in hostile territory, once their scheduled SEAL conditioning and training began the next day.

Early the following morning, Powers called his office and made arrangements to inform the Board of Directors of his employer, the Thompson Electronics Corporation, that he would personally be going along on the test cruise of he *USS Fertilance* to observe first hand the seaborne evaluation of the SIGINT/ECM (Signals Intercept/Electronic Counter Measures) the company had developed for the SEAL Team. It had been placed on one of the new Serpentine Class patrol boats, and he would be boarding the ship in Jacksonville, Florida.

The extensive evaluation would be conducted over a period of four weeks, and the multi-million dollar contract that could be awarded to Thompson, if the tests proved favorable, were worthy of top level attention from the company. Bob Lewis would be accompanying him, as the importance certainly justified the presence of a second senior executive, who could also oversee corporate security. While all of the other preliminary testing had included representatives of the various technical departments from Thompson involved in the weapons' system development, this was the ultimate "final exam". The remaining Directors were thrilled and delighted at the same time.

Nothing felt as good as expansive breakthrough technology that could be profitably marketed commercially. The U.S. Government always paid "top dollar", as did the closest U.S. allies who also were allowed to share in this latest defense technology. Had any of them realized what the real intent of the cruise was, their reactions would certainly have been far different. Although, on a personal basis, several might have supported the effort to get rid of the monster known to the world as José Ocho Garriana. None of them, however, would have wanted David Powers to put his life on the line on such a dangerous mission, which obviously should have been left to the professionals.

CHAPTER 26

UBON RATCHATHANI, THAILAND

Ubon Ratchathani, Thailand, stood near the head of the waterway that ultimately led to the fertile Mekong Delta region of South Vietnam, where it spilled out into the South China Sea. Long the stronghold of the three major warlords who controlled the heroin trade in the area, it was only thirty-six miles North of the so-called, "Golden Triangle", the point where the countries of Laos, Burma and Thailand came together in one sharp tri-corner. The innocuous village of nearly twenty-thousand inhabitants was also home to the well armed and dangerous armies controlled by two of the warlords. The Golden Triangle region, along with Sicily, was the source of nearly fifty percent of the world's supply of heroin and marijuana, the remainder coming from a number of diverse regions including the Bekaa Valley in Syria, India, Pakistan, China and Turkey. There were striking similarities to other major drug trafficking centers of the world, although these might not be readily apparent to a casual observer.

On the surface, marauding bands of well-armed soldiers loyal to their warlords controlled the drug trade within the immediate areas they dominated. U.S. and other Western intelligence services, however, had long acknowledged that, like Shining Path and other armed groups in Latin American and elsewhere, these armies could not sustain themselves and control vast networks of drug centered commerce without the complicity of local governments. Bangkok, Thailand for example, located at the mouth of the Gulf of Thailand, had been the center of major regional international commerce for several

237

decades. Containing branches of several major international banks and businesses, it served as the financial conduit for much of the Golden Triangle's drug trade, as Cardazanna, Colombia did for that area, Palermo for the Sicilian heroin trade, and Hong Kong, inevitably would, for China's worldwide trafficking in heroin. Bands of marauding soldiers, each loyal to a feudal warlord, simply could not accomplish all of this by themselves. The $100 billion a year in heroin and marijuana trade emanating from the Golden Triangle required the same types of "safe haven" and banking accomplices as would be needed anywhere else in the world.

One of the central elements of "Operation Snow Bird" was to strike at the leaders of four of the major drug trafficking centers in the world. To accomplish this, British SAS (Special Air Service) and United States SEAL Team units had been given the assignment of assassinating the three generals controlling the three major organizations in the Golden Triangle area. Two of the three, General Lieu Than and General Hi Phong, were headquartered in the immediate vicinity of Ubon Ratchathani. 3rd SAS, under the command of Lt. Colonel Roy Barkley, would attack the stronghold while 5th SAS, commanded by Major Guy Howard, would provide backup and cover.

The British SAS units were no strangers to this part of the world, having fought brilliantly successful counter-insurgency campaigns against the Malaysian insurgents in the past. While trained to fight anywhere, they were particularly adept at fighting in the harsh jungle conditions found around Ubon Ratchathani.

SEAL Team Three, one of the U.S.'s West Coast teams, would carry out the third assault against General Ong Keng in the area around Thatabarivat, Cambodia. Since Thatabarivat was located alongside the waterway leading south to the Mekong, SEAL Team Three's basic orientation to water made the unit perfect for the job. All three attacks were to take place simultaneously, in order to prevent the three armies from co-ordinating a joint counter attack, or from providing reinforcements to one another.

Due to the exceptionally thick foliage found around the village of Ubon Ratchathani, and the fact that the nearest area suitable for parachute landing was more than twenty-five miles away and located far too close to major Thai population centers, HALO (high altitude, low opening) parachute jumps into the target area were ruled out by the British high command. After carefully evaluating the terrain and using detailed intelligence information provided by both MI5 and the CIA, the SAS decided to stick to some of their most tried and true tactics. British Sea King Helicopters would drop a total of sixteen men between the Tonle Sap Great Lake in Cambodia and the Mun-Chi waterway connecting Ubon Ratchathani to the Mekong River Delta. The men would proceed overland to the Mun-Chi River and split into four groups. Two three man sniper units would each be assigned one of the two primary targets, and each would be protected by a five man SAS fire squad.

It had been determined by the British officers that a large unit assault, no matter how well conceived, would almost certainly fail due to the fact that, in addition to each of their personal armies consisting of nearly three thousand heavily armed, dedicated soldiers, the two men were looked upon as folk heroes akin to Robin Hood, by the thousands of ordinary citizens living in the surrounding area. In addition, since starting a major regional War was not the desired outcome, a small unit sniper attack made the most sense.

Half of the men would paddle about fourteen miles upriver during the night in the two man kayaks for which the SAS and its sister unit, the SBS (Special Boat Service), had become famous, in order to avoid detection. The other groups would make their way overland to the target area. Two of the men from each of the overland groups would pre-position themselves in the target area to provide assistance in calling in the sniper fire. All of the men involved would have to rely on every fiber of stealth, skill, conditioning and intense concentration that the years of arduous training had prepared them for.

The action had been rehearsed many times in wilderness area in British Columbia that possessed many similarities in terrain to that found around Ubon Ratchathani. Since the village of Thatabarivat was located three miles south of where the SAS units would enter the river, SEAL Team Three would launch its operation approximately twenty-four hours later, also under cover of darkness, the next night.

A three man sniper team would be dropped from a C130 Hercules aircraft utilizing the horizontal and silent gliding capability of the new MK91 UA parachutes. This enabled the men to silently glide the sixteen miles from the air drop point to the target. The James Bond-like operation would leave the drug dealers scratching their heads, wondering where their assailants had come from. A four man, heavily armed SEAL Team fire squad would be dropped into the same area to provide back-up. All three units, the SAS elements, the SEAL Team sniper squad, and the fire team, would be extracted by pre-positioned helicopter pickup. Back-up on top of back-up contingencies existed for all facets of the combined operation, including simultaneous bombing strikes as required to be launched by aircraft aboard the aircraft carrier *USS Kittyhawk* stationed in the South China Sea.

Now that the U.S. and British governments, as well as the Israelis, had determined that in many parts of the world drug terrorists and local governments had become one and the same, they were less concerned about the hostile reactions of these narco-terrorist governments than in the past. If these governments no longer wished to curb what were tantamount to declarations of a drug war against the West, they would have to live with the consequences of the West doing the job for them and eradicating illegal drugs within their countries. It was an agonizing reality with which Western governments had finally come to grips. The issue of what constituted declared overt acts of war had been unresolved ever since the Japanese attack against Pearl Harbor.

The issue had interfered with the conduct of American

Foreign Policy and had become crystallized during the Vietnam War. The conflict over when a country is in a war situation has existed for nearly fifty years. Finally, the United States government, along with several of its allies, had acknowledged that drug deaths perpetrated by drug lords were no less acts of war than the attack on Pearl Harbor had been. It was a horrible reality that at last was being dealt with.

Every element had been carefully considered in advance, including the precise location of the three sniper units. Since the maximum accurate range of the .50 caliber sniper rifle used by both the SAS and SEAL Team was eight hundred fifty yards, or approximately one-half mile, staff planners had carefully selected three locations for each of the three sniper teams, one primary and two back-up. All known variables from cover, to weather, to terrain had been meticulously considered prior to choosing each location. Final satellite confirmation of latitude and longitude coordinates would ensure the absolute precision of the snipers' locations. Since Western intelligence had agents inside the three drug organizations, the precise location of the targets would be known at the desired time. Nothing had been left to chance.

Three dead Thai, Laotian and Cambodian generals, their heads blown apart by exploding .50 caliber bullets, would attest once and for all to both the superior technology and collective resolve possessed by the industrialized Western nations. These governments had apparently finally decided who the real enemy was and just how dangerous the immediate threat to their collective survival truly was. At precisely 7:20 a.m., local time, August 9, 1992, the lives of the three warlords were violently ended, and twenty-four highly trained, dedicated, brave SAS and SEAL Team troops were safely extracted from the target areas, without leaving either a trace or any casualties. The rest of the world was left to ponder what really happened and most importantly, the drug lords and their accomplices now realized that they were no longer invulnerable. While their bestiality and money would continue to frighten local

241

populaces and even governments into submission (or buy their loyalty), they could no longer count on the Western governments simply rolling-over or continuing to ignore the reality of the threat against them. Perhaps they would one day learn that whatever their unlimited money could buy, it could not necessarily blunt the national resolve of certain countries. Everything had its limits, including the patience and passivity of many Western governments.

CHAPTER 27

LITTLE CREEK, VIRGINIA

D avid Powers lay exhausted in his room at the Hilton Inn, which was located adjacent to the Little Creek Naval Amphibious Base. He looked at the brightly-lit digits of the clock radio on the table next to his bed, it was 4:15 a.m. To his anguish, he realized morning was rapidly approaching. It was his eighth morning after a condensed physical, technical and emotional "Hell week" prior to the "vacation" in Cardazanna. He grinned as he remembered how the Commander couldn't conceal his doubts as to whether he and Lewis would get through the mission without ending up in a cardiac ward. Yet, here he was, still at it and his heart hadn't failed him yet, although, at this moment he wouldn't bet his wife a shopping trip to Paris on it. Every bone in his body ached, and he wondered whether he would be able to continue breathing. But his thoughts turned to the issue of his major concern of the day—how in fifteen minutes he would have to get his feet off the bed and onto the floor.

Powers was well aware that while normal SEAL training required runs over both soft sand and rough terrain of more than twenty miles, Commander Thomas had set a five-mile objective in a thirty-minute lapsed time as a realistic minimum. Powers found himself extremely thankful he had kept himself somewhat fit, despite his desk job. He was able to reach this goal on the sixth day. However, his celebration was cut short when Thomas, supposedly his friend, upped it to a new seven-mile, forty-nine minute run.

Commander Thomas had put a great deal of thought into how he was going to take these two middle aged civilians and turn them into two fine-tuned fighting machines. He came up with a daily routine that included: intensive running and weapons training. The weapons training included the firing of hundreds of rounds from three assault weapons: the HK P9 M13 9mm semi-automatic pistol with silencer; the HK MP5 9mm submachine gun also silenced; and the Remington Model 870 12-gauge pump-action shotgun. While a SEAL's routine training required proficiency in a dozen or more weapons, Commander Thomas decided that these three weapons would be adequate for anything the men might encounter during their mission.

Powers, willing to try anything at this point, was deeply immersed in his version of yoga—in other words, staring blankly at the wall across from his bed—when the wake-up call from the front desk broke through his concentration. It was exactly 4:30 a.m. The moment had come. Not quite taking the anticipated half-hour, Powers managed to get his aching body out of bed and dress while moving around the room his body's screams turned to whispers. As he glanced in the mirror, he noted with satisfaction that he appeared far more trim and firm than eight days ago. He smiled to himself, wondering whether he was imagining things. Then he saw his few gray hairs in the mirror. Brought back to the reality of his 47 years, he realized the quick reflexes of his youth, of twenty odd years ago, were gone forever.

But he remembered the true reason for his being there as he flashed back to the vision of his son's broken body in the hospital. He must concentrate on self-confidence. Without this, he could lose the sharp mental edge he needed to complete the job ahead. He must remain focused. He kept repeating this as he finished getting ready to meet Bob Lewis. Nothing must stand in the may of removing Ocho Garriana from this life and transporting him to the next. He stepped on the scale located just inside the bathroom door and realized he had lost thirteen pounds, returning him to his "fighting weight" of 187 pounds. Maybe the good old days were not gone forever! Regaining a

244

slight spring in his step, Powers placed a towel around his neck, picked up his sun glasses and proceeded to the elevator where he met Bob Lewis coming out of his room.

Powers looked at Lewis with envy. Lewis looked as if he just come off a week-long Caribbean cruise. He greeted Powers with a chipper, "Good morning. It's going to be a great day. I'm starved!"

The two exited on the ground floor, crossed the lobby and proceeded outside to the waiting, rented, blue sedan occupied by Commander Thomas. Powers got in the front while Bob Lewis entered the rear. Dale Thomas, still on separation leave and entitled to use Naval facilities, was staying in the Bachelor Officer's Quarters (BOQ) located on the base. He picked the two men up each morning at precisely 4:45 a.m. for the 5:00 a.m. scheduled run. As soon as both doors closed, Commander Thomas started the car and proceeded to the base. He seemed almost jubilant this morning,

"I hope you two are ready to meet a new guest. We're going to give the *Vindicator* Boat a spin right after breakfast." Commander Thomas grinned broadly as he gazed over at Powers seated next to him.

"Dave, how are you feeling?"

Despite his cheerful attire, the Commander was extremely serious about their workouts. One man falling behind due to a lack of conditioning could put every man's life in jeopardy. "You should be approaching what we call the pink of condition now."

Powers' answer helped to alleviate his concern.

"Dale, I feel great. Every goddam bone, muscle and tissue aches, but amazingly I feel twenty years younger."

There was no further conversation as the Commander guided the sedan into the entrance to Gate 7 at the Naval Base, acknowledged the salute of the Marine sentry posted at the guard shack, then drove to a relatively secluded beach located at the rear of the base. Parking the car, the three men exited and began their individual 10-minute stretching. As though on cue, Commander Thomas placed his towel on the hood of the car. Starting to run backwards, he was transformed from a respectful, caring friend, into his role as a commander of men.

"Okay, gentlemen....let's go. Our vacation has just begun....at a jog!"

The Commander then turned, jogged towards the beach and proceeded to lead the men on their seven-mile run. The white sand glistened as it reflected the rays of the sunrise. The only sounds that could be heard were the rhythmical crashing of the ocean waves onto the shore and the sea gulls screeching as they sought their morning meal. The course led up and down rugged sand dunes where, like quicksand, the soft terrain seemed to grab the men's feet at every stride. The men continued across land that became increasingly more difficult. Seven miles of a SEAL run was probably equivalent to twelve or so miles on a more traditional terrain.

Precisely 48 minutes and 22 seconds later, the run ended back at the sedan. The three men's chests heaving, sweating profusely, their cardiovascular systems strained for breath. The three men slowly circled the car for several minutes, hands placed on hips, cooling down their muscle strained bodies. They also gulped from the bottles of water provided by Commander Thomas. At exactly 06:00 local time, Commander Thomas directed the men to the car where he proceeded to drive them to the BOQ for breakfast.

After a five minute drive to the BOQ, the tired but enthusiastic aging warriors entered the low slung gray brick building. Picking up trays and silverware they passed along the food line packing their trays with everything that would fit. They ferociously ate the foods they would need to fuel their bodies with strength and build the much needed muscle tone and were done in fifteen minutes. This was a relative luxury for Commander Thomas, who was given only sixty seconds to throw down a meal during his early BUD-S Training nearly twenty-seven years earlier. Since he had often jokingly reminded his friends of this fact, Lewis and Powers did not abuse the extra time. When they were done, Commander Thomas announced it was time to go and meet a very important member of their team.

"Well, guys, it's time to meet the *Vindicator* Boat!"

Commander Thomas again drove the car back to the rear of the Naval Base, but before the usual turn made each morning for their run he continued on, turning several blocks down, heading towards the water. The men could see six parallel piers directly in front of them with a variety of small Naval craft docked on both sides. While Powers was not immediately familiar with all of them, they appeared to be a mixture of patrol craft, Zodiac boats and somewhat larger crafts that seemed very similar to the Riverine Swift boats utilized early in the Vietnam War. Both he and Bob Lewis knew better than to ask the commander any detailed questions, since the general capabilities of what they were viewing obviously were classified. Classified data included maximum speeds, drafts, carrying capacities, weapons platforms, electronics capabilities, etc.

Several men dressed in various forms of active duty SEAL uniforms, including shorts and T-shirts, long khaki pants and shirts, many with the camouflage patterns that had become associated with the unit, were busy working on the boats. Powers noted a sign designating the unit as SBS8, or Support Boat Squadron 8. None of the men seemed to notice the arrival of the three of them, since salutes to men in running clothes were considered too formal by the SEALs and not required.

Commander Thomas turned onto the main walkway to the six piers. Thomas, Lewis and Powers noticed three armed sentries directly ahead of them, all carrying HK automatic weapons. The three snapped to attention as the Commander approached, and after returning the salutes, the three sentries moved aside to allow the men to continue down Pier Six. At first, Commander Thomas' guests saw nothing and couldn't figure out why the sentries had been posted. Suddenly, the Commander pointed downward. At first Lewis and Powers, looking to where the commander pointed, could only see two

247

lines coming up from the water. Each looked like a miniature anvil, typical of all such tie down paraphernalia in the United States Navy. Still, even standing on their toes and looking down from the pier, the men could see nothing. Commander Thomas, now at the edge and still pointing directly downwards spoke,

"Gentlemen, please introduce yourselves to the *Vindicator* Boat! In the coming weeks you will develop a love/hate relationship with this craft. However, the love part is most important since it is the primary platform from which we will conduct our operation."

Finally, Powers' gaze caught sight of an extremely low slung, narrow, long, sleek-looking grayish craft. While his gaze caught sight of what were apparently machine gun stations, no other protrusions were apparent. A rope ladder led from the pier directly down to the boat, where two SEAL crewmen waited. Commander Thomas, saying nothing, climbed down the rope and motioned for them to follow. As they moved closer to the boat, Powers guessed it could be not more than two or three feet in total height, meaning it could maneuver in extremely shallow water, perhaps no deeper than a few inches. The hull was covered all around except for an opening towards the rear large enough to accommodate perhaps a dozen SEALs. Since both Lewis and Powers had been high school football stars, they could not help notice what appeared to be National Football League rib pads located among the other equipment in the boat, Standard Navy issue international orange life preservers, always present within any group of experienced SEALs could also be seen, along with an assortment of weapons, including what was obviously a large-caliber sniper rifle with a large telescopic sight, matte black color and bi-pod.

The two SEAL crew members, GM3 Thomas Smith and BM1 Horace Jones, approached Commander Thomas' two associates. They each helped them on with the requisite equipment. The rib pads came first, then the life preservers. The life preservers were exceptionally bulky so the two men could not possibly figure out why they also needed rib pads. Both knew the answers would shortly be forthcoming and contemplated the possibility of being less than pleased. Commander Thomas had already put on his gear and, in turn, checked Powers and Lewis for the straps proper fit, and location. He then addressed one of the SEALs, GM3 Smith,

"Gunnersmate Smith, would you please tell my two trainees everything they would ever want to know about the *Vindicator* Boat and why in God's name they have to dress-up like NFL players."

"Yes sir, Commander. The reason for the rib pads is that each member of the crew must sometimes lie flat in the boat, holding onto the hand holds located along the gunnels, although standing or seated positions are okay during an engagement. Lying flat is required to make our silhouette as low as possible to avoid detection while approaching or leaving the target area at extremely high rates of speed. The continuous smashing against the bottom of the boat, even in calm water, could break every one of your ribs. Only the driver is allowed to sit, and he must take extra precautions or his spine could easily be crushed. The boat carries a full compliment of weapons, all cushioned in customized foam-line cases than can withstand anything, and when the target area is reached and the boat stops, it functions as an extremely stable weapons platform."

He pointed his finger along the gunnels and continued, "For flexibility, layouts are based on the appointed mission, so please note the various mechanisms to accommodate the MK 11, Model 14, .50 caliber sniper rifle, grenade launchers, AR 15's, 40mm mortars, and 25mm automatic guns. Are there any questions?"

Finally, Powers could no longer contain his innate curiosity and held up his hand, immediately acknowledged by a nod of Gunners Mate Smith's head.

"Guns, what in hell powers this thing?"

GM3 Smith glanced at Commander Thomas for permission to answer what was obviously a highly classified question. The Commander nodded his acquiescence and GM3 Smith spoke.

"It's powered by two engines large enough to power battle tanks, equipped with sound mufflers and highly complex sound deadening foam. The noise basically mixes with normal sounds of the ocean."

Powers, obviously impressed, asked no more questions. He got the point that this boat was designed to run as silently as possible, allowing it to sneak right up on an enemy target. Since the technology during his time was relatively prehistoric compared to silent boats, satellite communications and large caliber gattling guns, he found today's capabilities absolutely awesome.

There was complete silence with the men first looking at each other, eyes opened wide, then at Commander Thomas. Responding to the silence the Commander stood up and addressed Gunners Mate Smith.

"Guns, please give our guests a ballistics lecture."

The Commander looked serious.

"Gentlemen, the model 60 machine gun fires 550 cyclical rounds per minute, the grenade launcher fires fifteen 40 millimeter grenades per minute, and the 25 millimeter gattling gun fires 60 rounds per minute."

David Powers was running a mental tally of what Gunners Mate Smith said, and could only imagine the impact 75 hand grenades and large caliber shells per minute would have on a hapless enemy. Added to hundreds of rounds of small arms ammunition, these rates of fire gave today's SEALs four to five times the firepower possessed by the SEALs of David Powers' generation.

Both he and Bob Lewis were amazed at these rates of fire. However, what neither man could have imagined was that today's weapons also had far more advanced and accurate aiming systems, making them absolutely lethal.

"Shall we take our guests for a little spin?" the Commander said.

Several minutes elapsed as each man was given extensive instruction on survival, such as the proper way to hold on. Powers had a feeling this would become very relevant almost immediately. Each man got into position, with Thomas at the controls. As though propelled by booster rockets, the craft literally flew from its moorings out towards the open water. As Thomas guided the boat along an inland waterway, the men were violently tossed against the sides and bottom of the boat. Powers was on the ride of his life and likened it to being in a rodeo, riding the biggest, baddest Bull in history. He was now operating on reflex autopilot, with no conscious thought processes. While he realized the boat was traveling at an extremely high rate of speed, he was unaware that the 70 MPH top speed enabled the craft to overtake anything on the water, as most small craft topped out at 35 MPH.

Almost eerily, there was virtually no sound, other than the water lapping against the craft as it bounced unforgivably up and down, smashing repeatedly against the water. Just as Powers and Lewis thought they would lose consciousness, Commander Thomas slowed the craft, driving it onto a beach which was surrounded by high weeds where it mercifully stopped.

The trainees were sick to their stomachs, dizzy, had blurred vision and felt as though everything around them was still shaking. Both felt like human blenders, their innards all scrambled, their sensibilities numb. Commander Thomas and the two other SEALs, were completely unfazed. Gently examining their guests for signs of any serious damage or injury they were pronounced alive and likely to survive. Commander Thomas then, unable to repress a slight grin, broke the news,

"Everything up to now has been the easy part. Now comes the real test. Having survived a run of several miles and a ride through Hell, you must retain enough mastery of your emotional, physiological and sensory being to do the job you came to do, which, simply put, is to shoot someone. This is what most people don't understand. But you don't just wake up, go outside and

251

start shooting. You might have to run fifteen miles, swim five, go on a forced march of twelve, be wet and freezing, and, within seconds of arriving, squeeze off a round that takes somebody out at several hundred yards. That's where civilians really don't get it. That is why we tend to separate the two worlds. Civilian and Military, and then again, separate the military part into SEALs and everyone else. Gentlemen, shall we proceed to the firing range?"

Both men, unable to speak, just stared at the Commander. At this moment they could not imagine walking, running, swimming or even taking an ambulance ride to anywhere.

Commander Thomas, having taken into account the recent pasts of both Lewis and Powers, had already anticipated this, and planned his landing where the SEAL Team weapons range was located only a brisk walk away. In the ensuing days, the *Vindicator* Boat rides were to gradually lengthen to 17 minutes out and 17 minutes back. After reaching their destination, for reasons neither Powers nor Lewis were made aware of, additional training sessions were added. Part of the exercises included a ten-minute firing exercise of the multiple weapons that were mounted aboard the *Vindicator* Boat. During these exercises, they would maneuver at a greatly reduced speed, in a zig zag pattern, firing at simulated patrol boat silhouettes as their targets. Despite the ear plugs provided, the deafening noise created by the incredible fire power left the men with temporary hearing loss. Both of them wondered how anyone facing such a fusillade of rapid fire from heavy caliber weapons could possibly be left alive, or how ships or other small objects could avoid being torn to pieces. Neither quite realized that on present day operations, human targets were not left alive and boats and other objects were in fact torn to pieces.

While neither satellite technology nor superior firepower could ever win battles, superiority in both combined with the training and superior characteristics of SEALs, always made any enemy the underdog. During the firing exercises, David Powers often thought back to his earlier training days of firing the M1

Garrand Rifle, BAR (or Browning Automatic Rifle) and the other somewhat antiquated weapons of the time. He wondered how anything could survive after facing this awesome firepower.

While it became obvious to Powers that the men were being prepared for both landborne and shipboard operations, his past SEAL training had taught him never to ask why.

After some prodding and encouragement, all of the men, carrying their mixture of weapons, arrived at the range. Awaiting them was GMC Todd Sanders, considered the expert within the SEAL Team in small arms training and use. It was rumored he could assemble and disassemble more than seventy-five U.S. and foreign type weapons blind-folded and, as a sniper, he had no equal. His long range "kill shots" from Vietnam to Beirut were legendary, several at ranges greater than a thousand yards. The men spent the next few hours firing several thousand rounds from a variety of weapons, including intensive training on sniping.

The men comprised a three-man team, with Commander Thomas firing the weapon and Powers and Lewis providing spotting support and security, respectively. The three traded roles, and Powers and Lewis were expected to attain proficiency in actually doing the shooting in case of any unanticipated injury to the other two team members. Commander Thomas emphasized over and over that this was not to be a Rambo-style operation. Rather, he hoped only a single exploding 50-caliber round would be necessary. Each individual's proficiency was necessary just in case the group got into trouble and had to fight its way out of a particularly tough spot.

Additional training was in radio communication protocol, first aid, land based navigation, swimming (just in case), and equipment cleaning and maintenance. Even the infamous "drown drill" was included during one particularly tough day at the pool, whereby Lewis and Powers had to ascend and descend, respectively, to and from the bottom of the pool while breathing in reverse. Such a capability was necessary in case the men were taken prisoner on a riverbank and had to escape, while tied hand and

253

foot by descending into the water. While only so much could be accomplished in two weeks, Commander Thomas wanted to insure that at least minimum proficiency was developed in skills that could help the men deal with 90% of the contingencies that might confront them.

At the end of their training, both Powers and Lewis had an endless list of questions they dared not ask, such as:

Since this action was not sanctioned by any branch of the government, what would happen if the operation turned into a disaster?

What if it were a success?

What if one or more of the men were wounded, killed or captured?

What if they missed Ocho Garriana?

Would any active duty Naval and/or SEAL personnel be accompanying them?

Finally, both men realized that in such matters you couldn't plan for every eventuality so some questions were perhaps just better forgotten.

This particular day ended with a trip through, under and over the obstacle course, the usual equipment checks and inspections, a three mile swim, and a couple of hours of battlefield trauma training.

At the end of the day, at just about the same instant, Lewis' and Powers' heads hit their pillows. It was 22:30 hours (10:30 PM to civilians) when their bodies were overcome with a fatigue akin to unconsciousness.

That night, Commander Thomas lay in his room with a peace of mind he had not felt since he and his new comrades had begun this impossible journey to Hell.

But, Lewis and Powers were honing their skills and, with their day of reckoning only six days away, their Commander was confident they would be capable of handling whatever lay ahead, though during parts of this past week there were times he doubted they would make it. Thomas always had respect for Powers and even Lewis (in the short time he had known him

254

personally), but he now had a new admiration for the inner strength these two men possessed. It was that inner strength that had brought them this far and he prayed it stayed with them for the rough times ahead. In the end, character and commitment overrode all else. It was his basic theory of life.

This evening, he could finally get a peaceful night's sleep. Closing his eyes, Thomas smiled as his thoughts of the resurrection of the old warriors lulled him to sleep. As General MacArthur once said, "Old soldiers never die, they just fade away." His two comrades were even resisting the luxury of fading away.

CHAPTER 28

BEKAA VALLEY,
SYRIA

Through the efforts of General Chaim Ben Lavan and Sir Robert Bretham Chapman, the Israelis had joined Operation Snow Bird and agreed to eliminate the heads of the largest drug organizations in Lebanon and Syria, and to destroy the major heroin processing plants in Syria, all under the cover of striking at the heart of Hezbollah, the violent military extremist faction of the PLO.

Israel's security and political problems were perhaps far more complex than either those of the British or Americans. For one thing, virtually every nation, either on Israel's border or in the immediate area, could be considered both hostile and a participant at some level in the drug terror unleashed against the West. In this region, more than anywhere else, the elements of legitimately constituted governments, drug trafficking organizations and terrorist groups were closely intertwined. It would therefore be difficult for the Israelis to launch punitive military action against any country or groups identified with only one of the three elements. In Lebanon, for example, Israel's military action ranged from strikes against civilian enclaves, almost always containing members of the PLO and other terrorist organizations, to those against isolated terrorist targets or even to attacks on drug organizations. But in most cases, these three categories of targets were inexorably tied together.

As dangerous as a strike against the drug factories in Syria seemed, elements within the Israeli cabinet wanted to go even further, including attacks deep inside Iran itself, for it was widely acknowledged within Western intelligence services, that Iran's government was the central element behind Hezbollah's murderous terrorism directed, not only against the Israelis, but other Western nations as well.

The assignment had been given to Sayeret Mat'kal, the most highly classified unit in the Israeli military, known in Israel as "The Chief of Staff's Boys." From Entebbe to Tunis, they had been major participants in virtually every top secret Israeli counter-terrorist operation. The Israeli government still does not acknowledge the existence of Sayeret Mat'kal. In 1991, they assassinated Abbu Abass, one of the leading PLO terrorists, at his home in Tunis, the location of PLO Headquarters. Their exploits, selectively leaked to the Israeli public, were truly legendary. They represented the "elite of the elite".

Mossad Intelligence indicated that Mustaffa El Khash, the head of the Sayad heroin cartel in Lebanon, would be in the city of Al-Moussia, Syria, to visit his Syrian counterpart, Sayer Ayud. The largest and most sophisticated heroin processing factories were located there. Far less sophisticated processing labs, considered expendable, were located at various places along the Bekaa Valley in Lebanon.

The Bekaa Valley runs almost seventy-five miles through Lebanon and into Northern Syria. Long a safe haven for terrorist organizations that operated throughout Beirut and its environs, the Bekaa Valley was the escape route for the PLO's extremist factions that often crossed the border into Syria after committing deadly terrorist attacks against Israeli forces in Lebanon, and civilians in Israel and elsewhere. The Syrian government, long on America's list of countries that backed and supported state-sponsored terrorism, always looked the other way as these groups sought safe haven on the Syrian side of the Bekaa Valley.

Normally, Israeli, U.S. and other counter-terrorist units

257

in hot pursuit of the guerrillas would stop at the border, since crossing into Syria was considered off-limits except in specific cases that were approved by the Israeli Prime Minister and the Cabinet. Such border crossings, even for a precisely defined military objectives, had the potential to result in a far wider conflict, and perhaps start World War III.

In recent years, with the destruction wrought on the Lebanese economy by the warring factions, heroin was grown openly in the Bekaa Valley on the Syrian side of the border. Periodically, NSA satellites would pick up the movements of tens-of-thousands of people in and around the valley during harvesting of the drug bearing crops. Instantaneous identification was necessary to avoid the conclusion that the Syrians or Lebanese armies were massing tens-of-thousands of troops to be used against the Israelis. While there was always relief when reconnaissance indicated that this wasn't the beginning of a border incursion that ultimately led to war, or a major invasion, there was horror at the reality of just how large the crop was if it required this amount of manpower to harvest it. Each harvest resulted in hundreds-of-millions, or billions of dollars of heroin shipments to the West, with the inevitable result of more crime, wasted lives, corruption and erosion of Western economies, institutions, and values.

While much of the high grade, raw opium crop was processed into heroin inside Lebanon, in the Bekaa Valley area, far larger and more sophisticated processing facilities were located across the border in Syria, making these operations that much more impregnable due to their greater distance from the Israeli border. Once the three Western intelligence agencies conveyed the almost overwhelming magnitude of the global drug problem to their respective heads of state, finally galvanizing them into action aimed at the top levels of the terrorist drug organizations and their sponsoring states, this illicit activity was, at least momentarily, slightly curbed. But as with all lucrative drug operations, after you take out the top kingpin, there is always another one vying to take over the business so his new group can earn the billions that are just waiting to be illicitly made.

The dilemma for Israel in attempting to combat the flourishing drug trade around her is that the PLO and other Syrian state sponsored terrorist organizations could easily launch retaliatory deadly attacks from next door territory in Lebanon already occupied and controlled by the nearly 40,000 Syrian Army troops in that country.

For Israel to effectively deter the drug trade she would have to enter Syrian territory and take aggressive military action against the drug cartels. If this happened, the international community would be in an uproar.

It was bad enough whenever Israel entered Syrian territory to combat terrorists—but there would be even louder protests against any Israeli action directed solely against the drug cartels on Syrian territory. As is the case elsewhere in the world, those in the top levels of the drug business are protected by their own corrupt governments, in the vast majority of countries.

Both the Syrian and Lebanese drug gangs had learned their lessons well, carefully studying both processing formulas and facilities located deep inside the Amazon Basin in Peru and Bolivia and in Palermo, Sicily. With chemists imported from the finest Western universities, the heroin being processed locally was considered to be of the highest quality in the world.

The Israeli mission, carefully defined by the Prime Minister after signing the equivalent of a U.S. President's Finding, was to assassinate both Mustaffa El Khash and Sayer Ayud, and to destroy the five largest and most sophisticated heroin processing facilities inside Syria. In addition, they were to inflict maximum damage against two major PLO terrorist bases, and against the terrorists themselves, located along the Northern end of the Bekaa Valley.

As in Latin America, the terrorists provided security for the drug traffickers and the enormous proceeds from the heroin, morphine base and marijuana trade helped finance the violent activities of the PLO, as similar activities financed the violent activities of Shining Path and like minded organizations located in other parts of the world. As usual, both operated with the explicit approval of the Lebanese and Syrian governments. Elimination of the top leadership of the Lebanese and Syrian cartels would continue the strategy of "striking at the heads of the Hydra" developed at the meetings of Mossad, the CIA and MI5 in Langley, Virginia, chaired by CIA Director John Nesmuth.

Since the Syrian city of Al-Mayad was only seven miles from the coast, the Israelis would use their naval commandos of Flotilla 13, the Ha'kommando Ha'Yami, to provide a two-pronged assault against the target. The Sayeret Mat'kal would be evacuated to the sea utilizing Bell 212 helicopters. Somewhat more traditional units of the Israeli defense force, or IDF, would attack and destroy the terrorist bases, also killing as many of the terrorists as they could. Since the two drug lords always traveled under the heaviest possible security the Israelis favored stealth and disguise to get in close to their targets.

During the assassination of Abbu Abass of the PLO in Tunis in 1991, the Sayeret Mat'kal soldiers were disguised as crippled beggars. On this occasion, they would appear as ordinary Syrian peasants. The plan was brilliantly simple. Two six-man commando squads would come ashore in the middle of the night by swimming in the dark more than four miles after being dropped off by Flotilla 13 boats. Removing their black swim suits and continuing on, dressed as local Syrians, they would enter the city of Al-Mayad before sunrise and set up their positions to await the arrivals of Mustaffa El Khash and Sayer Ayud. One squad, commanded by Lt. Col. Ehud Yigal, would eliminate the Syrian, and the other, commanded by Major Yossef Levy, would take out the Lebanese.

Both squads were extremely heavily armed, with AK 47's, Negev 5.56mm light machine guns, Gililon 5.56mm assault rifles with laser aiming lights, and Galil sniper rifles. The Israeli snipers were deadly at a thousand yards. In addition to

260

the two six man squads, several male and female Mossad agents were to successfully infiltrate the immediate area and surround the compound of Mustaffa El Khash, posing as local employees at restaurants and shops in Al-Mayad. Three other groups of Ha'kommando Ha'Yami and Sayerot Mat'kal commandos were to proceed to the five designated heroin-processing plants in preparation to launch their coordinated attack. The tactic of rapid and maximum fire in the shortest possible time favored by the Israeli high command was again to be utilized in the Bekaa Valley phase of Operation Snow Bird.

A final report would be filed later detailing the events of the operation. It would read, in part:

"At precisely 8:47a.m., local time, the two limousines carrying the Lebanese drug lord, Mustaffa El Khash and his bodyguards could be seen by the Israelis approaching the restaurant in Al-Mayad that would host the meeting of the two men. It was located immediately adjacent to the compound housing Mustaffa El Khash, his family, top aides and security detail. Less than 30 seconds later the three Mercedes limousines, carrying the Syrian drug lord, Sayer Ayud, arrived from the opposite direction. Nearly twenty heavily armed security personnel could be seen by the Israelis, lining the approaches to the Chezar Restaurant, several dressed in Syrian army uniforms. The sniper in Lt. Col. Ehud Yigal's squad watched his target through the sixteen power scope on top of his Galil rifle, while the one in Major Yossef Levy's squad squinted into his. Exactly thirty-five seconds later, as in the Golden Triangle mission, one shot each to the heads of Mustaffa El Khash and Sayer Ayud ended the lives of the heads of the Syrian and Lebanese drug cartels. In addition, during the ensuing thirty seconds, Israeli commandos detonated claymore mines and fired over a thousand rounds of ammunition and hand grenades into the cadre of twenty security personnel, killing sixteen of them and wounding the remaining four.

Due to the suddenness of the attack and the intensity of the automatic weapons fire, there was very little return fire,

261

and only two members of the Israeli forces suffered superficial wounds. In the resulting chaos, the Israelis boarded the four pre-positioned Bell 212 helicopters and were flown out of Syria and over the Mediterranean, where they were lowered onto IDF naval craft for the high speed journey back to Israel. Similar operations were launched against the five heroin processing plants where high explosives and heavy concentration of grenades and automatic weapons literally blew the factories and their inhabitants into pieces. Israeli raids launched against the two PLO bases killed thirty-seven terrorists and destroyed several tons of ammunition and high explosives, rendering the bases useless for at least several weeks."

The message was crystal clear. Western resolve and military and technological capabilities were the only effective weapons in the drug war. Short of this, the battle could only be gradually lost by the West, with insignificant damage inflicted upon those who sought to destroy Western societies through drug assaults that were tantamount to acts of war. Within the worldwide partnerships existing between governments, terrorists and drug organizations, individuals in the drug trade would have to think twice before being promoted to the top jobs, and no-one under them would be safe or out of reach. There was no other known effective deterrent and the elected leaders of at least three major Western governments were beginning to acknowledge this terrible reality. While the constitutional, legal, moral and other dimensions of this strategy still had to be addressed at the highest levels of government in the industrialized world, nothing else attempted by law enforcement groups seemed to work.

One only had to look at the extent of the green, amber and red lights all across CIA Director Nesmuth's world map to see just how deadly serious the drug problem had become. It could never be fought by wishful thinking alone and failed strategies or fantasies hoping that the population would "just say no."

CHAPTER 29

PALERMO, SICILY

The fourth element of Operation Snow Bird was to be a joint operation between British SAS units and the Italian Carbinieri. While total secrecy was a mandatory element in the preceding actions directed against both Asian warlords and Bekaa Valley terrorists, it was particularly critical here.

It was certainly no secret that the Italian Mafia, purveyors of most of the world's heroin trade, had bought several high ranking politicians, judges and law enforcement officials within that country. It was even rumored that so many members of the legislature were on the Mafia's payroll that they could control the outcome of voting on any legislation affecting the heroin traffickers. Other than rewriting the Colombian Constitution and infiltrating the directorate of Canada's intelligence service, this entrenched Mafia power structure posed the greatest threat to the West. Who would have ever imagined that the drug cartels could gain control of major law enforcement elements of the governments of Canada and Italy, two of the larger, more economically advanced Western nations? One could only imagine what would happen if the trend continued. And why would it not continue given the immense power and unlimited financing of the drug cartels? A worldwide domino effect—with one major country after another being undermined by the drug lords—has become inevitable. It has already been demonstrated that with the kind of money that these drug kingpins have at their disposal, they can infiltrate and corrupt any law enforcement agency anywhere they wish to do business.

263

Of course, major democratic, pro-West elements still existed within the Italian government, and the directors of the CIA and MI5 had developed a very close working relationship with them. Francisco Bertucci, the head of Italy's Intelligence Service (the Carbinieri) was committed to destroying the Mafia's influence within the heart of Italy's government. A true patriot, he could no longer control his rage and disgust at the Mafia's blatant assassination of dozens of high-ranking Italian judges and police officials. This was the retaliation for their individual efforts in trying to curb the Mafia's excesses, including the violent control of a substantial part of the global heroin trade. He had long ago realized that they would never be stopped by following the rules of law and constitution that governed Italy's judicial system. It was time for an "eye for an eye". The Italian Prime Minister, Augustino Feragammo, had signed Italy's equivalent of a Finding, but other than two or three members of his inner circle, the plans for the assassination of the heads of the four crime families were kept absolutely secret.

Carbinieri surveillance constantly tracked the whereabouts of Carlos Gioualla, Salvatore Rico, Luigi Salvadori and Franco Constanzo, the Godfathers of the four Italian crime families that controlled the worldwide heroin trafficking out of Palermo, Sicily. Long ago Francisco Bertucci's most trusted agents had penetrated these crime families at all levels and now had men working as bodyguards, drivers, and even advisors to the four chieftains.

Unlike the other operations, Carbinieri agents were already working immediately next to their targets on a daily basis. While all of this was certain to create a flap within the Italian Press, it was still decided to utilize the assistance of SAS units to insure that the top level leadership of the cartels realized they were now dealing with unified responses to their activities. Judicial niceties would finally give way to the violent and terrible realities of a war being fought to the death.

A total of sixteen Italian speaking SAS troops were detailed to work inside Palermo with the Carbinieri paramilitary units and sixteen more would provide backup and transportation in and out of the country. Francisco Bertucci's intelligence sources were superb, allowing for a fairly normal planning cycle. The SAS units would all enter Sicily utilizing civilian transport to avoid undue suspicion. The men entered in groups of no more than three, disguised as crew members aboard freighters, truck drivers, tourists and even members of the clergy. In each instance, based on the previous barbarism of the Italian drug lords, including the detonation of car bombs that killed dozens of innocent victims along with the wives and children of their targeted victims, eliminating them was the primary objective and this was to be accomplished at any cost, although family members and other innocents were to be spared if at all possible. Italy's Intelligence Service had finally decided that the ends, in fact, did justify the means.

Carlos Gioualla was killed by 27 9mm rounds fired at him from close range by two of his bodyguards. Several months ago these same bodyguards were the only two of the seven security personnel with him to survive a brazen assault inside his compound by four Italian-speaking men of unidentified origin firing HK 9mm submachine-guns.

Salvatore Rico died in an explosion at his mansion. What remained looked as though it had been hit by a nuclear weapon. Fortunately, his wife and six children were not at home at the time, although nearly two dozen bodyguards, advisors and other employees died in the blast.

As Luigi Salvadori opened his car door, a car bomb as powerful as those recently detonated in Beirut blew him, his driver and four bodyguards into pieces. An entire city block near his office was leveled and three innocents also died as a result of the blast.

Franco Constanzo walked out of the front door of his twenty-two room mansion and was greeted by two men disguised in the sort of clothing worn by his innermost circle of personal bodyguards. They opened fired with Bernelli semi-automatic shotguns, cutting the man's torso in half. Two other accomplices, alleged to be members of one of the other crime families, killed three other members of his security detail in a fusillade of automatic weapons fire.

All of the SAS units safely returned to their headquarters at the Hereford Barracks, where the men coldly and jokingly conversed in Italian as they re-created the individual assassinations. While Mafia crime families used fear as their primary weapon, to subjugate much of the Italian populace, the SAS units here were used to dealing with the monsters produced by each generation of humanity during the more than fifty years of their existence. The members of the participating Carbinieri units realized they had just eradicated the most immediate and violent threat to their society since the days of Mussolini. Unfortunately, they could not really share this secret with the rest of Italian society.

In addition to reporting on the gruesome deaths of the four Mafia crime bosses, the media reported the destruction of several heroin processing facilities located throughout Palermo. The press was particularly specific in reporting the unprecedented magnitude of the explosions and carnage. A piece of debris no larger than a small rock was all that remained of one particularly large heroin processing facility.

John Nesmuth received the phone call on his secure line from Francisco Bertucci, his counterpart within the Italian security service, with mixed emotions. While delighted at the news of the demise of the four heads of Italy's heroin cartel, he realized that the only unfinished element of Operation Snow Bird was the United State's commitment to assassinate José Ocho Garriana. Now that he had been forced by his superiors to terminate the operation against Garriana that had been assigned to Carl Roget, he felt more frustrated and hand-tied than at anytime in his career. With all overt or covert avenues now totally blocked, the desperation he felt caused a sudden rush in his head, accompanied by nausea. What could he do? He had no answer.

The United States government was in the deepest foreign policy trouble in its history as the duplicity within its intelligence services caused by the media's publicizing of the CIA's participation in the drug business was virtually strangling the country. What was the remaining moral basis for conducting the nation's foreign policy? With little moral high ground left on which to base it's actions, and too much public scrutiny of past illegal activity, what was the United States government to do?

The beginning of an answer was gently rolling back and forth, riding on top of the whitecaps of the Atlantic aboard the *USS Fertilance* as it made its way from an East Coast Naval Base to the Amazon River Basin.

CHAPTER 30

APRIL, 1993
(SOMEWHERE IN THE ATLANTIC OCEAN)

The *USS Fertilance* was the third of a new class of Naval vessel especially designed for the conduct of Naval Special Warfare, or SPECWAR, it's code within the United States Navy. The "Serpentine" class vessels, 175' long, carried a crew of 24 regular Navy personnel and could accommodate sixteen fully equipped SEALs.

The *USS Fertilance* itself had been named after a poisonous, highly lethal snake found in the Andean Ridge. Although the name was provocative to the United States Navy's more traditional elements, the lethal capability of the vessel was exactly what SPECWAR elements had in mind when they thought of the name. The boat had the latest in electronics and security gear and its specially designed automatic winch, mounted on the ship's fantail, enabled it to off-load an even smaller, very high speed craft aboard which the SEALs could stealthily proceed upriver along extremely shallow inland waterways.

The *Fertilance* was proceeding along an east by southeasterly course with an initial heading of 116.4 degrees at its cruising speed of 21 knots. The men had boarded the ship at the Jacksonville, Florida Naval Base and were enroute to its first fueling and replenishment stop at the Roosevelt Roads, Puerto Rico Naval Station. The ship itself was capable of cruising in waters only eight feet deep. It had been specifically designed for operations along waterways like those found in Latin America, in and around countries such as Peru, Colombia and

Bolivia. It was certainly clear that Navy SEALs would be a central element in fighting the drug wars of the future and equipment for the unit was being designed with other drug missions in mind.

Included in the array of electronics equipment was night vision scanning gear that allowed the crew to see anything in total darkness within a full sight range of 360 degrees and electronic monitoring equipment that enabled it to eavesdrop on all voice communication for several miles. Most of the crew members were fluent in Spanish, providing additional capabilities to disrupt cartel operations in the Andean Ridge countries.

While both Lewis and Powers awoke one morning to a rendezvous with Coastal Patrol boats of SBU 38 (Special Boat Unit) out of Puerto Rico, they assumed the new small craft hoisted aboard the *USS Fertilance* was, in fact, the *Vindicator*. Unknown to them, the new boat was yet a third craft that had been specially fitted with sponsors and radar arch. Due to the need for operational deception, the radar cross section of this craft would "paint" or create artificial radar images that could range from the smallest fishing trawler to one indicating a vessel as large as an aircraft carrier. In order to provide the highest possible levels of deception and avoid raising suspicion within the cartel, it was decided to program an average-sized trawler about 220 feet long. As far as the cartel's radar watch was concerned, the vessel they were tracking from Florida to the coast of Colombia posed no immediate threat.

Behind the scenes, Commander Thomas' separation leave had been interrupted by sympathetic "ears" throughout the Special Warfare community. Since Commander Thomas had been so intently involved with much of the new technology developed for the SEAL Team, nobody thought anything was unusual about the sixty-day extension signed by Admiral Blankenship, authorizing the Commander to personally supervise the final evaluation of the highly classified Thompson Electronics SIGINT/ECM gear.

"Leaks" were discreetly encouraged throughout the U.S. government, informing anyone listening in, including the thousand eyes and ears of the Cardazanna Cartel, of the normal, peaceful intent of the various ships' activities. The cartel paid a lot of money for any useful information related to the movement of any United States military units towards their shores. In fact, Juan Espinoza had received indications from people purportedly with Central Intelligence Agency connections, that an element outside the normal U.S. military chain of command might be enroute to the area. This was dutifully passed along to José Ocho Garriana, who ordered his informants to be particularly vigilant about any non-U.S. military interlopers. Espinoza reveled in the praise he received from his boss about this particularly highly classified tidbit of intelligence information.

Also behind the scenes, word was put out to do nothing about the NSA intercept regarding David Powers' knowledge about José Ocho Garriana. The FBI's Counterintelligence units realized somebody was asking them to look the other way so the sympathetic "ears" within their community did nothing to investigate the sources of his information. Clearly, something of gigantic proportions was up! Since nobody really knew much of anything, "plausible denial" was working in overdrive for all concerned, from the President, to Admiral Blankenship, to the Directors of the FBI and CIA. In fact, only one living person knew the whole story, and as far as the U.S. military was concerned, that person, Commander Thomas, was busy supervising the seaborne testing of highly classified equipment aboard the *USS Fertilance*! What was unfolding would demonstrate to the entire world that a real war on drugs could indeed be fought. The issue was national will, not military or human capability.

This particular evening, David Powers, Commander Thomas and Bob Lewis were sipping coffee from cups emblazoned with the ship's logo, a coiled, reddish snake with a three-pronged implement reminiscent of a pitch fork running through it. An enlarged map was spread across the table in the open galley at which the men were seated. They shared the table with two members of the crew, Lt. John Dilullo and BM1 Thomas Oloff. Unlike larger and more conventional Naval vessels, there were no separate officer's wardroom or Chief Petty Officer (CPO) quarters, so the galley was used by all hands aboard, both officers and enlisted men, the ship's crew intermingled with the SEALs.

The gentle swells, combined with the warmth of the summer evening and the salty air, brought Powers back nearly thirty years to his first stint in the Navy aboard the Destroyer *USS Parks*. The combination of motion, human and cooking odors, oily fumes, and sounds of the ocean, were sensory feelings never forgotten by anyone who had experienced them. The five men were engaged in an animated conversation comparing Naval vessels of previous generations with those of today. Lt. Dilullo looked at his watch, realized it was 7:45 p.m. local time (19:45 hours Navy time) and politely excused both himself and BM1 Oloff to assume the next bridge watch commencing in 15 minutes at 20:00 hours. After the two members of the crew departed, the three men returned their attention to the map and the operation to be directed against José Ocho Garriana in less than ninety-six hours. Commander Thomas pointed his finger at the map and moved it along the course plotted on the chart by the ship's Navigator, Lt. (jg.) George Bronson, also the *USS Fertilance*'s Executive Officer. He explained the routing to the other two men,

"As you can see, we are proceeding on an initial heading of one one six point four degrees in an East by South Easterly course from where we boarded in Jacksonville, Florida, heading towards Roosevelt Roads, Puerto Rico, covering a distance of approximately one thousand nautical miles. After refueling, we will proceed on a West by South Westerly course of two hundred thirty-five point five degrees to the entrance of the Panama Canal in Colon, Panama. After passing through the Canal, and exiting it in Panama City, we will head East by

Northeast on a heading of sixty-nine point three degrees, which will take us the remaining two hundred fifty-seven miles to our rendezvous point at the head of the Magdalena River off the coast of Colombia." He looked up, continuing, "Are there any questions so far?"

Since nothing particularly exciting was contained in the navigational briefing, both men silently shook their heads from side to side, indicating there were no questions. Actually, both were anxious for Commander Thomas to get to the rendezvous point and beyond, where they knew the real action would occur.

Commander Thomas smiled and continued to look up at the two men while he continued,

"Bob, I don't mean to be quoting you out of context, but national security prohibits me from telling you anymore on this sensitive subject until we reach the rendezvous point."

Both men burst out laughing at the irony of what their mentor had just told them. Over the years Powers had related to Commander Thomas several times the story of how FBI Agent Lewis continually kept him in the dark using this same euphemism about "national security" when they were both involved in the nuclear terrorist matter at the Modular Products plant.

The comic relief was almost too much to bear, and Commander Thomas continued to look on with amusement as both men laughed hysterically. The Commander glanced at his watch, and said goodnight to this friends.

CHAPTER 31

Colon Air Force Base, Panama

The huge C17 Starlifter slowly taxied to the Eastern end of the longest runway on the United States Air Force base located outside Colon, Panama. Being the largest aircraft in the U.S. Air Force's logistics command, it would require every possible foot of runway to get airborne. The gigantic engines roared as maximum power and thrust were applied by Colonel John Brewer, the aircraft's Commander. Seated next to him at the controls was Major Hubert Dahlgren and his hands mirrored the movements on the throttle made by the Colonel. Staff Sergeant Joseph Piccardi, the Loadmaster, was also seated in the cockpit, as was Major Jeffrey Reardon, the navigator. The two way communication, between Red Fox Two Three, the aircraft's call sign, and home plate one, the control tower, continued uninterrupted over the headphones worn by the crew, even as the C17 lunged forward as maximum power was applied,

"Home plate one, this is Red Fox Two Three, over...."

"Red Fox Two Three, this is Home plate One, over...."

"Require initial turn instructions, over...."

"Red Fox Two Three, turn right to course one niner zero degrees, speed three sixty knots, over...."

"Repeat copy, Home plate One, turning right to one nine zero, speed three sixty knots, over...."

"Roger, Red Fox Two. Instructions confirmed, out."

The aircraft looked larger than life as it became airborne and banked to the right to begin its climb out and initial turn. At that moment, Staff Sergeant Piccardi removed his headphones, unbuckled his seat belt, stood up, and turning to the rear, opened the cockpit door to enter the gigantic cargo hold.

The top secret cargo was known only to a few, and as far as the entire flight crew was concerned, this was merely another joint training exercise involving units of the special operations command headquartered in Tampa, Florida. The *Vindicator* Boat, a low slung high speed craft utilized to insert SEAL Team elements into inland waterway operational areas, was positioned immediately over the main cargo doors located in the center of the aircraft's belly. Several SEALs could be seen cleaning and checking equipment, their intense appearances highlighting just how seriously these matters were taken. It seemed to Sergeant Piccardi that all Navy SEALs cared about was their equipment. Then again, since their lives depended on the reliability of everything they carried, why not care about it? So intent were the SEALs on the task at hand that none of them looked up, either when the Sergeant entered the cargo bay, or returned to the cockpit, carefully closing the door behind him.

Since training flights of C17's and other aircraft originating in Panama and flying along the coast of Colombia and the other Andean Ridge Nations were fairly routine, the "eyes and ears" of the Cartel paid little attention to this one, particularly since the aircraft was flying alone. Approximately three hours later, after reaching and cruising at its normal altitude of 35,000 feet, the plane gradually descended to an altitude of only four thousand feet and slowed it's speed to 140 knots as it approached the headwaters of the Magdalena River, located some thirty miles in a Westerly direction from the location of the aircraft. Since this was the absolute bare minimum altitude and speed required to keep the giant aircraft aloft, every member of the crew strained in intensity to insure no mistake that would cause a fatal stall and loss of lift. While much of the world's military focused on maximum performance that strained the limits of present day technology, the minimum performance capabilities of aircraft such as the C17 and C130 Hercules were far more important for insertion and other maneuvers required of Navy SEALs and other special operations units. As the plane began to ascend back to an altitude of five thousand feet, the SEAL jumpmaster, BMC Lance Allen, checked the six cargo chutes that would be utilized to drop the *Vindicator* from the C17's cargo hold. At exactly four thousand feet, a manual hand signal was conveyed from Aircraft Commander Colonel John Brewer, through Sergeant Piccardi, to BMC Allen to start the jump. At precisely the same instant, the *Vindicator* exited through the main doors, the chutes opening almost simultaneously.

Within seconds, the sixteen SEALs also exited through the main cargo doors, free-falling to the pre-designated altitude of two thousand five hundred feet under the strobe of the cartel's radar. Each man utilized the newest MTIX free-fall parachutes. The only thing visible on the radar was the C17 ascending back to its normal cruising altitude. Within minutes, the SEALs had boarded the *Vindicator* and were speeding towards the pre-positioned rendezvous point at the head of the Magdalena River, where they would be linking up with the other mission elements headed towards them aboard the *USS Fertilance*. Other than the SEALs themselves and Commander Thomas, no one knew they were there. The element of surprise was now their major weapon.

David Powers had slept the sleep of the near dead. The emotional anticipation, the physical exertion expended in trying to return a fifty-year-old body to its early twenties condition, and the gentle rolling of the ship acted the same as the strongest sleeping pill. The deep sleep was interrupted by a gentle tap on the shoulder and the voice of BM2 Lewis Jones, "Good morning, sir, it's zero five forty-five and our rendezvous is in forty-five minutes."

Powers blinked and was looking into the muted red night lens on the flashlight of the Boatswain's Mate. Oddly, in the middle of the most advanced military technology in the world, the same muted red lens had been used to alert Navy men to their missions for more than fifty years. It took only a few seconds for his vision to adjust, and the foggy outline of the man next to him became increasingly clear as the seconds went by. Powers thanked the man, who politely turned and left the forward sleeping area, silently closing the door behind him. He looked at his own watch, which indicated 05:47 local time. As he dressed, his mind wandered to Phoenix, where it would be sometime in the middle of the preceding night. He wished he could have rolled over and hugged his wife, or made love to her. He was quickly brought back to the present, however, as he smelled the early morning breakfast aromas so typical of United States Navy ships. He would do anything for a cup of coffee! Boatswain's Mate Jones had thoughtfully left a steaming cup of black coffee in a mug emblazoned with the logo of the *USS Fertilance*. Now fully awake, the anticipation that the operation against José Ocho Garriana would commence in only one half hour made his mind race.

Since Commander Thomas told him to appear on the bridge at 06:30 hours carrying nothing but the clothes on his back and a watch, he would shave, shower and dress as carefully and meticulously as he ever had in his life. He had absolutely no idea (and he had not dared to ask) why each man was to report without any equipment whatsoever. He realized that a highly classified surprise lay in store for him, but had no idea what it could be. Powers did not know whether he should be euphoric, absolutely scared to death, or both. As the warmth of the steamy shower pounded his inner senses, his mind returned to neutral, tender, loving thoughts of Maggie. These quickly receded to the background and were replaced by the reality of surviving the present. The brief daydream about his wife provided a rather pleasant interlude to the quite normal fear of the unknown, particularly an unknown bound to be both extremely violent and just as dangerous to his continued existence.

At precisely 06:28 local time, David Powers made his way up the sharply angled ladder on the port (left) side that led from the main deck to the bridge. In addition to the four uniformed men comprising the bridge watch, Commander Thomas, Bob Lewis and two other Navy SEALs, MM3 Wilfred Ziegler and BMC Harrison Kienow were also present. Commander Thomas introduced everyone and suddenly pointed to the starboard side. At first, David Powers couldn't see anything. Suddenly, out of the mist, at a distance of about forty yards, he could make out the silhouette of a low, long boat, or at least he thought it was a boat. The scene was eerily reminiscent of early Hollywood movies, where some prehistoric monster emerges from the water surrounded by the mist and begins to move towards the ship that has spotted it. Powers reflected that it looked like something out of Jules Verne's "Twenty Thousand Leagues Under the Sea." As the boat came closer, Powers could still not see anything on the boat's surface, the dark gray hull was windowless, and had no apparent open deck area. No personnel could be seen, and the craft was absolutely silent. Power's heart started racing. What in God's name was this? As the vessel pulled up alongside the *USS Fertilance,* a hatch opened, and two men climbed out to greet the astonished civilian visitors. Commander Thomas, by now grinning from ear to ear, returned the salute from the two uniformed SEALs, and while gesturing for the others to follow, spoke, "Gentlemen, meet he U.S. Navy's secret Stealth boat!"

David Powers had long heard the rumors of a highly secretive Naval vessel, invisible to radar, undetectable by listening devices such as sonar, and even invisible to the human eye except at extremey close range. He was too astonished to speak, and after shaking hands with the two new men, followed Commander Thomas down a hatch, and took a seat next to the man. All he could see, besides the Commander seated next to him, were Bob Lewis seated next to a SEAL in front of himself and Thomas, and two other SEALs seated immediately behind them. No weapons were evident, and there was absolutely no sound as the craft sped away for it's rendezvous with the *USS Vindicator*. Unknown to Powers, an "All clear" signal had been flashed to Juan Espinoza who had relayed it personally to José Ocho Garriana that the fishing trawler tracked by the cartel's radar posed no immediate threat, since it had stopped and anchored nearly thirty miles off the coast of Colombia. Who could imagine that the West's arsenal included an invisible boat, that could neither be seen or heard? Who else could imagine that even civilian ships tracked by radar would turn out to be something altogether different, such as U.S. Navy military craft, not at all what they appeared to be on the radar screen?

Even David Powers had not yet figured everything out when approximately one hour later the Stealth boat rendezvoused with the *Vindicator* craft. The hatches were opened, and the group along with pre-positioned cases of weapons and other equipment were transferred to the *Vindicator* for the final assault against the most feared drug lord in the world. After the transfer was completed, the invisible boat disappeared into the haze, making Powers almost believe he had dreamed it all. Strangely, as the *USS Vindicator* took them upriver, Commander Thomas never referred to the invisible trip. David Powers almost became convinced that, in fact, it hadn't ever occurred!

CHAPTER 32

CARDAZANNA, COLOMBIA
THE NEXT DAY

José Ocho Garriana had a meeting scheduled later that morning with Lyle Mendoza, the President of Banco Commercialle Rojas (BCR), Mexico's second largest commercial bank, aboard Ocho Garriana's palatial yacht, the *"Carmenito"*. The ship, normally anchored at an isolated heavily secure corner of the Port of Cardazanna, was guarded around the clock by more than twenty of his best security personnel. The *"Carmenito"* was more like a miniature cruise ship, and had no equal in the world, even among the handful of the world's truly most wealthy and powerful individuals. Nearly 300 feet in length, equipped with twenty-two staterooms, each appropriate for a king, queen or other royalty, the luxurious appointments challenged the imagination. The ship also had two separate lavishly appointed conference rooms, each of which would accommodate meetings of up to thirty people. Solid gold fixtures, marble floors, period antique original furniture specific to each stateroom, the world's best navigation and secure communications gear, the finest diesel propulsion units available in the world, were only the tips of the iceberg.

It was a trophy appropriate for someone who both considered himself, and was also considered by many others, to be the most powerful and feared man in the world. The crew of one hundred twenty-four were trained to attend to every guest's whim, wish or dream. The compliment of security personnel assigned for cruising duty totaled an additional thirty, all the same caliber as those routinely assigned to personally guard the top man himself. The ship cruised at twenty-two knots and had a top speed of slightly over thirty. A helicopter landing pad was located topside in the middle of the vessel. Normally used to bring distinguished visitors to the "*Carmenito*" while the ship was underway, the helicopter could also be used by the top man himself for a speedy getaway, in the unlikely event that other security precautions failed or proved to be inadequate.

The main dining area could accommodate all forty-four guests in one sitting, and a visitor once remarked that it was reminiscent of the royal family's private dining room in Buckingham Palace. It probably was purposely designed that way. A private cinema, several intimate lounge areas, a show floor, private gambling and card rooms and a world class library completed the facilities. No ruler of any country on Earth, including the Gulf states, could claim anything even close. While nobody on the outside knew for sure, the "*Carmenito*" was rumored to have been built in a Danish shipyard at a cost exceeding three hundred million dollars.

Due to the almost total seclusion and privacy, many of Ocho Garriana's most important business meetings were conducted aboard the yacht as it cruised out of Cardazanna along the Magdalena River. There were many reasons for this, particularly security considerations that included the river's enormous width, exceeding two miles at several points. This permitted an additional security compliment of four well armed former Colombian Navy Patrol Craft, secretly acquired from the French, to cruise with the "*Carmenito*". The eighty two foot long boats, part of the latest "Escadrille" class flotilla of French Naval vessels, were the equal of most boats of this class in the world. The wide river provided a great deal of maneuvering room in case of unanticipated security problems. Nothing was left to chance. Not even Ocho Garriana, however, could imagine what was in store for him this morning. At precisely 10:00 a.m., the "*Carmenito*" slowly left its mooring area, accompanied by the four patrol craft, only Ocho Garriana and Lyle

Mendoza were aboard. The two were discussing several billion dollars of investments in Mexico by Ocho Garriana that were being laundered through Banco Commerciale Rojas, under the personal supervision of Mendoza himself.

Approimately one hour later, the lookouts on the "Carmenito" began to run towards the bow as they spotted a small, high speed craft rapidly approaching Ocho Garriana's luxurious craft.

The USS Vindicator was commanded by BMC Lewis Twilley. Twilley, at 29, the youngest Chief Boatswain's Mate in the United States Navy, was a twelve year Navy Veteran. Born and bred in Aurora, Colorado, Twilley was the Colorado AA State Heavyweight Wrestling champ in 1981, his final year at Aurora West High. An extremely bright, rugged outdoors type, Twilley knew he wanted to be a Navy SEAL since boyhood, and turned down several college athletic scholarships to enlist. He spanned the generations of all Navy Chief Boatswain's Mates. At 6'2", 218 pounds, his heaviy muscled arms and neck strained as he turned the Vindicator from side to side while continuously closing on the two Colombian Naval patrol craf that were attempting to position themselves between the "Carmenito" and the Vindicator. Twilley had closed to under three hundred yards when the sixteen other members of SEAL Team Four already aboard the boat, their two civilian "gests" and six members of the boat crew all opened up with their weapons.

Powers thought to himself that this situation was reminiscent of the old duel between the heavily armed "Monitor" and "Merrimack" gunboats facing off during the Civil War nearly one hundred and thirty years before. The Vindicator had six 25mm gattling guns, all shipboard mounted with portable electric generators, a dozen CAR hand fired weapons, 40mm grenade launchers (model 203) firing both high explosive and flechette rounds, which were supplemented by the lightweight M60 machine guns carried by the rest of the crew. In all, the equivalent of four hundred hand grenades rained down upon the patrol craft, along with more than two thousand rounds of small arms fire and three hundred heavy caliber projectiles from the 25mm gattling gun. Even a destroyer or light cruiser would have been torn to pieces and sunk with only the smallest pieces of debris remaining.

The two patrol boats looked like an ox that had been torn apart by the pihrannas of the region or a large log that had been processed through a saw mill. The boats and their crews resembled wooden chips and ground up pieces of human remnants. There were floating cemeteries on each side of th *Vindicator* as it passed between the decimated remnants of the two "Escadrille" class boats.

Th *Vindicator* continued to speed towards the yacht, that by now was trying to run away at its full speed of thirty knots. At nearly 100% faster, th *Vindicator* closed the distance very quickly. Ocho Garriana's security detail could be seen running along the hand rails on the top deck, positioning themselves to return the fire, while Security Chief Juan Espinoza, was chasing after them, wildly swinging his machete like a Zulu chieftain. He almost hacked one of his men in half who was not shooting and reloading fast enough for his liking. Behind the *Vindicator*, an occasional water crane or sea gull would light upon a small piece of the flotsam and jetsam debris from the demolished patrol crafts. This was all that remained in the *Vindicator*'s wake to indicate that only moments before two "Escadrille" class vessels had also shared the waters.

At approximately three hundred yards from their target, the SEALs and *Vindicator* crew opened fire, as the security detail did their best to shoot back.

José Ocho Garriana had no chance to get away from his doomed vessel. His escape helicopter, always carried aboard the vessel to permit a quick exit while his guards fought off any assailants, didn't have a chance to even get the motor started. It, too, was torn to pieces in the initial fusillade, only seconds before the main craft itself was obliterated by point blank fire from the *Vindicator*.

In less than five minutes, only sinking, burning debris was left of the *"Carmenito"*. The vessel had been ripped to pieces by a barrage of 40mm grenades, 25mm high explosive rounds, and thousands of rounds of automatic small arms fire. The *Vindicator* actually possessed the firepower of a light cruiser of WWII vintage, and with concentrated fire on the 300 foot yacht, only small pieces of minced debris remained. The once magnificent vessel now looked like Hell, an apt reference to the next port of call for the *"Carmenito's"* passengers.

After circling the flaming wreckage and seeing nothing left alive, the *Vindicator*'s crew turned the boat and sped away from the destruction towards their next rendezvous.

The following morning, newspaper headlines around the globe carried reports of the deaths of José Ocho Garriana and Lyle Mendoza. Due to the unprecedented devastation of the attack, with little wreckage and no survivors, reports included speculation about a possible twenty-plane raid of American attack aircraft and even rumors of the detonation of a tactical nuclear weapon.

The local media actually believed these were the only explanations for how the unpenetrable defenses of their legendary drug kingpin, José Ocho Garriana, could have been breached. A strong protest was launched by the Colombian government against the United States and delivered to the Secretary of State in Washington by Colombia's diplomatic representative to the U.S., Ernesto Fonces Valinuevella.

The United States' response was to totally deny any involvement and request formal evidence proving U.S. complicity. As there were no official orders ever given to any branch of the U.S. Military for a mission of this kind, the State Department was enraged at these unfounded accusations.

No evidence was presented by the Colombian government to substantiate their charges. Arguments raged within the Colombian legislature as to whether any should be provided if it were found. Wasn't this man little more than a drug dealer and not the national hero that some local newspapers had depicted to the outside world? And, besides, who had the equipment to dive in the two-mile-wide river, teeming with pirhanna, to look for anything?

The desire of the Colombian legislature to distance itself from Ocho Garriana steadily increased as the reality of what had transpired on the river became ever more apparent in the ensuing days.

Again running his mental total, David Powers calculated that the level of almost unbelievable firepower he had just witnessed was at least five to ten times what could have been fired from comparable riverborne platforms of his day. Present day aiming technology that permitted shipboard weapons to consistently remain on target probably increased the effectiveness of the firepower to twenty times or more than it had been during the Vietnam era. He recalled Swift Boat operations against the Vietcong where twin .30 caliber machine guns, rifle grenades fired one at a time, and a single heavy .50 caliber machine gun were considered overpowering by the U.S. Navy's adversaries.

He could only imagine what might have been if the firepower he'd just witnessed had been brought to bear along the Mekong River Delta in those days. He also speculated about the level of future technology that would be required during the next decade to provide yet another quantum leap from today's incredible rates of fire.

The answer was too outrageous to even be estimated. Neither could the end results.

CHAPTER 33

ABOARD THE *USS FERTILANCE*
TWO DAYS LATER

David Powers and Commander Dale Thomas were seated in the ship's galley, sipping hot coffee, each immersed in very deep, extremely personal thoughts. Each felt the muted euphoria from the successful completion of their mission. Both realized there were still unfinished agenda items. But Powers and Thomas had fallen into an exhausted thirteen-hour sleep after the *Vindicator* had rendezvoused wit *USS Fertilance* and been hoisted aboard by the highly sophisticated winch located on the ship's fantail.

USS Fertilance and her sister ship, *USS Copperhead,* were now steaming at twenty knots, returning to the Jacksonville, Florida port from which both had come. Powers looked up from his thoughts and coffee cup, and the letter he was reading from his son, Jeremy, newly promoted to full Lieutenant and now the Operations Officer of SEAL Team Two. Commander Thomas instinctively looked up from his coffee cup, realizing that it was time to complete the unfinished business that existed between the two men.

"Dale, there's something we have to talk about."

Powers' somber tone provided an even bigger clue to what lay ahead. The man continued, "Since none of us can have our cake and eat it too, it's clear to me that the electronics tests failed miserably. Isn't it clear to you as well?" Commander Thomas was uncertain how to respond to his friend, although he certainly knew where the conversation was leading. He wanted to leave Powers with some leeway.

"I'm not sure, David. Why are you so convinced?"

Powers responded, "It has to fail, Dale, because everyone must have plausible denial. There can be absolutely no official connection between us in the future. It can never be said that yourself, or the United States Navy, or SEAL Team, were somehow connected to commercial interests that might have benefited from what happened here. A profit link between myself, and my company, on the one hand, and you, the Navy and SEAL Team, on the other, would be a disaster."

The strong, unambiguous tone with which the words were spoken made Commander Thomas realize that, in fact, there was no moral ambiguity inherent in Powers' position, the man had absolutely meant what he said. Commander Thomas moved from the immediacy of the present to his concern for David Powers' future with the Board of Directors of the Thompson Electronics Corporation.

"Won't the failure of the tests and your company's SIGINT/ECM electronics gear get you into serious trouble with your Board of Directors? Since they don't know what happened here, how can they make a judgment that is in any way separate from whether or not you are representing your company's best interests? Won't they demand details of how and why it failed? Couldn't you get fired?"

It was apparent to Powers that Commander Thomas was deeply concerned for his well being, that if he wanted a way out, Thomas would, in fact, help him find one. Perhaps Thomas' alluding to what had transpired during the past several days meant he would permit Powers to tell his Board of Directors some details of what had really happened, although Powers would have none of it.

"Dale, this is just a short term setback. If I lose my job over the temporary failure of this one new product, the Board had no confidence in me anyway. It would have just been a matter of time before they found another reason to get rid of me."

Commander Thomas again realized that ridding the

world of José Ocho Garriana had been done within the absolute moral certainty of the Code of Honor by which these two men and most of those around them had lived their entire lives. The issue now resolved, Commander Thomas returned to his deepest private thoughts about a future not tied to the United States Navy. David Powers' emotions again returned to Phoenix, where he would be reunited with his supportive family. After all he'd been through, this would be far more important than any decision made by the Thompson Electronics Corporation's Board of Directors.

Powers had one more unrelated question.

"Dale, what was all that bullshit about sniping and the other stuff when you knew all along that the plan was going to be the one we used?"

Thomas' look said it all.

"To protect against unauthorized leaks so there would have been no chance that Garriana could have possibly learned what was coming."

Powers fully understood and didn't feel betrayed by being so obviously misled.

CHAPTER 34

Purchase, New York

The four FBI agents looked up excitedly as their blue 1993 Oldsmobile Cutlass approached the mansion at the end of the winding country road leading to the palatial residence of Mirriam Wilson and her husband. The agents took greater delight in arresting people of Mirriam Wilson's station in life than more traditional criminals such as members of organized crime or terrorists. Perhaps it was the hypocrisy of this ilk that particularly irritated and disgusted the agents.

Each of the four agents knew that while Mirriam Wilson lived a lavish public life as bank president and socialite, she was coming ever closer to making their personal most wanted list due to her numerous violations of Federal bribery, conspiracy and currency laws. She actually made them sick to their stomachs, particularly as they got within sight of the mansion and its decadent opulence. They knew how she really earned the tens of millions of dollars necessary to support this lifestyle.

Agent Howard Carr, seated on the passenger side in the front seat, looked at his watch, and without preamble, told the other agents, almost as an afterthought,

"Quarter to six, right on time."

The three other agents nodded their agreement, as agent Leo McQuade slowed the car and pulled it over to the right hand side of the driveway, about thirty yards from the main entrance to the house. Agent McQuade positioned the Olds in a small clump of trees to avoid detection. Operation "High Digit" as it was code named, was the FBI plan to shut down money laundering operations headed by high profile, high net worth, socially prominent individuals such as Mirriam Wilson. Simultaneously, all across the country, at mansion residences comparable to Mirriam Wilson's, other FBI agents in groups of two and four were arriving as a part of operation "High Digit". Nearly fifty individuals had been indicted as part of one of the largest and most complex FBI investigations in history. In order to increase the embarrassment and make the point even more strongly that individuals as powerful, wealthy and socially prominent as Mirriam Wilson were not above the law, as many of the arrests as possible were to be made at the homes of these individuals, and at mealtimes or during social functions, to impact as many associates or family members as possible. Unknown to the general public, the amount of damage being done to the U.S. economic system by these individuals was infinitely more serious than the damage inflicted by street gangs and other more visible criminal elements of society. Whatever the cost, the damage being wrought by kingpins like the Mirriam Wilson's of the world had to be stopped by whatever means necessary.

None of the agents spoke during the inevitable buildup of anticipation that preceded this type of an operation. After a few minutes passed, agent Carr picked up his arm and again glanced at his watch. It was now 5:58 p.m., local time. He simultaneously reached for the door handle as he again addressed his fellow agents, the excitement and anticipation in his voice both perceptible,

"Let's go!"

The other three agents opened their doors in unison and proceeded in pre-arranged order towards the front door. Agent Lawrence Hill, who had been sitting in the rear left seat, led the other three and began to circle to the rear of the residence. In the FBI, just as in local and state law enforcement, backup is essential. As the other three walked up the stairs leading to the front door, they positioned themselves almost automatically in the manner that each had either rehearsed or performed countless times since joining the Bureau. Agent Deborah Smith edged over to one side of the door, her back to the house, facing the

289

enormous expanse of manicured acres in front of the home. Agent McQuade, carefully mirroring the maneuvers of Agent Smith, moved to the same position on the other side of the door. By this time, the shadow of Agent Hill could be seen disappearing behind the house, and after allowing a few moments to pass that would ensure Agent Hill's proper backup position at the rear door, Agent Carr, the driver, knocked three times on the front door, and moved back a discreet distance in case drawing his weapon became necessary. Although Mirriam Wilson was considered a serious criminal within the FBI, she was not considered violent, and the agents did not want to scare friends or family members by menacingly entering the residence with drawn guns. Nonetheless, the feel of the cold steel of each one's Berretta model 92s 9mm automatic inside the standard issue blue wind breakers with large yellow FBI letters in block print on the back, was comforting indeed.

Inside the residence, Mirriam Wilson was hosting one of the typical dinner parties that she had become famous for. The most socially prominent residents of Westchester County, New York vied for her exclusive invitations. Agent Hill, now positioned as a backup at the rear door, could observe two maids dressed in black uniforms with crisply starched white aprons going about the many chores associated with so lavish an affair. At precisely the same moment, hearing the rather loud knocks, the four guests all glanced towards the front door as one of the maids diverted from her duties to answer the door. She appeared visibly startled as she instinctively backed away from the imposing figure standing just outside the door. Agent Carr spoke in a low pitched yet firm tone as be addressed the maid,

"Mirriam Wilson, please. I'm Agent Howard Carr of the Federal Bureau of Investigation." The full formal title of the agency was used in such instances rather than the more well known euphemism, "FBI". Helen Murphy, the maid, was a college student from Dublin, Ireland who still spoke in the thick native brogue of her native country. While an FBI agent knock-

ing at the door would have a visibly emotional impact on who-
ever answered, this maid was singularly unperturbed. In fact,
she did little to shield the matter from her mistress' guests. She
returned to the cavernous dining room and announced to the
entire assemblage, "Mrs. Wilson, there's a Mr. Howard Carr
of the Federal Bureau of Investigation here to see you."

Mirriam Wilson, her husband and their four guests literally froze in their places, each stopping what he or she had
been doing, failing to even return to normal positions. Mirriam,
for example, had a fork full of vegetables halfway from her
plate to her mouth, and for a few seconds that seemed like
eternity did not even put the fork down. It was as though the
moment had been frozen in time. After several seconds of silence, everyone present placed his or her utensils on a plate,
gently dabbed his or her mouth with the Irish linen napkins
used for such specil occasions, placed the napkins down, and
leaned forward, clasping their hands together in breathless
anticipation and fear of what might happen next. Everyone
was absolutely motionless. Although Helen Murphy could not
quite figure out what was going on, she realized it was important and began to understand that the FBI was not just some
local bowling club or social organization.

Mirriam Wilson, whose life of rehearsed social graces had
prepared her for almost any situation imaginable, instinctively
knew she was in deep trouble, but her social skills prevented
her from showing it. Although her heart was most likely in her
mouth, she turned the quarter circle or so necessary to face her
guests, politely smiled as she backed her chair away from the
table, and quietly excused herself while getting up.

By that time, the figures of two other individuals could
be seen standing on the porch behind and on either side of
Agent Carr, who had stepped into the foyer separating the
front door from the dining room. Carr's suit jacket was open,
and Mirriam could plainly see the shoulder holster holding his
9 millimeter automatic as he reached into the opposite side of
the jacket for his FBI badge and identification. Mirriam could

feel the almost electric pulses of hot flashes pulsing up and down her body, a cold sweat began to ooze from what felt like every pore, and she could visibly see what appeared to be black and red dots clouding her vision. She felt as though she were about to pass out, and secretly wished she would, to add to the uncontrollable drama of the moment. The imposing agent spoke, "Mirriam Wilson, I am Agent Howard Carr of the Federal Bureau of Investigation."

Wilson could barely distinguish the words, that seemed to blend together with the staccato flashes reflecting off the man's silver FBI badge, which he was now holding in plain sight.

"You are under arrest for multiple violations of Federal Law, including mail and wire fraud, multiple Federal currency violations, conspiracy, illegally transporting stolen money across State and National...."

At that moment, Mirriam Wilson, leaned back against the wall, fainted, and began slipping to the floor.

"....borders as well as seventeen separate charges for violations of the RICO statutes, the Federal conspiracy and racketeering laws."

While Mirriam Wilson did not yet know that the charges, if proven true, carried possible prison sentences of life plus hundreds of years, Agent Carr had begun to approach her now prostrate figure, and the other two agents rushed into the house as they observed her slipping to the floor. Although the FBI agents had some knowledge of the basic first aid required in this situation, two of the guests, one of whom was a prominent neurosurgeon, hurried over and knelt over the fallen body of the host, while another ran to the kitchen to dial 911. The scene was becoming chaotic, and might have even had a comic dimension had it not been so pathetically serious.

Agent Deborah Smith, wishing neither the possible liability of needlessly injuring the suspect or of unnecessarily punishing her, called for additional medical backup. The doctor in attendance left the house to get his medical bag, accompanied by agent Leo McQuade who was ready to lend assistance as well as to keep the man under appropriate surveillance. By the time the breathless doctor returned with his FBI shadow, sirens from both the FBI and the EMS ambulances were heard growing closer. Agent Smith had already begun to administer first aid to Mirriam Wilson, and had covered her in a blanket.

The husband of the hostess sat in a chair, cradling his head in his arms, sobbing hysterically. His whimpering was soon drowned out by the mixed sirens speeding up the circular driveway, their flashing emergency lights shimmering across the walls. The two ambulance crews ran in to find their patient wrapped in a blanket, fully conscious and sobbing away. As unobtrusively as possible, Agent Smith bent the suspect's arms back, snapped on handcuffs, and led her out of the house under her own power. Agents McQuade and Hill positioned themselves in front and in back of the woman. This brusque procession filed past the startled guests and the shocked ambulance crews.

The guests nervously stood by, not knowing what to do as they had never been in the presence of an FBI drug raid before. Most were horrified and knew nothing of their hostesses dirty secret source of wealth. They were more worried about their potential liability for just being in attendance at her party and, worse yet, whether their names would appear in the newspapers.

Mirriam Wilson, the seemingly omnipotent, impeccable bank president and socialite, was led away to begin an ordeal that would end with an eighty-seven year prison sentence in the federal penitentiary at Levenworth, Kansas.

At least she would not be alone in repaying society for her terrible abuses of the system. Forty-six other equally prominent individuals from such diverse fields as medicine, law, professional sports, academia and the arts, and coming from fine suburbs like Bel Air, Grosse Pointe, Easthampton, Greenwich and Winettka, would all be given federal prison sentences totaling more than 1,000 years.

CHAPTER 35

LANGLEY, VIRGINIA
EPILOGUE

The three intelligence chiefs of the U.S., UK and Israel had assembled once again, and for the last time regarding their special project, Operation Snow Bird. Their post-mortem analysis determined that this had been the most successful joint counter-drug operation in the history of the alliance between the three nations. And this time they managed to expand their scope of operations to include the covert assistance of several other nations, such as Italy, Germany and Canada, that wished to cleanse their societies of the cocaine scourge.

While considerably more violent and perhaps less subtle than previous joint action, Operation Snow Bird had nonetheless accomplished its objectives and delivered the unmistakable message to anyone at or near the top levels of power within the drug apparatus itself: participation in drug trafficking to the West will lead to death or prison.

It was a blustery, snowy day outside as the three old warriors settled into their chairs, their faces glowing eerily from the fire burning in the fireplace of the CIA Chief's office. Director Nesmuth rose from his place, walked over and stoked the fire. He then poured a glass of brandy into the crystal brandy snifters placed on the very ornate pure silver tray that had been painstakingly hand-crafted and was a gift from the British Prime Minister. General Chaim Ben Lavan proposed a toast after lifting his glass of brandy from the tray,

"May the Snow Bird fly away forever, never to return its poisonous scourge to the earth."

The other two men enthusiastically clanked their glasses together, the three snifters being held aloft as one. Each stared at his glass and after taking a sip, returned the snifter to its rightful place on the sparkling silver tray. Sir Robert Bretham Chapman turned to his friend John Nesmuth.

"So, John, what will you be doing now that you're joining the world of the retired?"

Nesmuth's two guests intuitively knew that the sudden retirement had something to do with Operation Snow Bird, but dared not ask what. Now that José Ocho Garriana had finally been sent to his maker, Director Nesmuth would be able to keep the dark secret of his alliance and deal making with this most despised human being. It was a relationship with the Devil which Nesmuth would take with him to his grave. He could barely contain the laugh that was rising from deep within, although any such overt emotion would surely tip off the other two intelligence directors that there was more to this operation than met the eye.

Nesmuth comforted himself with the rationalization that, no matter how bad Ocho Garriana had been, the secret intelligence information obtained about Shining Path and other violent drug and terrorist organizations worldwide was surely worth the small price he paid by trading information and not targeting Garriana's operation as aggressively as the U.S. had gone after those of his competitor cartels. The fact that such short term intelligence gains carried an increasingly larger long term price was of no consequence to the retiring CIA Director, who was content to bask in the glow of the enormous success of Operation Snow Bird.

Nesmuth turned to the questioner,

"Well, my wife and I built a beautiful place along the Maine Coast where we can spend summers. We have a place in Arizona where we'll spend the winters, plus we plan to travel a lot, hit the lecture circuit and, of course, I'll write my memoirs—in which you two will play the prominent roles you deserve."

Both men began to nervously edge forward in their chairs, protesting the remotest possibility that their roles and their countries' roles in Snow Bird might ever be revealed. After all, the operation involved outright assassinations and various violations of international law. Nesmuth held up his hand, already anticipating their concerns, his mischievous grin broadening....

"Don't worry, my friends, the very existence of Operation Snow Bird flew away with General Ben Lavan's toast. Rather than devote too many pages of my future book to the two of you, it would be more interesting to the average reader to discuss the enormous changes that have taken place in the world of intelligence.

Can you imagine, even Colonel Oleg Kamanoski, the KGB's highest ranking operative in Latin America, is beginning to cooperate with us now?"

The two men leaned back in their chairs with palpable relief, picked up their brandy snifters again, and returned their host's smile.

"So, John, what is your assessment of the operation that never occurred?" asked General Bar Lavan.

Having anticipated the question, Director Nesmuth returned to the back lit chart with multi-colored light bulbs on which the original plan had been outlined so many months before. Many of the countries on the map now contained a fourth bulb of a totally different color. He picked up and carried with him the same pointer that had been used the first time around and began an informal debriefing.

"If you remember, there were three different colored light bulbs the first time we met to plan Operation Snow Bird. We have now added a fourth. Blue identifies those countries that have been largely cleansed of the cancer that illegal drugs inflicts on their society."

With a flip of a switch, an impressive number of blue light bulbs came on all over the world map, with nearly half the nations that previously had red and amber lights (indicating serious drug infestations) now showing blue. Previous problem countries now in the blue included Italy, Thailand, Burma, Canada, Spain and several others. The display was impressive, and the two visitors reveled in their success, nodding in delight as Director Nesmuth reeled off the name of one country after another, describing their "before" and "after" profiles as drug users, traffickers or producers.

The MI5 Director spoke with unchecked glee,

"The liberals will agonize over the human rights we trampled on while eliminating these mass murderers. The conservatives?

They will say that we risked too many lives and spent too much time finessing the mission when we should have come in with Harrier Jets, B52s and cruise missiles and simply nuked the bastards back to the Stone Age. The way they see it, countries who flood us with the rat poison of drugs should be treated like bloody rats.

If Operation Snow Bird doesn't have the long-term effects I envisage, if softness and vulnerability sink in once again at the highest levels of our governments, then perhaps when the drug cartels again proliferate as a new generation of drug criminals move in to fill the lucrative void we have created, we may have to resort to crude military strikes like that instead of our brand of laser surgery."

The room went silent with the prospect of facing the same problem at some time down the road. The brandy snifters created a montage of shadowy patterns as the glow of the fireplace reflected against the walls. Suddenly, General Ben Lavan spoke up.

"Has anybody ever thought about legalizing what we have done?

Can't we have international laws upgraded to prevent rogue nations and corrupt mini-states from exporting so much misery?

If the nations who are victimized by this narco-terror get together out in the open, we would not have to hear about massive bombing missions in fifty countries and risking terrorist retribution and perhaps even nuclear showdowns with lawless criminal nations.

We all know that it is only a matter of time before one of the drug kingpins bribes his way into securing a nuclear weapon which will either be used to blackmail us or, worse yet, used on our people."

While the men clearly understood the wisdom of Ben Lavan's sentiments, each of them knew that the so-called developed nations were nowhere near the level of unambiguous moral vision required to legally and openly declare real war on the drug cartels and order the assassination and outright destruction of major drug operatives across national borders.

No, the men agreed that the legal, moral and religious issues were too complex to ever allow something like Operation Snow Bird to go above board. They also realized that legalizing cocaine and other illicit drugs was not even a discussible option for most of the same reasons.

The inner warmth generated by the brandy, the glowing fire and the successful completion of their mission turned the mood far more philosophical than usual. After a few more comments, John Nesmuth got up and stated what all three were clearly thinking.

"Are these really our choices?

Will our nations delude themselves by continuing to fight unwinable "Wars on Drugs" while expecting to lose several million to drug addiction and crime each year, or worse yet, will we sit back and wait for one of these powerful, angry, crazy cartel billionaires to buy a nuclear weapon to confront us with?

There surely is a third alternative, gentlemen, and that's where we come in. We are hired to do what we do when a nation in crisis has no apparent alternative to the two extremes of doing nothing or doing too much. We are the people who do anything necessary, who give our reputations and who are disposable when things go wrong—and if need be we give our lives. And we do all this so our countries can plausibly say they have done nothing.

The silence in the room said it all.

Meanwhile, in an underground laboratory hidden from satellite surveillance a team of Eastern European scientists are hard at work for their new employers in an Andean Ridge nation. The synthetic drug they are developing stimulates the brain's release of dopamine like nothing ever produced before.

Because the substance is highly addictive, projected profits from this illegal drug should exceed the billion dollar mark in the first year of reconnecting old distribution channels. Soon.....a new generation of young people will be inflicting great damage on themselves and their societies.....

The illusion of victory is never ending.

SOURCES AND RESOURCES

There are a variety of resources available for no cost from federal and private organizations for anyone wishing to attain a broader understanding of the present drug problem in the United States. This includes information on what is, or is not, being done about it:

1. Executive Office of the President, Office of National Drug Control Strategy. This organization publishes the President's annual statement on drug control strategy. The 1997 issue is available.

    Drugs and Crime Data Center and Clearing House
    (DCDCC)
    1600 research Blvd.
    Rockville, MD 20850
    Tel. 800/666-3332

2. A 1992 report entitled, "Drugs, Crime and the Justice System," with periodic updates through 1996 is available. This is an extremely thorough report on all facets of the drug problem, including what drugs are produced where, which countries are involved, etc. It is available from:
    Bureau of Justice Statistics Clearinghouse
    Box 6000
    Rockville, MD 20850
    Tel. 800/732-3277
    (There is also a fax on demand service)

3. SAMHSA (Substance Abuse and Mental Health Services Associations) has several informative publications, including:

National Household Survey on Drug Abuse
Trends in the Incidence of Drug Use in the U.S. 1919-1992
Preliminary Estimates from the Drug Abuse Warning Network

SAMHSA Office of Applied Studies
5600 Fishers Lane, room 16C-05
Rockville, MD 20857
Website: http:fwd/fwd/www.SAMHSA.GO2

4. The Drug Enforcement Agency (DEA) furnishes extensive data and a large number of informative publications
including:

The NNICC Report: an annual inter-agency report covering the worldwide supply of illegal drugs to the United
States. It is prepared in conjunction with twelve federal
agencies including: Customs, the FBI, Department of the
Treasury, U.S. Coast Guard, Department of State, Department of Defense, Internal Revenue Service, CIA, National Institute on Drug Abuse, Immigration and Natu-
ralization Service and the Office of National Drug Control Policy.

Drug Enforcement Agency
Office of Public Affairs
Washington, D.C. 20537
Tel. 202/307-7977

The author suggests that anyone desiring a broad overview of
the various issues related to counter-drug activity should consult the publications above.

Index

Norriega, Manuel, *123*
Drug Producing Areas, *63*
  Amazon River Basin, *25, 44-50,63, 168, 228, 267*
  Burma, *38, 237, 297*
  China, *38, 91, 142-144,150, 154, 237-238,*
    Hong Kong, *142, 144, 154, 195, 238*
  Golden Triangle, *39, 154, 237, 238, 261*
  Italy, *39, 44*
  Laos, *38*
  Lebanon, *38, 153, 154, 256-259,*
  Syria, Bekaa Valley, *153-154,158, 237, 256-263*
  Thailand, *38*

F

Foreign Intelligence Services
  KGB, *61-64,68-69,74*
    Kamanoski, Colonel Oleg, *63-64,68-75*
French Intelligence, *65*
  Broughes, Jacques, *67-68*

H

Helicopters, *72-73*
  Bell, *262*
  Sea King, *239*

M

Money Laundering/Banks, *128,136, 146, 158, 197, 204, 288*
  BCCI, *157, 201*
  BCR, *279*
  FGB, *124-126,133, 140-141,195-198,202-204*

P

Personalities
  Ben Lavan, General Chaim, *34-44, 152-161, 294-300*
  Blankenship, Admiral William, *83-85,89*
  Bretham Chapman, Sir Robert *34-44, 152-161, 294-300*
  Chaubenais, Jon Paul, *125-129,*
  Cor. Dale Thomas, *113*
  Felipe, Roberto, *130-132,195-196*
  Lewis, Bob, *86, 90, 94-95,103, 114-115,*
  National Security Advisor, *51*
  Nesmuth, John, *35-44,117-123,152-161,190-194,*
  Powers, David, *82, 85, 87, 91-92,97-114,*
  Powers, Lt. (jg) Jeremy, *26, 46-50,66, 68, 74, 76, 77, 80, 96, 102*
  Powers, Maggie, *84, 87, 89, 94, 96*

Appendix

Excerpts From the 1997
"National Drug Control Strategy Report"

Trends in Youth Drug Use

The most alarming trend is the increasing use of illegal drugs, tobacco, and alcohol among youth. Children who use these substances increase the chance of acquiring life-long dependency problems. They also incur greater health risks. Every day, three thousand children begin smoking cigarettes regularly; as a result, a third of these youngsters will have their lives shortened.[12] According to a study conducted by Columbia University's Center on Addiction and Substance Abuse, children who smoke marijuana are eighty-five times more likely to use cocaine than peers who never tried marijuana.[13] The use of illicit drugs among eighth graders is up 150 percent over the past five years.[14] While alarmingly high, the prevalence of drug use among today's young people has not returned to near-epidemic levels of the late 1970s. The most important challenge for drug policy is to reverse these dangerous trends.

Early drug use often leads to other forms of unhealthy, unproductive behavior. Illegal drugs are associated with premature sexual activity (with attendant risks of unwanted pregnancy and exposure to sexually-transmitted diseases like HIV/AIDS), delinquency, and involvement in the criminal justice system.

Overall Use of Illegal Drugs. In 1995, 10.9 percent of all youngsters between twelve and seventeen years of age used illicit drugs on a past-month basis.[15] This rate has risen substantially compared to 8.2 percent in 1994, 5.7 percent in 1993, and 5.3 percent in 1992 — the historic low in the trend since the 1979 high of 16.3 percent. The University of Michigan's 1996 *Monitoring the Future* study found that more than half of all high school students use illicit drugs by the time they graduate.

Cocaine Use Among Youth. Cocaine use is not prevalent among young people. In 1996, approximately 2 percent of twelfth graders were current cocaine users. While this figure was up from a low of 1.4 percent in 1992, it was still 70 percent lower than the 6.7 percent high in 1985. Among twelfth graders in 1996, 7.1 percent had

ever tried cocaine — up from the 1992 low of 6.1 percent but much lower than the 1985 high of 17.3 percent. However, during the past five years, lifetime use of cocaine has nearly doubled among eighth graders, reaching 4.5 percent in 1996.[16] A similar trend is identified in the 1995 National Household Survey on Drug Abuse, which showed a drop in the mean age for first use of cocaine from 23.3 years in 1990 to nineteen in 1994.[17]

Heroin Use Among Youth. Heroin use is also not prevalent among young people. The 1996 *Monitoring The Future* study found that 1 percent of twelfth graders had used heroin in the past year, and half of 1 percent had done so within the last thirty days. Encouragingly, both figures were lower than the 1995 findings. However, the 1996 survey showed that the number of youths who ever used heroin doubled between 1991 and 1996 among eighth and twelfth graders, reaching 2.4 percent and 1.8 percent respectively.[18]

Marijuana Use Among Youth. Marijuana use continues to be a major problem among the nation's young people. Almost one in four high school seniors used marijuana on a "past-month" basis in 1996 while less than 10 percent used any other illicit drug with the same frequency. Within the past year, nearly twice as many seniors used marijuana as any other illicit drug.[19] Marijuana also accounts for most of the increase in illicit drug use among youths aged twelve to seventeen. Between 1994 and 1995, the rate of marijuana use among this age-group increased from 6 percent to 8.2 percent (a 37 percent increase). Furthermore, adolescents are beginning to smoke marijuana at a younger age. The mean age of first use dropped from 17.8 years in 1987 to 16.3 years in 1994.[20]

Alcohol Use Among Youth. Alcohol is the drug most often used by young people. Approximately one in four tenth grade students and one third of twelfth graders report having had five or more drinks on at least one occasion within two weeks of the survey.[21] The average age of first drinking has declined to 15.9 years, down from 1987's average of 17.4 years.[22]

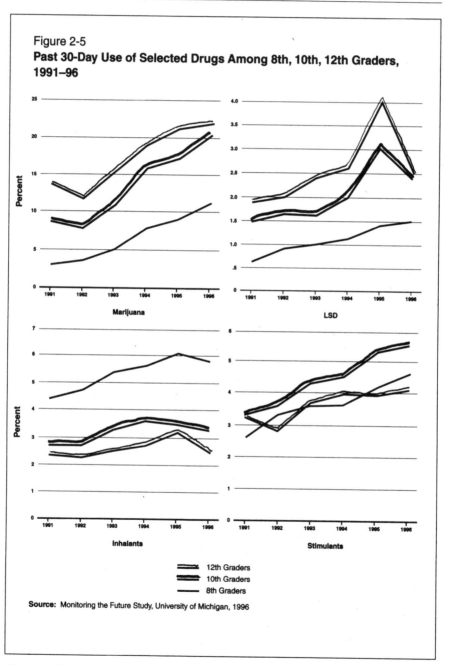

Figure 2-5
Past 30-Day Use of Selected Drugs Among 8th, 10th, 12th Graders, 1991–96

Marijuana

LSD

Inhalants

Stimulants

12th Graders
10th Graders
8th Graders

Source: Monitoring the Future Study, University of Michigan, 1996

Tobacco Use Among Youth. Despite a decline in adult smoking, American youth continue to use tobacco products at rising rates. In 1996, more than a third of high school seniors smoked cigarettes, and more than one in five did so daily. These percentages are greater than at any time since the 1970s.[23]

Other Illicit Drug Use Among Youth. After marijuana, stimulants (a category that includes methamphetamine) are the second-most-commonly used illicit drug among young people. About 5 percent of high school students use stimulants on a monthly basis, and 10 percent have done so within the past year. Encouragingly, the use of inhalants — the third-most-common illicit substance — declined among eighth, tenth, and twelfth graders in 1996. LSD however, was used by 8.8 percent of twelfth graders during the past year.[24]

Consequences of Illicit Drug Use

The social and health costs to society of illicit drug use are staggering. Drug-related illness, death, and crime cost the nation approximately $66.9 billion. Every man, woman, and child in America pays nearly $1,000 annually to cover the expense of unnecessary health care, extra law enforcement, auto accidents, crime, and lost productivity resulting from substance abuse.[25] Illicit drug use hurts families, businesses, and neighborhoods; impedes education; and chokes criminal justice, health, and social service systems.

Health Consequences

Drug-Related Medical Emergencies Are at a Historic High. The Drug Abuse Warning Network (DAWN), which studies drug-related hospital emergency room episodes, provides a useful snapshot of the health consequences of America's

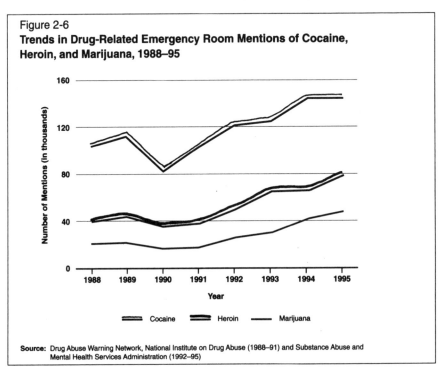

Figure 2-6
Trends in Drug-Related Emergency Room Mentions of Cocaine, Heroin, and Marijuana, 1988–95

Source: Drug Abuse Warning Network, National Institute on Drug Abuse (1988–91) and Substance Abuse and Mental Health Services Administration (1992–95)

drug problem. In 1995, DAWN estimated that 531,800 drug-related episodes occurred — slightly more than the 518,500 incidents in 1994. The 1995 figure marks the first time in the past five years that drug-related emergency department episodes did not rise significantly.[26]

DAWN also found that cocaine-related episodes remain at a historic high. Heroin-related emergencies increased between 1990 and 1995 by 124 percent. While no meaningful change occurred in the number of methamphetamine-related episodes between 1994 and 1995, a marked increase did occur between 1991 and 1994 when the figure rose from five thousand to nearly eighteen thousand.

Nearly 40 percent of deaths connected with illegal drugs strike people between age thirty and thirty-nine, a group with elevated rates of chronic problems due to drug abuse.[27] Overall rates are higher for men than for women, and for blacks than for whites.[28] AIDS is the fastest-growing cause of all illegal drug-related deaths. More than 33 percent of new AIDS cases affect injecting drug users and their sexual partners.[29]

The Consequences of Heroin Addiction are Becoming More Evident. Heroin-related deaths in some cities increased dramatically between 1993 and 1994 (the most recent year for which these statistics are available). In Phoenix, heroin fatalities were up 34 percent, 29 percent in Denver, and 25 percent in New Orleans.[30] The annual number of heroin-related emergency room mentions increased from 34,000 in 1990 to 76,023 in 1995.[31]

Maternal Drug Abuse Contributes to Birth Defects and Infant Mortality. A survey conducted between 1992 and 1993 estimated that 5.5 percent, or about 221,000 women, used an illicit drug at least once during their pregnancy.[32] Marijuana was used by about 2.9 percent, or 119,000; cocaine was used by about 1.1 percent, or 45,000.[33] Infants born to mothers who abuse drugs may go through withdrawal or have other medical problems at birth. Recent research also suggests that drug-exposed infants may develop poorly because of stress caused by the mother's drug use.

These children experience double jeopardy: they often suffer from biological vulnerability due to prenatal drug exposure, which can be exacerbated by poor caretaking and multiple separations resulting from the drug user's lifestyle.

Maternal substance abuse is associated with increased risk of infant mortality or death of the child during the first year of life. An in-depth study of infant mortality conducted on women receiving Medicaid, in the state of Washington from 1988 through 1990, showed an infant mortality rate of 14.9 per one thousand births among substance-abusing women as compared to 10.7 per one thousand for women on Medicaid who were not substance abusers.[34] In addition, this research indicated that infants born to drug-abusing women are 2.5 times more likely to die from Sudden Infant Death Syndrome (SIDS).

Chronic Drug Use is Related to Other Health Problems. The use of illegal drugs is associated with a range of other diseases, including tuberculosis and hepatitis. Chronic users are particularly susceptible to sexually-transmittable diseases and represent "core transmitters" of these infections. High risk sexual behavior associated with crack and injection drug use has been shown to enhance the transmission and acquisition of both HIV and other STDs.

Underage Use of Alcohol and Tobacco Can Lead to Premature Death. Eighty-two percent of all people who try cigarettes do so by age eighteen.[35] Approximately 4.5 million American children under eighteen now smoke, and every day another three thousand adolescents become regular smokers.[36] Seventy percent of adolescent smokers say they would not have started if they could choose again.[37] In excess of 400,000 people die every year from smoking-related diseases — more than from alcohol, crack, heroin, murder, suicide, car accidents, and AIDS combined.[38]

Alcohol has a devastating impact on young people. Eight young people a day die in alcohol-related car crashes.[39] According to the National Highway Traffic Safety Administration, 7,738 intoxicated drivers between the ages of sixteen and twenty were fatally injured in 1996.[40] The younger an individual starts drinking and the greater the intensity and frequency of alcohol consumption, the greater the risk of using other drugs.[41] Two and-a-half million teenagers reported they did not know that a person can die from alcohol overdose.[42]

Drug Abuse Burdens the Workplace. Seventy-one percent of all illicit drug users aged eighteen and older (7.4 million adults) are employed, including 5.4 million full-time workers and 1.9 million part-time workers.[43] Drug users decrease workplace productivity. An ongoing, nationwide study conducted by the U.S. Postal Service has compared the job performance of drug users versus non-users. Among drug users, absenteeism is 66 percent higher, health benefit utilization is 84 percent greater in dollar terms, disciplinary actions are 90 percent higher, and there is significantly higher employee turnover.[44]

The workplace can function as a conduit for information on substance-abuse prevention and identification both to adults — many of whom, as parents, are not being reached through more traditional means — and to youth who are employed while attending school. The threat of job loss remains one of the most effective ways to motivate substance abusers to get help. The workplace provides many employees (and families) who seek help for a substance-abuse problem with access to treatment. Since evidence shows that substance-abuse treatment can reduce job-related problems and result in abstinence, many employers sponsor employee-assistance programs (EAPs), conduct drug testing, or have procedures for detecting substance-abuse and promoting early treatment.

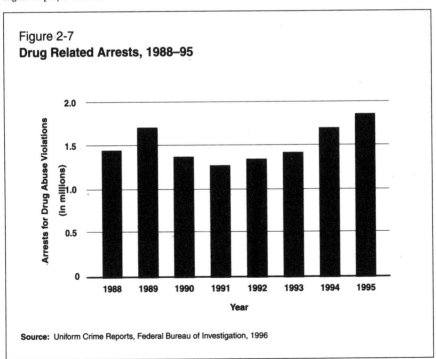

Figure 2-7
Drug Related Arrests, 1988–95

Source: Uniform Crime Reports, Federal Bureau of Investigation, 1996

The Cost of Drug-Related Crime

Drug abuse takes a toll on society that can only be partially measured. While we are able to estimate the number of drug-related crimes that occur each year, we can never determine fully the extent to which the quality of life in America's neighborhoods has been diminished by drug-related criminal behavior. With the exception of drug-related homicides, which have declined in recent years, drug-related crime is continuing at a strong and steady pace.

Numerous Drug-Related Arrests Occur Each Year. In 1994, state and local law enforcement agencies made an estimated 1.14 million arrests for drug law violations. The largest percentage of these arrests were for drug possession (75.1 percent).[45]

Arrestees Frequently Test Positive for Recent Drug Use. The National Institute of Justice Drug Use Forecasting (DUF) program calculates the percentage of arrested individuals whose urine indicates drug use. In 1995, DUF data collected from male arrestees in twenty-three cities showed that the percentage testing positive for any drug ranged from 51 percent to 83 percent. Female arrestees ranged from 41 percent to 84 percent. Among males, arrestees charged with drug possession or sale were most likely to test positive for drug use. Among females, arrestees charged with prostitution, drug possession or sale were most likely to test positive for drug use. Both males and females arrested for robbery, burglary, and stealing vehicles had high positive rates.[46]

Drug Offenders Crowd the Nation's Prisons and Jails. At midyear 1996, there were 93,167 inmates in federal prisons, 1,019,281 in state prisons, and 518,492 in jails.[47] In 1994, 59.5 percent of federal prisoners were drug offenders[48] as were 22.3 percent of the inmates in state prisons.[49] The increase in drug offenders accounts for nearly three quarters of

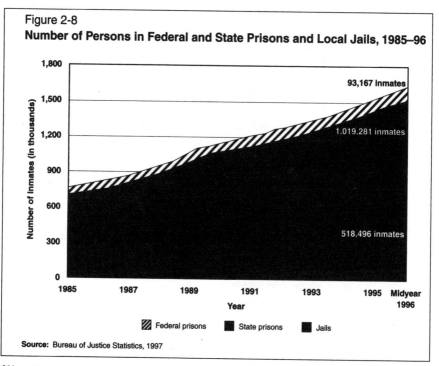

Figure 2-8

Number of Persons in Federal and State Prisons and Local Jails, 1985–96

93,167 Inmates

1.019.281 inmates

518.496 inmates

Number of Inmates (In thousands)

Year

Federal prisons   State prisons   Jails

Source: Bureau of Justice Statistics, 1997

Figure 2-9
Drug Use* Among Booked Arrestees, 1995

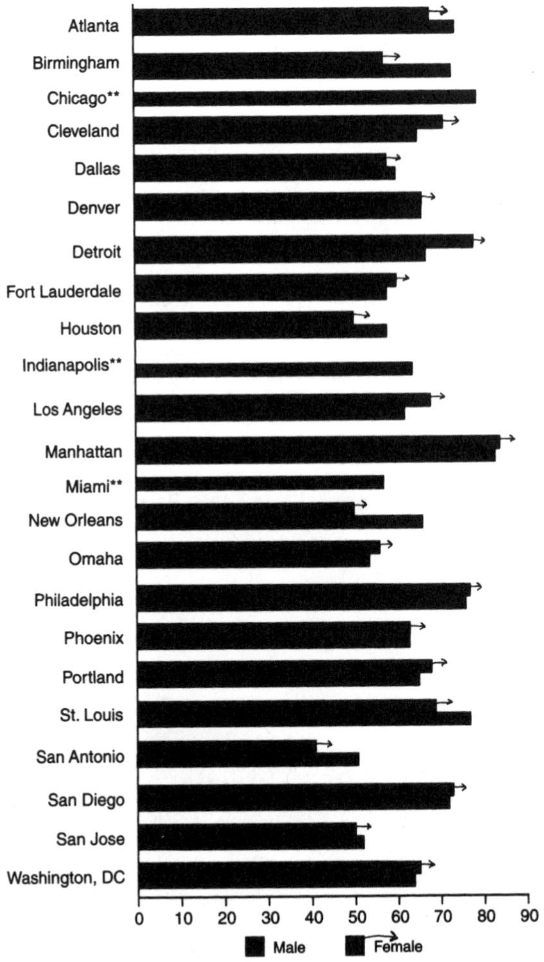

Atlanta
Birmingham
Chicago**
Cleveland
Dallas
Denver
Detroit
Fort Lauderdale
Houston
Indianapolis**
Los Angeles
Manhattan
Miami**
New Orleans
Omaha
Philadelphia
Phoenix
Portland
St. Louis
San Antonio
San Diego
San Jose
Washington, DC

0 10 20 30 40 50 60 70 80 90

■ Male   ■ Female

* Tested positive on urinalysis
** Data are not collected on female arrestees

Source: Drug use Forecasting Program, National Institute of Justice, 1996

the total growth in federal prison inmates since 1980. Most drug offenders are imprisoned for possessing more drugs than possibly could be consumed by one individual distributing drugs or committing serious crimes related to drug sales. In 1995, for example, only 4,040 people were sentenced in federal courts for marijuana-related charges; 89.1 percent of those offenders were facing trafficking charges.[50]

Inmates in Federal and State Prisons were often under the Influence of Drugs when they Committed Offenses. A 1991 survey of federal and state prisons, found that drug offenders, burglars, and robbers in state prisons were the most likely to report being under the influence of drugs while committing crimes. Inmates in state prisons who had been convicted of homicide, assault, and public

order offenses were least likely to report being under the influence of drugs. With the exception of burglars, federal prison inmates were less likely than state inmates to have committed offenses under the influence of drugs.[51]

Offenders Often Commit Offenses to Support Drug Habits. According to a 1991 joint survey of federal and state prison inmates, an estimated 10 percent of federal prisoners and 17 percent of state prisoners reported committing offenses in order to pay for drugs.[52]

Drug Trafficking Generates Violent Crime. Trafficking in illicit drugs is often associated with violent crime. Reasons for this relationship include competition for drug markets and customers, disputes among individuals involved with illegal

Figure 2-10
Drug-Related Murders, 1988–95

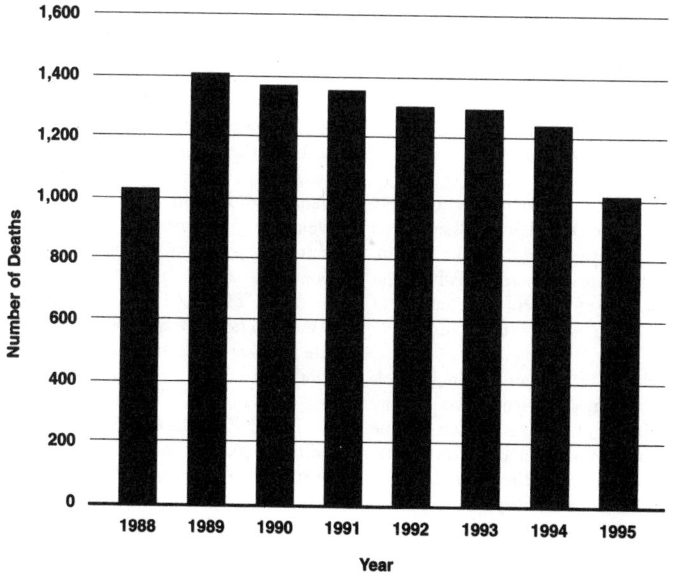

Source: Uniform Crime Reports, Federal Bureau of Investigation, 1996

drugs, and the location of drug markets in disadvantaged areas where legal and social controls against violence tend to be ineffective. The proliferation of lethal weapons in recent years has also made drug violence more deadly.

Drug-Related Homicides Have Declined. There was a steady decline in drug-related homicide between 1989 and 1995. The Uniform Crime Reports (UCR) indicated that of 21,597 homicides committed in 1995 in which the circumstances of the crime were known, 1,010 (or 4.7 percent) involved drugs. This figure was significantly lower than 7.4 percent in 1989.[53]

Money Laundering Harms Financial Institutions. Money laundering involves disguising financial assets so they can be used without the illegal activity that produced them being detected. Money laundering provides financial fuel not only for drug dealers but for terrorists, arms dealers, and other criminals who operate and expand criminal enterprises. Drug trafficking generates tens of billions of dollars a year; the total amount of money involved cannot be calculated precisely. In September 1996, the Internal Revenue Service (IRS) estimated that 60 percent of the money laundering cases it investigated during that fiscal year were drug-related.[54]

Illegal Drugs Remain Available

Illegal drugs continue to be readily available almost anywhere in the United States. If measured solely in terms of price and purity, cocaine, heroin, and marijuana prove to be more available than they were a decade ago when the number of cocaine and marijuana users was much higher.

Cocaine Availability. Colombian drug cartels continue to manage most aspects of the cocaine trade from acquisition of cocaine base, to cocaine production in South America and transportation, to wholesale distribution in the United States. Polydrug trafficking gangs in Mexico, which used to serve primarily as transporters for the Colombian groups, are increasingly assuming a more prominent role in the transportation and distribution of cocaine. Wholesale cocaine

distribution and money laundering networks are typically organized into multiple cells functioning in major metropolitan areas. Domestically, retail level sales are conducted by a wide variety of criminal groups. These sellers are often organized along regional, cultural, and ethnic lines that facilitate internal security while serving a demand for drugs that permeates every part of our society.

Gangs — including the Crips, Bloods, and Dominican gangs as well as Jamaican "posses"— are primarily responsible for widespread cocaine and crack-related violence. The migration of gang members and "posses" to smaller U.S. cities and rural areas has caused an increase in drug-related homicides, armed robberies, and assaults in those areas. According to the National Narcotics Intelligence Consumers Committee (NNICC) Report, the price and availability of cocaine in the United States remain relatively stable. In 1995, cocaine prices ranged nationally from $10,500 to $36,000 per kilogram. The average purity of cocaine at the gram, ounce, and kilogram level also remains high. Purity of the gram (retail level) in 1995 was approximately 61 percent while purity per kilogram (wholesale) was 83 percent.[55]

Heroin Availability. Heroin continues to be readily available in many cities. Nationally, in 1995 wholesale prices ranged from $50,000 to $260,000 per kilogram. This wide range reflected such variables as buyer-seller relationship, quantity purchased, frequency of delivery, and transportation costs. Data obtained from DEA's Domestic Monitor Program, a retail heroin purchase program, indicates that high-purity Southeast Asian heroin dominates the U.S. market. However, the availability of South American heroin has increased steadily, reflecting the fact that Colombian traffickers have gained a foothold in the U.S. heroin market.[56]

The NNICC Report also reveals that heroin purity levels have risen considerably. In 1995, the average purity for retail heroin from all sources was 39.7 percent nationwide, which was much higher than the average of 7 percent reported a decade ago. The retail purity of South American heroin was the highest of any source, averaging 56.4 percent nationwide and 76 percent in New

York City, a major importation and distribution center. Heroin purity was generally highest in the Northeast where a large percentage of the nation's users live.

Marijuana Availability. Marijuana is the most readily available illicit drug in the United States. While no comprehensive survey of domestic cannabis cultivation has been conducted, the DEA estimates that much of the marijuana consumed in the United States is grown domestically. Cannabis is frequently cultivated in remote locations and on public lands. Major outdoor cultivation areas are found in Tennessee, Kentucky, Hawaii, California, and New York. Significant quantities of marijuana are also grown indoors. The controlled environments of indoor operations enable growers to use sophisticated agronomic techniques to enhance the drug's potency. The majority of the marijuana in the United States comes from Mexico, much of it being smuggled across the southwest border. However, marijuana shipments from Colombia and Jamaica are increasing.

Marijuana production and distribution in the United States are highly decentralized. Trafficking organizations range from complex operations that import the drug, grow it domestically, and trade within the U.S., to individuals cultivating and selling at the retail level. High quality marijuana is widely available in all parts of the United States. Prices vary with quality and range from forty to nine hundred dollars per ounce.[57] Over the past decade, marijuana prices have dropped even as the drug's potency has increased.

Methamphetamine Availability. Domestic methamphetamine production and trafficking are concentrated in the western and southwestern regions of the United States. Clandestine methamphetamine laboratories operating within Mexico and California are primary sources of supply for all areas of the United States. Mexican polydrug trafficking groups dominate wholesale methamphetamine distribution in the United States, saturating the western U.S. market with high-purity methamphetamine. These groups

have also become a source of supply for Hawaii, threatening to displace traditional Asian suppliers.

LSD Availability. LSD in retail quantity can be found in virtually every state, and availability has increased in some states. LSD production facilities are thought to be located on the West Coast in the northern California and Pacific Northwest areas. A proliferation of mail-order sales has created a marketplace in which distributors have no personal contact with buyers.

Availability of Other Drugs. PCP production is centered in the greater Los Angeles metropolitan area. Los Angeles-based street gangs, primarily the Crips, continue to distribute PCP to a number of U.S. cities through cocaine trafficking operations. MDMA — a drug related to methamphetamine and known by such street names as Ecstasy, XTC, Clarity, Essence, and Doctor — is produced in west Texas and on the West Coast. It is distributed across the country by independent traffickers through the mail or commercial delivery services. MDMA is often sold in tablet form with dosage units of 55 to 150 milligrams. Retail prices range from six to thirty dollars.[58]

In 1995, an influx of flunitrazepam (Rohypnol) tablets reached the Gulf Coast and other areas of the United States. Manufactured legally by Hoffman-LaRoche in Colombia, Mexico, and Switzerland, Rohypnol has been reported to be combined with alcohol and cocaine, and is becoming known as the "date rape" drug. Illegal in the United States, it sells wholesale for a dollar a tablet and retail from $1.25 to three dollars a tablet.[59]

While Progress Has Been Made, More Remains to be Done.

We have made progress in our efforts to reduce drug use and its consequences in America. While America's illegal drug problem is serious, it does not approach the emergency situation of the late 1970s or the cocaine epidemic in the 1980s. Just 6 percent of our household population age twelve and over was using drugs in 1995, down from 14.1

Figure 2-11

Marijuana: Disapproval and Perceived Harmfulness of Regular Use Compared with Past 30 Day Use Among 12th Graders, 1996

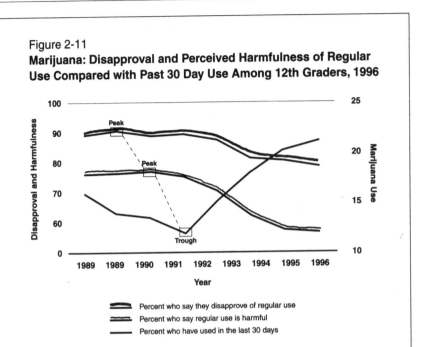

Source: Monitoring the Future Study, University of Michigan, 1996

percent in 1979. Fewer than 1 percent were using cocaine, inhalants, or hallucinogens. The most-commonly-used illegal drug was marijuana, taken by 77 percent of drug users.[60]

As drug use became less prevalent through the 1980s, national attention to the drug problem decreased. The Partnership for a Drug-Free America suggests that an indicator or that decreased attention was the reduced frequency of anti-drug public service announcements (PSAs) on TV, radio, and in print media. Our children also dropped their guard as drugs became less prevalent and first-hand knowledge of dangerous substances became scarce. Consequently, disapproval of drugs and the perception of risk on the part of young people has declined throughout this decade. As a result, since 1992 more youth have been using alcohol, tobacco, and illegal drugs.

A disturbing study prepared by CASA suggests that adults have become resigned to teen drug use. In fact, nearly half the parents from the "baby-boomer" generation expect their teenagers to try illegal drugs.[61] Forty percent believe they have little influence over teenagers' decisions about whether to smoke, drink, or use illegal drugs. Both of these assumptions are incorrect. Parents have enormous influence over the decisions young people make.

We Must Act Now to Prevent a Future Drug Epidemic

The United States has failed to forestall resurgent drug use among children in the '90s. This problem did not develop recently. The 1993 *Interim National Drug Control Strategy* highlighted the problem of rising drug use among American youth, quoting the 1992 *Monitoring The Future* study which found that eighth graders and college students were "... reporting higher rates of drug use in 1992 than they did in 1991. Further, fewer eighth graders in 1992 perceived great risk with using cocaine or crack than did eighth graders in 1991." The continuation of these trends has been substantiated by every significant survey of drug use since 1993.

Our challenge is to reverse these negative trends. America cannot allow the relapse we have experienced to signal a return to catastrophic illegal drug use levels of the past. The government has committed itself to that end; so have non-governmental organizations such as Community Anti-Drug Coalitions of America (CACDA); the Partnership for a Drug-Free America (PDFA); Columbia University's Center on Addiction and substance-abuse (CASA), the National Center for the Advancement of Prevention (NCAP), the Parent's Resource Institute for Drug Education (PRIDE), and many others. Working together, we can succeed.

Endnotes

1. Substance Abuse and Mental Health Services Administration, *Preliminary Estimates from the 1995 National Household Survey on Drug Abuse* (Rockville, Md.: U.S. Department of Health and Human Services, 1996).

2. The Gallup Organization, *Consult with America: A Look at How Americans View the Country's Drug Problem, Summary Report* (Rockville, Md.: March 1996).

3. Substance Abuse and Mental Health Services Administration, Preliminary Estimates from the 1995 National Household Survey on Drug Abuse.

4. Rand Corporation, *Modeling the Demand for Cocaine* (Santa Monica, Calif.: Rand Corporation, 1994).

5. W. Rhodes, P. Scheiman, and K. Carlson, *What America's Users Spend on Illegal Drugs, 1988-1991* (Washington, D.C.: Abt Associates, Inc., under contract to the Office of National Drug Control Policy, 1993).

6. National Narcotics Intelligence Consumers Committee, *The NNICC Report 1995: The Supply of Illicit Drugs to the United States* (Washington, D.C.: Drug Enforcement Administration, August 1996).

7. Office of National Drug Control Policy, *Pulse Check, National Trends In Drug Abuse* (Washington, D.C.: Executive Office of the President, Spring 1996).

8. Substance Abuse and Mental Health Services Administration, *Preliminary Estimates from the 1995 National Household Survey on Drug Abuse.*

9. *Ibid.*

10. National Institute of Justice, *1995 Drug Use Forecasting, Annual Report on Adult and Juvenile Arrestees* (Washington, D.C.: U.S. Department of Justice, 1996).

11. Office of National Drug Control Policy, *Pulse Check, National Trends In Drug Abuse* (Washington, D.C.: Executive Office of the President, Spring 1996).

12. Substance Abuse and Mental Health Services Administration, 1995 National Household Survey on Drug Abuse, unpublished data.

13. J.C. Merrill, K. Fox, S.R. Lewis, and G.E. Pulver, *Cigarettes, Alcohol, Marijuana: Gateways to Illicit Drug Use* (New York, N.Y.: Center on Addiction and Substance Abuse at Columbia University, 1994).

14. Lloyd Johnston, *Monitoring the Future Study - 1996*, press release (Ann Arbor, Mich.: University of Michigan, December 1996).

15. Substance Abuse and Mental Health Services Administration, *Preliminary Estimates from the 1995 National Household Survey on Drug Abuse.*

16. Lloyd Johnston, *Monitoring the Future Study - 1996*, press release.

17. Substance Abuse and Mental Health Services Administration, *Preliminary Estimates from the 1995 National Household Survey on Drug Abuse.*

18. Lloyd Johnston, *Monitoring the Future Study - 1996*, press release.

19. *Ibid.*

20. Substance Abuse and Mental Health Services Administration, *Preliminary Estimates from the 1995 National Household Survey on Drug Abuse.*

21. Lloyd Johnston, *Monitoring the Future Study - 1996*, press release.

22. Substance Abuse and Mental Health Services Administration, *Preliminary Estimates from the 1995 National Household Survey on Drug Abuse.*

23. Lloyd Johnston, *Monitoring the Future Study - 1996*, press release.

24. *Ibid.*

25. Dorothy P. Rice, Sander Kelman, Leonard S. Miller, and Sarah Dunmeyer, *The Economic Costs of Alcohol and Drug Abuse and Mental Illness: 1985*, report submitted to the Office of Financing and Coverage Policy of the Alcohol, Drug Abuse, and Mental Health Administration (San Francisco, Calif.: Institute for Health & Aging, University of California, U.S. Department of Health and Human Services, 1990).

26. Substance Abuse and Mental Health Services Administration, *Preliminary Estimates from the Drug Abuse Warning Network, 1995 Preliminary Estimates of Drug-Related Emergency Department Episodes*, Advance Report Number 17 (Rockville, Md.: U.S. Department of Health and Human Services, August 1996).

27. U.S. National Center for Health Statistics, *Alcohol and Drugs: Advance Report of Final Mortality Statistics, 1989, Monthly Vital Statistics Report, Vol. 40, No. 8, Supplement 2* (Hyattsville, Md.: U.S. Department of Health and Human Services, 1992).

28. Centers for Disease Control and Prevention, *Monthly Vital Statistics Report, Advance Report of Final Mortality Statistics, 1994*, Vol. 45, No.3., Supplement (Hyattsville, Md.: U.S. Department of Health and Human Services, September 30, 1996).

29. Centers for Disease Control and Prevention, *HIV and AIDS Trends, Progress in Prevention* (Hyattsville, Md.: National Center for Health Statistics, 1996).

30. 1994, *Drug Abuse Warning Network, Statistical Series, Series 1, No. 14-B, Annual Medical Examiner Data.*

31. Substance Abuse and Mental Health Services Administration, *Preliminary Estimates from the Drug Abuse Warning Network, 1995 Preliminary Estimates of Drug-Related Emergency Department Episodes*, Advance Report Number 17.

32. National Institute on Drug Abuse, *1992-93 National Pregnancy & Health Survey: Drug Use Among Women Delivering Livebirths* (Rockville, Md.: U.S. Department of Health and Human Services, 1996).

33. *Ibid.*

34. L. Schrager, J. Joyce, and L. Cawthon, *Substance Abuse, Treatment, and Birth Outcomes for Pregnant and Postpartum Women in Washington State* (Olympia, Wash.: Washington State Department of Social and Health Services, 1995).

35. Office on Smoking and Health, *Preventing Tobacco Use Among Young People, A Report of the Surgeon General* (Rockville, Md.: Center for Disease Control and Prevention, U.S. Department of Health and Human Services, July 1994).

36. Substance Abuse and Mental Health Services Administration, *Preliminary Estimates from the 1995 National Household Survey on Drug Abuse.*

37. American Cancer Society, *Facts About Children and Tobacco Use* (Atlanta, Ga.: American Cancer Society, 1997).

38. J.M. McGinnis and W.H. Foege, "Actual Causes of Death in the United States," *Journal of the American Medical Association*, Vol. 270, No. 18, (Chicago, Ill.: 1993), pp. 2207-2212.

39. Center for Substance Abuse Prevention (CSAP), *Teen Drinking Prevention Program* (Rockville, Md.: U.S Department of Health and Human Services, 1996).

40. National Highway Traffic Safety Administration, *Fatal Accident Reporting System* (Washington, D.C.: U.S. Department of Transportation, July 1996).

41. Center for Substance Abuse Prevention (CSAP), *Teen Drinking Prevention Program.*

42. J.C. Merrill, K. Fox, S.R. Lewis, and G.E. Pulver, *Cigarettes, Alcohol, Marijuana: Gateways to Illicit Drug Use.*

43. Substance Abuse and Mental Health Services Administration, *Preliminary Estimates from the 1995 National Household Survey on Drug Abuse.*

44. National Institute on Drug Abuse, *Research on Drugs and the Workplace: NIDA Capsule 24* (Rockville, Md.: U.S. Department of Health and Human Services, 1990).

45. Federal Bureau of Investigation, *Crime in the United States; 1995: Uniform Crime Reports* (Washington, D.C.: U.S. Department of Justice,1996).

46. National Institute of Justice, *Drug Use Forecasting, Annual Report on Adult and Juvenile Arrestees 1995.*

47. Bureau of Justice Statistics, *Prison and Jail Inmates at Midyear 1996* (Washington, D.C.: U.S. Department of Justice, January 1997).

48. Bureau of Prisons (Washington, D.C.: U.S. Department of Justice), unpublished data.

49. Bureau of Justice Statistics, *Correctional Populations in the United States, 1994*, (Washington, D.C.: U.S. Department of Justice, June 1996).

50. K. Maguire and A.L. Pastore, eds., *Sourcebook of Criminal Justice Statistics 1995* (Washington, D.C.: Bureau of Justice Statistics, U.S. Department of Justice, 1996).

51. Bureau of Justice Statistics, *Comparing Federal and State Prison Inmates, 1991* (Washington, D.C.: U.S. Department of Justice, September 1994).

52. *Ibid.*

53. Federal Bureau of Investigation, *Crime in the United States; 1995: Uniform Crime Reports.*

54. Internal Revenue Service, unpublished data.

55. National Narcotics Intelligence Consumers Committee, *The NNICC Report 1995: The Supply of Illicit Drugs to the United States.*

56. *Ibid.*

57. *Ibid.*

58. *Ibid.*

59. Office of National Drug Control Policy, *Fact Sheet: Rohypnol* (Rockville, Md.: Drugs and Crime Clearinghouse, September 1996).

60. Substance Abuse and Mental Health Services Administration, *Preliminary Estimates from the 1995 National Household Survey on Drug Abuse.*

61. Luntz Research Companies, *National Survey of American Attitudes on Substance Abuse II, Teens and Their Parents* (New York, N.Y.: Center on Addiction and Substance Abuse, September, 1996).

Books of Related Interest

SEAL TEAM COMBAT MISSIONS: *Search and Destroy*
by Mark Roberts, Chief Jim Watson.
Only a top military fiction writer and a founding member of SEAL Team Two could have joined forces to pack this much action and ordnance battling "Charlie" in the Mekong Delta. The first in an exciting new SEAL series.
ISBN 1-56171-328-7 $4.99

COMPROMISED: *Clinton, Bush and the CIA*
by Terry Reed and John Cummings.
Reed, a CIA asset turned into a fugitive for opposing government drug trafficing, presents damning evidence placing Governor Bill Clinton and Vice President Bush directly in the Iran-Contra loop, complete with a trail of Contra training, money laundering,and dealing with Oliver North and even the U.S. Attorney General, etc. ISBN 1-56171-249-3 $23.95

THE MAFIA, CIA & GEORGE BUSH by Pete Brewton.
If you thought the S&L scandal rocked the Bush administration, you've got to read what this investigative journalist has uncovered about the former president, a circle of Texas cronies and billionaires, the Mafia and covert CIA assistance. The US taxpayers lose out to the tune of half a trillion, while the criminals get richer! ISBN 1-56171-203-5 $22.95

THE BAMBOO CAGE: *The True Story of American P.O.W.s in Vietnam*
by Nigel Cawthorne.
The government claims that over 2,000 American soldiers missing in action in the Vietnam War are dead. The author fought for documentation from the CIA, the Pentagon and even the authorities in Hanoi to prove otherwise. Revealed here are the cruel and illegal secrets the U.S. government doesn't want you to know. ISBN 1-56171-241-8 $5.99

TARGET AMERICA: *Terrorism in the U.S. Today* by Yossef Bodansky.
Can we breathe easy now that the World Trade Center terrorists are behind bars? Not according to the Director of the Republican Task Force on Terrorism & Unconventional Warfare of the U.S. Congress. Terrorist groups from Islamic and Balkan countries are primed to strike. ISBN 1-56171-269-8 $5.99

- -

Send Payment in U.S. Dollar to:
S.P.I. Books 136 West 22nd St. New York, NY 10011 USA
Order by phone: 212 / 633-2023 or Fax 212/ 633-2123
Please send the following book(s) listed on attached sheet.
I enclose $_____ (For postage and handling please add $2.50 for the first book, and $.75 for each additioal book. For Canada add $5.00, Europe add $10.00.)
Checks or money orders accepted, for credit card orders please fill out the line below:
___ MC or ___VISA # _____Exp. Date_____
Name:_____
Address: _____
Allow 4 to 6 weeks for delivery.
You may use a copy of this order form or a seperate sheet.